T0313773

Praise for *Learning Systems Thinking*

The book sells itself short. "Your life is not about to get easier"—yes, it is. You'll learn how to stop making things worse by trying to make them better.

—*Kent Beck, chief scientist, Mechanical Orchard;*
author of Tidy First?

When changing code becomes easy enough,
yet changing software only gets harder—it is time for this book.

—*Jessica Kerr, symmathecist*

As with the best learning books, the learning set out in this book isn't about instruction; it's about being shown the road, the map, and the stories you may come to tell. Deeply insightful, reassuringly practical, delightfully real, and staggeringly well written.

—*Kevlin Henney, independent consultant, trainer, and*
thought provoker; editor of 97 Things Every Programmer Should Know
and co-editor of 97 Things Every Java Programmer Should Know

This book is a reality call: we need to face the fact that modern software development is a complex endeavor that we can't fully control and plan. Diana does an exemplary job of giving us language and practices to help us improve our approaches.

—*Dr. Eduardo da Silva, independent consultant on*
sociotechnical architecture modernization

Montalion has captured the warp and woof of systems thinking. I was particularly encouraged by her focus on the role systems thinking plays in business success. Read this book, share it with your team, and be ready to think differently.

— *Mike Amundsen, writer, speaker, trainer, and author of* RESTful Web API Patterns and Practices Cookbook

Diana offers us a book with practical insights and tools for the quest of designing, building, and maintaining software. It is definitely not a linear journey! Also, her jokes rock.

— *João Rosa, independent consultant and Team Topologies valued practitioner*

The perfect tool to expand your thinking, *Learning Systems Thinking* is essential reading for anyone with hard problems to solve.

—*Alexandra Paskulin, technical writer*

For sustainable cultural transformation in software development, understanding and collaboratively designing the system is crucial. Diana Montallion's provides software engineers with a pragmatic approach, equipping them with the tools needed to collaboratively pivot a system for change.

— *Kenny Baas-Schwegler, independent software consultant, tech lead, and software architect; coauthor of* Collaborative Software Design

Learning Systems Thinking is essential for anyone thinking about thinking. This isn't just a book to read; it's a guide to changing how you think, offering practical advice and real-world examples to help you create more impactful software systems.

—*Avraham Poupko, principal architect at Forescout Technologies*

This is a rescue manual for anyone trapped in the morass of linear thinking that cripples software delivery. Journey into perspectives and practices that can powerfully reshape your imagination, your work, and perhaps even your organization, in radically nonlinear ways.

—*Paul Rayner, author of* The EventStorming Handbook *and founder of the Explore Domain-Driven Design conference*

Learning Systems Thinking provides insightful practices to creatively tackle and make an impact on nonlinear, sociotechnical challenges. It enables everyone to have conversations and create decision-informing models, whilst dancing with uncertainty.

—*Dawn Ahukanna, design principal and front-end architect*

As you become more experienced, your intuition grows about what works, yet you do not always know exactly why. *Learning Systems Thinking* will help you understand most of the whys and give you extra tools and vocabulary for clearer thinking.

—*Andrea Magnorsky, programmer;*
creator of Bytesize Architecture Sessions

In an increasingly complex and unpredictable world, linear deterministic thinking by the few is no longer sufficient. The full power of all the people in an organization, the whole system, must be fully engaged to be able to adapt and thrive.

—*Trond Hjorteland, IT consultant with Capra Consulting*
and sociotechnical practitioner

Learning Systems Thinking
Essential Nonlinear Skills and Practices
for Software Professionals

Diana Montalion

Beijing · Boston · Farnham · Sebastopol · Tokyo

Learning Systems Thinking

by Diana Montalion

Copyright © 2024 Mentrix Group LLC. All rights reserved.

Published by O'Reilly Media, Inc., 1005 Gravenstein Highway North, Sebastopol, CA 95472.

O'Reilly books may be purchased for educational, business, or sales promotional use. Online editions are also available for most titles (*http://oreilly.com*). For more information, contact our corporate/institutional sales department: 800-998-9938 or *corporate@oreilly.com*.

Acquisitions Editor: David Michelson
Development Editor: Shira Evans
Production Editor: Clare Laylock
Copyeditor: Liz Wheeler
Proofreader: Kim Wimpsett

Indexer: WordCo Indexing Services, Inc.
Interior Designer: David Futato
Cover Designer: Karen Montgomery
Illustrator: Kate Dullea
Chapter-Opener Image Designer: Lisa Maria Moritz

July 2024: First Edition

Revision History for the First Edition
2024-07-11: First Release

See *http://oreilly.com/catalog/errata.csp?isbn=9781098151331* for release details.

978-1-098-15133-1

[LSI]

Table of Contents

Part II.   You Are a System of Thinking

Part III. We Are a System of Thinking

Part IV.   Designing a System of Thinking

Preface

It became apparent that communications and computing served each other so intimately that they might actually become the same thing.
    —Tracy Kidder, *The Soul of a New Machine* (Little, Brown and Company)

From Nowhere to Everywhere

Sixteen years ago, I owned an independent bookstore, Mooncougar Books, near the University of Montana in Missoula. The building once housed Freddy's Feed and Read, where you could nibble tofu shepherd's pie while browsing books by local authors. Eight years after Freddy's closed, I bought the business from the penultimate owner in a long line of struggling booksellers.

On July 20, 2007, twelve kids were nestled in the second-floor reading nook, wearing pajamas and reading *Harry Potter and the Deathly Hallows*. At midnight, the book was officially released, and they left to continue reading it at home. Downstairs on the purple counter, there were Read Banned Books buttons in a basket next to the bookmarks. The next morning, the enticing smell of Bears Brew coffee seeped in through the door shared with the coffee shop.

The bookstore, and Missoula itself, was surrounded by 1.6 million acres of national forest land. During time off, I'd shrug on my backpack and disappear into that forest, hiking alongside fresh moose tracks. I rode my motorcycle (BMW F650, for the gearheads) across hundreds of miles of logging roads, sleeping in a tent overlooking the valley while the occasional bear sniffed at my stuff.

Everywhere, indoors and out, I was reading.

One afternoon, I was avoiding boring inventory work, reading an essay by Anne Patchett published in (if memory serves) *Real Simple* magazine. Beauty, she said, depends on our geography. She wasn't beautiful in preppy Massachusetts towns. She wasn't beautiful in towns where black eyeliner and tattoos were common. As that article progressed toward the Big Reveal, the place where she felt truly beautiful, I knew exactly where we were going—the Bitterroot Valley. Where I lived. In the Bitterroots, being fresh-air tousled, friendly, and smart with some mud on your boots was beautiful. I rarely wore makeup, unless Chapstick counts.

Who you were, authentically, mattered. In winter, getting up the mountain to home mattered. (Learning to put chains on your tires so you didn't slide off the mountain mattered.) In April, not getting stuck in mud mattered. Every shift in weather, especially during fire season, mattered. Bears mattered and moose occasionally meandered into my yard. My dogs played hide-and-seek with the deer. (I didn't know deer played hide-and-seek, did you?)

Reading and learning mattered. People said that Missoula had the highest per capita percentage of waitresses with master's degrees. People mattered. When those waitresses asked you how you were, they actually wanted to know.

In Missoula, 16 years ago, there wasn't technology. Not compared to, say, every town in the Northeast US. Before moving there, I'd studied programming and web engineering. In Montana, I had dial-up internet access. (Remember when we called the internet on the phone?) After a year or so of living down in the valley, I moved up a mountain and had no internet access at all.

Turns out, when you stretch a wire up the side of a mountain to provide phone service, it won't (later) carry the internet to you. Amazon's home page, such as it was then, took almost six minutes to load. Sure, I could check my email, if I was very patient, but basically I was cut off. I didn't mind. I had internet access in the bookstore. There was a receptor attached to the second-floor roof, installed in winter, that stopped working when the leaves came back.

At home, I was surrounded by trees and wind and time to write. I did more writing then, though I didn't publish much. I was the source of my own entertainment. Books and words, mountains and rivers.

Life wasn't all peaceful and idyllic. There were dysfunctional interpersonal dramas, heartbreak, and difficult decisions to make. The relational part of my life was a mess. Still, when I remember Missoula, I remember beauty. For many years, I planned to return when I could afford to stay.

(Missoula has broadband internet access now.)

Eventually, an internet service provider came up the mountain and sunk a tall metal pole into wet concrete near the hot tub. The installer stuck a receiver on top of the pole and pointed it toward a new transmitter. I bet you can guess what happened next....

Within a month, I had moved into Second Life, a virtual world of endless...enjoyment? Creativity? Time squandering? I rediscovered being plugged in. I say *redisc*overed because before Montana, there was Merentha, a text-based role-playing game my son and I spent too many hours exploring together. One afternoon, he, as a centaur, had taken me, a half-elf monk scholar, for a ride on his back to places where I could hunt dragons. I needed their skin to make sturdier gloves.

Missoula evenings became less about reading books; mornings became less about writing. I refilled my coffers from digital oceans. I surfed. Increasingly, I connected with people elsewhere. The rich beauty, the endless possibility, of Montana faded into the (boring) distance.

sigh

I don't know, writing this now, which decision was the chicken and which was the egg. After a local competitor refurbished and expanded their bookstore in some wonderful but impactful-to-me ways, I closed the store. I sold my inventory to Powell's in Portland, Oregon. Visits there still feel like visiting a loved one buried in a cemetery.

One winter weekend, in the midst of closing the bookselling business, I rented the Star Meadows Guard Cabin from the Forest Service in Whitefish, Montana. I'd recently finished a yearlong, creative nonfiction writing mentorship with Diana Hume George (which remains one of my most valuable investments). Simultaneously, I was building custom software (retrospectively, for shockingly little money) and mastering PHP, the programming language that, up until recently, powered most internet software. I brought Kelly James-Enger's book *Six-Figure Freelancing* (Improvise Press) determined to make a choice. Writing or programming? I was the only "techie" I knew in Missoula, which felt increasingly frustrating. The digital world was speeding up—I could hardly keep up from the middle of the forest.

From Software to Systems

Six months later, I moved to Austin, Texas. I'd never been to Austin, but my Spreadsheet of Relevant Statistics told me that it was The Place to Be if you wanted to ride the wave of tech into the next decade. I choose to ride that wave.

Spoiler alert: it was the place. I rode the wave. And here I am…

…living 90 minutes north of New York City, in a big house on four acres with my also-a-techie husband, three dogs, two cats, a ferret named Merry, and eleven chickens. I've written code for smallish and medium-sized websites. I've written code for Really Big digital properties. Nowadays, I architect systems of interdependent software and cloud-native platforms for entire organizations.

I've helped build and design the digital traps that entangle your attention. I give talks and trainings at conferences, wearing those fancy headsets. I (sometimes) create healthy, happy teams that enjoy solving hard problems together. I pay more in annual income tax than I earned selling books in Montana.

When I first arrived in Austin, I built tools for clients like TXMPA, a nonprofit advocacy group that brings millions of film dollars into Texas. I spent a weekend, alone, moving lists of differently structured data into their new CRM (people information) software. The expertise I developed led to a meeting with a professional services team. I joined, and we built big websites. I became deeply involved in open source.

Big websites, at the time, generally meant installing a piece of open source software and extending it with (lots of) PHP. We built themes for styling, code that organized colors and fonts (we endlessly debated fonts). We hosted it all in a LAMP stack (software that runs the software that runs the software) with load balancing in front and controller/agent MySQL database configuration in back. Over time, we added hundreds of modules. To scale the software for high-traffic sites, we added caching (Varnish).

It was, often, complex and innovative work. Even though I could model the architecture of most features on a single page.

Analyzing a problem or feature request and then writing code to resolve or deliver it was enjoyable and addictive. Sometimes frightening, like when I added many lines of code to the Donate to Wikipedia process, enabling donors to pay with a credit card. Millions of dollars ran through that code. I threw up before launch, but everything went fine. The internal code review from Tim Starling remains my favorite ever. Across multiple initiatives and client teams I've worked with, the feedback I got from others has made the code stronger. Made me stronger.

Meanwhile, the world around us—the internet—was growing into the complex information graph it was perhaps never intended to be. Less about a document, or web page, and more about the relationships among all information. People were less interested in visiting a website and more interested in getting relevant information in whatever context they occupied, on whatever device they were using.

The digital gardens we planted grew into an interconnected web of interdependent information systems. I was with *The Economist* when they made the Big Jump toward a serious digital presence. I was with them again, 10 years later, when a single article had 40+ destinations (website, app, Facebook, etc.) and there were multiple types of media being created (including films). New destinations and system-level challenges were arising daily despite there being no infrastructure (yet) to support them.

Nowadays, my teammates and I build information systems. I work across multiple teams building multiple platforms constructed from multiple cloud-native services interacting asynchronously with multiple types of software that interdepend. The theme layer is now its own (decoupled) piece of software that morphs depending on the context (device, location, individual) it's serving. There is rarely only one frontend piece of software. The backends consist of multiple instances of editing or data-organizing software, in some cases over 200 instances. In between, there are platforms, weaving software and services together with Kafka streams, infrastructure as code, container orchestration, and data schemas defining what was once simply "content on a web page."

The complexity of everything has increased.

I am not alone. Most technology teams are attempting digital transformations, in one form or another.

Scaling now means "distribute information from multiple sources to nearly infinite people, products, and platforms." To model this for you, I need interconnected pages of models. There's a lot more caching.

The coronavirus pandemic forced most organizations to rethink customer interactions, remap user journeys, and redesign data flows to give information significantly more visibility. Under the surface was a shift from serving requests for web-based information to the need for asynchronous event-based interactions.

Television, like the internet, has shifted toward information platforms in your pocket. Technology is everywhere; everything is technology; everyone is involved. Technologists are learning to speak every language—tech, marketing, business, product— simultaneously. We are continuously deploying, building data firehoses, moving from monolith to microservices, modernizing. This involves transforming DevOps workflows with continuous deployment and integrating design systems into those workflows. We are adopting practices like Domain-driven Design and Team Topologies to help us create new mental models.

In other words, we are reconstructing the fabric of digital space-time.

Here is where I almost burnt out and quit IT, imagining that life as an accountant or landscape architect would be preferable to systems architecture.

That transformation—from thinking in software to thinking in systems—is an iceberg almost every initiative hits. And when they fail, transformation initiatives don't just sink, they sink spectacularly. And they drag down the hope and joy that powered them in the first place.

It's exhausting.

There is a lot of blame. There is a lot of drama. There's a lot of bull&*#$. This book is born out of the bull&*#$.

We've been amassing a pile of reasons for our failings since the "software crisis" began in the 1960s, as complexity was increasing. Then, since, and now, the reason is the same: *we can't change our thinking fast enough to keep up.*

The skills we need no longer fit the stereotypical Lone Supernerd coding while eating pizza at 2 a.m. *No one can do it alone.* Technology skills (alone) are not enough.

We don't think in systems. To move from software to systems, we need to think differently (together).

Technology Design Is Communication Design

Once again, I have arrived at a crossroads in my life. Here I am…writing. The choice I made in Montana, a career in communication or a career in technology, was not, and should never have been viewed as, a dichotomy. My journey from nowhere to everywhere, from software to systems, has led me to one inevitable conclusion: *technology design is communication design.*

> Organizations, who design systems, are constrained to produce designs which are copies of the communication structures of these organizations.
>
> —Conway's Law (*https://oreil.ly/rFa1g*)

We build what we think. We structure thinking through communication, and then we craft it into something actionable. Communication is how we think together. The structure and flow of information, in our own minds, with other people and as organizations, creates the sociotechnical systems, the integration of people and technology, that are the core of our work.

Whatever else we think we are doing, we are always, also, designing systems. Wherever we imagined we were heading with our digital transformations, we have arrived. Information technology is no longer elsewhere. Systems are right here, woven into the fabric of our days, our lives. They influence our decisions and shape our mental models.

We are immersed in the digital world, like I once was in Second Life. We have all traveled away from a friendly conversation with the waitress and into a global, always-on, digital pageant.

My technology career has long since surpassed any dream I had when I left Montana. When I'm quiet and honest, I also know that I went deep into the disease as well, like a drunk who isn't entirely sorry for everything that happened before she got sober. But, mostly, I would have preferred making choices without all the delusion. Mistakes have also been my teachers on a journey that has led me here: advocating for topics that aren't, necessarily, popular at tech conferences. (Where's the Kubernetes chapter?!) Yet, my day-to-day experience suggests they are essential IT topics.

We ignore them at our peril.

I entered my STEM career through the linear, logical door of programming internet software. I abandoned the messy, creative uncertainty of nature and words for the solidity of cities and software engineering. Then I found myself in the hall of mirrors that is systems.

This is the risk everyone in STEM, perhaps everyone in life, takes. We choose a path and end up right back in the middle of the forest. Because everything is a system. Everywhere we are part of those systems.

We need to think in and communicate about systems.

Conventions Used in This Book

The following typographical conventions are used in this book:

Italic
> Indicates new terms, URLs, email addresses, filenames, and file extensions.

 This element signifies a tip or suggestion.

 This element signifies a general note.

Supplemental Material

This book will mention and quote systems thinkers, past and present, who have contributed the knowledge we need. You can find them in the evolving digital library (*https://systemslibrary.com*). You can also recommend more resources! If you'd like to join the emerging community of SystemsCrafters, you can find us at *https://mentrix.systems*.

O'Reilly Online Learning

 For more than 40 years, *O'Reilly Media* has provided technology and business training, knowledge, and insight to help companies succeed.

Our unique network of experts and innovators share their knowledge and expertise through books, articles, and our online learning platform. O'Reilly's online learning platform gives you on-demand access to live training courses, in-depth learning paths, interactive coding environments, and a vast collection of text and video from O'Reilly and 200+ other publishers. For more information, visit *https://oreilly.com*.

How to Contact Us

Please address comments and questions concerning this book to the publisher:

O'Reilly Media, Inc.
1005 Gravenstein Highway North
Sebastopol, CA 95472
800-889-8969 (in the United States or Canada)
707-827-7019 (international or local)
707-829-0104 (fax)
support@oreilly.com
https://oreilly.com/about/contact.html

We have a web page for this book, where we list errata, examples, and any additional information. You can access this page at *https://oreil.ly/learning-systems-thinking*.

For news and information about our books and courses, visit *https://oreilly.com*.

Find us on LinkedIn: *https://linkedin.com/company/oreilly-media*.

Watch us on YouTube: *https://youtube.com/oreillymedia*.

Acknowledgments

From Diana

> In systems, relationships produce effects. The individual parts do not, by themselves, generate impactful outcomes. Relationships do. *Learning Systems Thinking* is living proof. This book is stronger, in every way, because I did not write it alone. Other people's valuable contributions are woven into every sentence.
>
> For 30 years, Lisa Wolfe has encouraged me to face my demons, believe in my work, and discover joy when I didn't believe joy existed. I say, and I mean it, she saved my life. Much of what I know about self-awareness, a key systems thinking skill, I learned with Lisa. Anna Granta, a brilliant neurodiversity coach, came into my life when writing felt impossible and helped me discover leverage points in my own brain.
>
> Andrew Harmel-Law pushed me when I needed pushing. He also made me safe, by reading each chapter first and hanging out with me in Discord. Together we navigated the ups and downs of creation. (You'll want to read his book next!) He also passed on Karsten Lettow's feedback as the first critical reader.
>
> As reviewers, Alex Paskulin, Vlad Khononov, and Jacqui Read had an immeasurably positive impact on everything you are about to read. They pointed to all the right changes. I rewrote whole chapters based on their excellent feedback. I never want to write anything without them again.

The O'Reilly team is a dream team. Melissa Duffield encouraged me to engage with her team. Before I even got started, I won the editor lottery. First with Louise Corrigan, then David Michelson. David helped me envision a book that mattered to write. When the draft was done, Clare Laylock shepherded the book through production and somehow made it feel like a party. Liz Wheeler was the best copyeditor I've ever experienced; I'm happy you'll experience her 800 improvements.

As development editor, Shira Evans spent a year working on this book with me. She also, perhaps more importantly, developed *me* as someone who could write it. I don't know, and don't want to know, what this book would have been without Shira. Books are a knowledge system, and Shira is the consummate architect. She's also wonderful to work with.

Lisa Moritz created the sketchnotes throughout this book. Her work was like magic, a rendering of each chapter that both delighted and inspired me. I know you'll have the same experience. Read her book or reach out to her. She's also a wonderful teacher.

Everything I've learned about systems, I learned with and through other people. Robb Lee, my partner in developing Mentrix. Stepan Protsak, whose engineering and software architecture skills are truly inspirational. Dawn Ahukanna, Andrea Magnorsky, and Tobias Goeschel, who developed workshops with me that expanded my practice of systems thinking. We all benefit from the wisdom of our forerunners mentioned in the text; Donella Meadows, Peter Senge, Russell Ackoff, Jay Forrester, Larry Prusak, Ann M. Pendleton-Jullian, Christopher Alexander, Mel Conway, and many others.

Wise people, fortunately for me, have shared their expertise and friendship. Will Doran, Jessica Kerr, Elizabeth Ayer, Mark Jacobs, Dominic Scimeca, Indu Alagarsamy, and Paul Rayner are a few of those wise people. The Witches in Tech, a group of brilliant technologists who encourage and support each other, are my professional family. (You, dearest witches, are my happy place.)

I am profoundly grateful to the community of people figuring out systems design and helping knowledge workers thrive. My constant, current, teachers include Eric Evans, Trond Hjorteland, Kenny Baas-Schwegler, Chelsea Troy, Nick Tune, Mathias Verraes, Kent Beck, Ruth Malan, Eduardo da Silva, and many others who are impacting the industry in positive ways. (I wish I could mention them all!) Vaughn Vernon was the person who said, "You should write a book on this," and thanks to him, here we are.

Systems thinking is inherently cross-functional, and some of my best teachers are not software developers. Robin Raven showed me how to think from a product development perspective. Rebecca Moss and Anna Miklasch taught me the power and art of facilitation. Phil Kenny taught me to think and communicate visually. Dr. Evelyn Thar mentors my pragmatic, business-savvy thinking, as a colleague and a dear friend. Pam Santilli reminds me that being a whole person, outside of tech, matters too.

And then, there's Dom. When this project consumed me, my husband Dominic Laycock walked our dogs, cooked me meals, read the chapters, managed our finances, listened to my ideas, and encouraged me to rest. While simultaneously helping enterprise teams resolve their DevOps issues. On the weekends, while I was working on the couch, Dom was working alongside me. He is a brilliant technologist, a respectful ally, a delightful friend, and my beloved partner. Anything I can do well, I can do because, as a system, Dom and I are greater than the sum of our parts.

If you are reading this book, you are part of the community improving our systems. I look forward to everything you will contribute. You are not alone. Systems work can be challenging, and thank goodness you are willing to join me. I need you. Without you, we won't succeed.

— Diana Montalion
New York, July 2024

From Lisa:

When Diana approached me about doing illustrations for her book, I was delighted in many ways. First, she recalled that I had drawn a sketchnote for her episode of "Softwarearchitektur im Stream"[1] in October 2022, focusing on "Nonlinear Thinking." It has been a long time since then. Diana, nonetheless, kept this in mind.

Second, I found the subject itself to be captivating and intriguing at that time, and Diana graciously provided me with the opportunity to check out the book prior to its official release.

It is a fantastic book. One can anticipate ample opportunities for reflection, numerous "aha!" moments, and lots of practical examples, thereby dispelling even the most skeptical critics regarding the merits of systems thinking. She has written a reference book that reads like a novel, and you won't want to put it down and will recommend it to all your friends.

Diana, thank you for including me in this great book project. It is an honor to be given this opportunity.

— Lisa Maria Moritz,
Author of "Sketchnotes in der IT"
https://www.sketchnotes.tech

---

1 Episode 137, "Non-linear Thinking with Diana Montalion" (*https://oreil.ly/b_fOk*), software-architektur.tv.

PART I

A System of Thinking

This book is unabashedly about abstract thinking and reasoning. It describes practices, principles, tools, and ways of looking at your circumstances that increase your capacity for doing hard things. Software professionals are increasingly faced with relationally complex circumstances; these circumstances require systems thinking. Software is becoming systems of software. Here, you'll find a system for thinking about systems.

We have been taught to think linearly. We need that skill to develop software. We also need to think nonlinearly and develop approaches that support us when our usual reductionistic approaches fail. As knowledge workers in the systems age, we are developing approaches that help us think about, and improve, the systems we design and deliver.

Our thinking generates the concepts that we rely on when designing our systems. When our concepts work together in harmony, supporting a system's purpose, they have integrity. Fred Brooks says that "conceptual integrity is the most important consideration in systems design." Without conceptual integrity, our software systems are built by "many good but independent and uncoordinated ideas." Whether we recognize it or not, the coherence and interconnectedness of our concepts shape our technological systems.

To think in systems and create conceptual integrity, you need to become adept at shifting your perspective. Practices like learning, modeling with others, and discovering the root causes of systemic challenges support this mental flexibility. In Part I, you'll be introduced to systems thinking, practice cultivating conceptual integrity, and discover the mindshifts that help you think in systems.

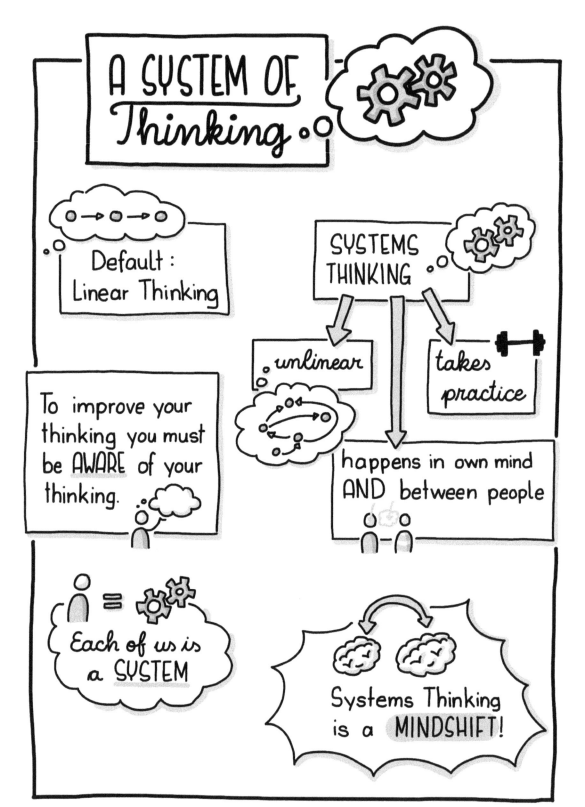

CHAPTER 1

What Is Systems Thinking?

Vision without systems thinking ends up painting lovely pictures of the future with no deep understanding of the forces that must be mastered to move from here to there.

—Peter Senge, *The Fifth Discipline* (Currency)

You might imagine that when you finish reading *Learning Systems Thinking*, you will have learned to think in systems. Nothing could be further from the truth. Systems thinking is a practice, a perspective, a framework, an emerging language…we could even call it a way of life.

Reading a book about tennis won't teach you to play tennis. You must go outside and play tennis. It's the same with systems thinking. Experience is needed to change your thinking. I hope that while you are reading this book, you will go outside and play with systems.

This book describes a system for thinking about systems. Reading it will give you context, guidance, vocabulary, and practices. What does a world in which I "think in systems" look like? How do I navigate toward it?

What do I do there? Why does it matter? What practices, principles, and tools will I need to be successful?

My favorite quick introduction to systems thinking is Figure 1-1.

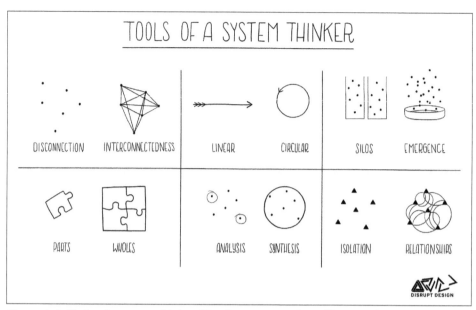

Figure 1-1. Tools of a system thinker (Credit: emmasegal.co, illustrator)

For technology professionals, this book is a journey from thinking about software to thinking about systems of software. It is also, perhaps more importantly, a journey away from reductionism and thinking about people and technology as separate entities.

It is a book about thinking. Because what we think, and communicate, is what we push to production.

Many of our approaches to developing software arose in the machine age. We cling tightly to the reductionist and mechanistic thinking they relied on. Forty years ago, our systems were primarily physical and mechanical. We read the printed newspaper, books from the library, letters in the mailbox. When we got lost, we asked a human for directions. In some ways, the type of thinking we needed, and were taught, fit our time.

Now we are in the systems age. We've created a vast, interrelated, and interdependent digital landscape of software to replace newspapers and libraries and postal mail and maps. Software shapes our online spaces, stores, and social experiences. Software structures infrastructure for other software.

Relational complexity, the number of variables we need to consider in order to make software decisions, is running riot. As software becomes systems of software, we have reached the limits of our traditional ways of thinking.

> In the Systems Age we tend to look at things as part of larger wholes rather than as wholes to be taken apart.
>
> —Russell L. Ackoff

This book is unashamedly about thinking. About abstract thinking. Many (many, many, many) times in my career, I have heard derision toward thinking (and communication), as if they're not matterful skills and activities. "That's too abstract. Make it concrete!"

I'm all for concrete. My house is built on a concrete foundation. But my stove and my bathtub and lawn and garden and dogs are not concrete. Concrete thinking is important, but it isn't *everything*. These things matter too: Creating concepts that guide our integrated decision making. Synthesizing multiple points of view. Looking under the surface of problems to discover their root causes. Transforming the mental models that structure our legacy software systems.

In the wilderness of systems, there is a lot less concrete.

Systems thinking expands our toolsets as knowledge workers. It steps us outside the constant, pointless culture war about architecture versus engineering as a practice. Systems are nondualistic—the choice isn't "ivory tower architect" versus "hands-on coder"…the choice is "which tool, practice, or approach will help us understand what we need to understand?"

Can you shift perspective and think differently?

The first step toward systems thinking is willingness. Willingness to see things differently, think deeply, practice self-awareness, and become curious about patterns and complexity. Willingness to change your mind and step into the unknown.

As Morpheus says to Neo in *The Matrix*:

> I can only show you the door. You're the one who has to walk through it.

Let's walk through the door together.

Linear Thinking Is the Default

> *[B]lack-and-white logic can sometimes work even for complex systems. But it ignores the ways in which parts interact with one another. Reductionism may serve to explain how a bird flies, but not how a flock of birds move in unison. It may describe internal combustion, but not traffic patterns. It may describe electric patterns in the brain, but not consciousness, and it's unlikely that anyone or anything—not even the world's most powerful computers— will ever fully analyze the interactions that make for healthy soil.*
>
> —Mark Bittman, *Animal, Vegetable, Junk* (Mariner)

We are taught to think linearly. Linear thinking is so ubiquitous, many of us don't recognize it as one type of thinking. We call it, simply, thinking: predictable, rational, repeatable, procedural, dualistic, top-down, and concerned with control. We rely on linear thinking to design, build and deploy, run, and maintain software.

Our experience in software has strengthened our linear thinking skills. Governed by our "if this, then that" causal thinking, we expect software systems to behave exactly as we intend them to behave, in all circumstances. In code, we speak a language designed to be unambiguous.

We expect the people who build software to behave in predictable, procedural, top-down controlled ways. Our preferred communication style reflects these expectations—straightforward, concrete, and concerned with control.

Linear thinking is reductionistic, understanding a whole by breaking it into parts. Object-oriented programming is reductionism. Software architecture approaches divide and conquer, "manage" complexity through modularity, and "decompose" problems into subproblems. We break software (or a system of software) into parts or components. We model boxes with lines between them. We fit people (teams) into those boxes.

When we outgrow that model, we re-create the boxes.

This book does not argue against linear thinking. Linear thinking isn't bad, and systems thinking isn't good, like the Witches of the East and North in *The Wizard of Oz*. We can't operate as knowledge workers without linear thinking. In some circumstances, excellent linear approaches are exactly what are needed! Linear thinking and approaches help us in a lot of ways:

- *Break down a complex problem* into its component parts so you can understand and solve it.
- *Analyze cause and effect.* Find the "bug" causing an unplanned effect. Design a change to produce a desirable effect.
- *Imagine the steps* involved in building something new *and take those steps*, adapting as you learn more.
- *Learn new programming languages*, tools, frameworks, rules, and processes. Apply those skills.
- *Identify weak ideas* and implementations, then work to improve them.
- *Iteratively build* new software behaviors, learning from the result.
- *Identify and follow best practices.* Change them as circumstances change.
- *Test ideas* to discover where they fail. Track valuable operational data.
- *Improve efficiency* by editing solutions until they are elegantly simple.

Linear and nonlinear thinking are interrelated. This book is a matterful addition to your bookshelf because linear approaches cannot resolve systemic issues.

We are in the systems era. As relational complexity increases, we need to think *differently*. Many of our challenges are systemic. We need to expand our skillset so we can think, communicate, and act as healthy systems.

Systems Thinking Is Nonlinear

Linear relationships are easy to think about: the more the merrier. Linear equations are solvable, which makes them suitable for textbooks. Linear systems have an important modular virtue: you can take them apart and put them together again—the pieces add up.

Nonlinear systems generally cannot be solved and cannot be added together. . . . Nonlinearity means that the act of playing the game has a way of changing the rules. . . . That twisted changeability makes nonlinearity hard to calculate, but it also creates rich kinds of behavior that never occur in linear systems.

— James Gleick, *Chaos: Making a New Science* (Open Road Media)

In a linear world, I would plant seven kale seeds, and 50 to 55 days later, I would harvest seven mature kale plants. When a rabbit nibbles one of my plants, I put a fence around the garden to keep rabbits out. They stay out. When the days become unusually hot, I know growth will take longer, so I adjust my expectations. This is the mindset we use when planning software initiatives.

In my actual garden, I sometimes get nine plants because kale is biennial and I planted some last year. Sometimes I get zero plants. When that happens, maybe it's rabbits; maybe it's deer reaching over the fence because their favorite foods are in low supply. Maybe there's been too much rain or not enough rain or too much heat in May or October. Maybe the soil doesn't have enough nitrogen or the cabbage worms or slugs ate them. Maybe the birds poked holes in the leaves while eating the snails who were eating the kale.

Most likely, the cause of zero plants is *some combination of these things*, impacting each other in difficult-to-predict ways. This, in its simplest form, is what we mean by nonlinear. Systems are not fully controllable and unpredictable. Relationships among parts impact what happens.

You may have built a single piece of software that, for the most part, operated in a relatively controlled environment. When I did that, I couldn't always predict what would happen when I pushed a change to production. But for the most part, I could mitigate the risk of unexpected outcomes.

For many of us, myself included, that time has passed. Software is everywhere, built on top of other pieces of software, interacting with multiple information sources, spanning the breadth of an organization with hacky bridges. New features are used in ways developers didn't intend. Modern software becomes "legacy" three minutes after we launch it. Software operates in ever-changing circumstances and depends on a flow of information in flux.

Some bad news: nonlinear approaches are invariably more difficult than linear ones. Your life is not about to get easier. Does this make you want to throw the book across the room? You already have so much to do. Now I'm telling you that nonlinear approaches involve doing the work *and* figuring out how to do the work *and* improving the ways we work *and* clarifying why the work matters *and* learning…all the time.

Learning all the time. Thinking deeply and also thinking deeply about thinking.

The good news is: you will become *more effective.* The work won't feel so much like work, which means you'll have more energy. Systems thinking *improves your capacity for doing difficult things.*

Nonlinear approaches increase signal and decrease noise.

In the world of information systems, we've built an entire digital ecosystem in less than 30 years. Software governs most of our human communication processes. That ecosystem is emergent…the sum is greater than the parts. Behaviors and trends arise from the relationships among the parts. The "like" button didn't just give Facebook users a quick way to comment; it transformed social constructs in unpredictable ways.

We are doing difficult things. We can't design nonlinear systems with linear thinking. For that, we need to expand our thinking toolset. We need to think in systems.

What Is Systems Thinking?

For those who stake their identity on the role of omniscient conqueror, the uncertainty exposed by systems thinking is hard to take. If you can't understand, predict, and control, what is there to do?

—Donella Meadows, The Donella Meadows Project (*https://oreil.ly/M6NwO*)

Nonlinear thinking is expressed in a myriad of forms. This book is called *Learning Systems Thinking.* That phrase, "systems thinking," has been defined in numerous, sometimes contradictory, ways across technology, business, and academia. The vocabulary to describe it is still emerging. Nonlinear thinking integrates more than systems thinking. Strategic thinking, for example, is systems thinking plus creative navigation toward change. Pattern thinking, parallel thinking, and systemic reasoning…all mean thinking in systems.

Learning teams are nonlinear thinking teams.

To some extent, it doesn't matter whether or not we share an unequivocal definition. The practices and the vocabulary we use to describe them are evolving. The definitions here will get us started. It's okay if they morph over time.

To define systems thinking, let's first consider what "system" means. Here are some definitions:

- A set of things working together as parts of a mechanism or an interconnecting network. (Oxford English Dictionary (*https://www.oed.com*))

- A system is a whole that consists of parts, each of which can affect its behavior and properties. The parts are interdependent. (Russel Ackoff (*https://oreil.ly/w8o6u*))

- An interconnected set of elements that is coherently organized in a way that achieves something (a goal). (Donella Meadows (*https://oreil.ly/9qjGG*))

- An arrangement of parts or elements that together exhibit behavior or meaning that the individual constituents do not. (The International Council on Systems Engineering (*https://oreil.ly/m5Obl*))

A system is also the set of principles or procedures according to which something is done; an organized framework or method. This is important because systems are sociotechnical. The principles and procedures people use and the framework or methods that structure our work are interrelated and inherently design our systems.

However else we define "system," it includes the ways we structure our thinking and approaches.

As software professionals, we are concerned with *software* systems. So for our purposes:

> A system is a group of interrelated hardware, software, people, organization(s), and other elements that interact and/or interdepend to serve a shared purpose.

Caution—this clear description gets muddy fast. Defining "purpose" depends on your point of view. Every piece of software serves a purpose. WordPress is a digital publishing tool. But that's not what I mean by purpose. Purpose is a property of the whole and doesn't inhere in any one component. What mission do the elements serve?

Imagine an organization whose mission is to tell the world about the health benefits of plant-based cooking. WordPress might be an element in that system. Other parts like social media publishing tools and Google Ads and an asset manager and recipe generation platforms might also play a role. The writer's labor in developing the information is an element in the system. As are the readers. Without the inputs (content) and outputs (consumers), the software doesn't serve a purpose.

Now that we've defined "system," what is "thinking"? Thinking has a surprising variety of definitions. When we are *systems thinking*, we use our minds to reason about something. Which is an interesting sentence…if I am using my mind to think, who is the "me" using my mind?

We aren't going to open a philosophical conundrum, delightful as that might be. But I do want to make the point that systems thinking is not only thoughts but also your awareness of thoughts. Thoughts that are intertwined with experiences, memories, judgment, and sensory information (like the look on someone's face).

In this book, we extend the definition of thinking to include structuring and communicating those thoughts. Whiteboarding is thinking. We don't simply think about code, we write code; we don't simply think about systems, we make artifacts. An artifact can be a document or a model, a Slack message or a conversation, anything that conveys thinking. In this way, systems thinking is hands-on.

What, then, is systems + thinking? Here are two "systems thinking" definitions:

> Systems thinking often involves moving from observing events or data, to identifying patterns of behavior over time, to surfacing the underlying structures that drive those events and patterns.
>
> —Michael Goodman, in Systems Thinker (*https://oreil.ly/2HDdj*)

> [Systems thinking] recognizes and prioritizes the understanding of linkages, relationships, interactions and interdependencies among the components of a system that give rise to the system's observed behavior. Systems thinking is a philosophical frame, and it can also be considered a method with its own tools.
>
> —The Alliance for Health Policy and Systems Research (*https://oreil.ly/JDTCb*)

In this book, I am defining systems thinking as a *practice*.

 Systems thinking is a system of foundational thinking practices that, when done together, improve nonlinear thinking skills.

Systems Thinking Is a Practice

The practices in this book don't represent the Definitive List of All Necessary Practices. Systems and nonlinear thinking are evolving, especially in the world of software systems, where we are just beginning to apply them. These practices are an excellent starting point, and you will discover more on your journey.

How we categorize the practices you'll find here doesn't really matter. For example, they blend "hard skills" and "soft skills" (in my experience, the soft skills are harder). Practicing will expand the thinking tools in your toolbox. Over time, practicing will improve your ability to apply these tools to "wicked" problems (problems with many interdependent factors that are in flux).

Systems thinking is a practice that happens in your own mind and among people. It restructures the thinking and communication processes around you, like the organizational structure at work. Practicing systems thinking inside of a linear-thinking organization is helpful but not transformational. We practice systems thinking alone, with others, and as a leadership practice.

The four parts of this book, and the chapters within each, are designed to introduce you to the capabilities of a systems thinker.

- Part I: Basic concepts and practices
- Part II: Working with your own mind
- Part III: Working with input from other people's minds and the system itself
- Part IV: Leadership in a nonlinear world

Through practice, you'll develop qualities that will enable you to do hard things with others and empower you to increase your value as a knowledge worker. We are all facing systems challenges—we need each other to figure out how.

Qualities of a Systems Thinker

There are no "12 Steps to Systems Thinking and the First One Will Surprise You!" listicles that will teach you everything you need to know in 10 minutes. There are no systems thinking whiteboard tests to pass or certification exams. You never finish learning about systems; they will teach you forever. So how do you know you are becoming good at systems thinking?

As you practice systems thinking skills, you will take on more complex challenges. With each new challenge, you will discover there is much more to learn. The paradox in systems thinking is that the more you know, the more you know that you don't know. We could say that the most valuable quality of a systems thinker is they know they don't know.

Here are some recognizable patterns and behaviors in people who think nonlinearly. People who are good at systems thinking regularly engage in some key actions:

- *Practice thinking.*
- *Recognize the difference between* reductionistic, analytical thinking *(linear) and* taking a systemic perspective *(nonlinear).* Discern when to apply one or the other (or both).
- *Describe solutions that are meaningfully connected to the context* and system-level purpose.
- *Know that people systems are inextricable from technical systems.* View challenges as inherently sociotechnical.
- *Shift perspective easily to explore challenges* from different points of view. Comfortably engage shifting mental models as circumstances change.
- When faced with recurring problems, *seek to understand the systemic structures* and feedback loops that block change.
- *Demonstrate high levels of self-awareness* and metacognition, especially about thinking patterns that are reactive, fallacious, or biased.
- *Avoid adding noise and blame,* recognize reactions, and shift toward responding.
- *Approach life with an "always learning" mindset.* Structure discovery, learning, and exploration with others proactively.
- *Communicate well-reasoned ideas, recommendations, and theories.* Articulate the reasoning behind conclusions.
- *Listen respectfully* and helpfully work with others to strengthen collective insights.
- *Understand how interrelated and interdependent parts act together to create patterns and processes.* Investigate the ways those patterns are reinforced.
- *Create conceptual models,* alone and with others, to guide impactful decisions. Have sufficiently diverse modeling techniques and use them improvisationally.
- *Accept that* uncertainty *is a natural, welcome, and inevitable part of life.*

As a systems architect, I do systems thinking full time, but you don't need to take that path. You can develop systems skills to complement your software-thinking skills. A complementary career ladder for most software professionals might look something like Figure 1-2.

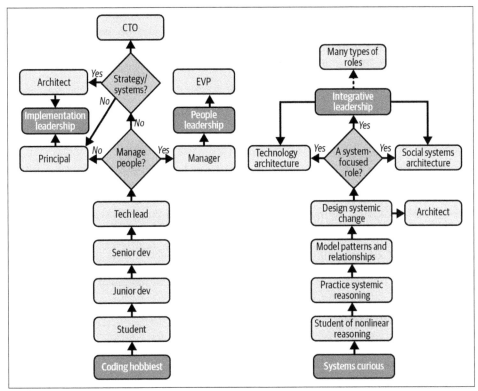

Figure 1-2. A career ladder for systems thinkers

Systems thinking is a mindshift, away from linear and reductionist approaches toward nonlinear ones. The "right" way to achieve this mindshift depends on your skills and circumstances. There are many right ways.

Chances are, you're already shifting. If you've adopted microservices or continuous integration or other interrelated software approaches, you've experienced some of this mindshift. If you do collective modeling, connect what you build to why it's valuable, or think about the relationships among software parts, you're thinking about systems. If you've improved patterns and processes in order to "fix" a recurring problem—systems thinking.

If you find that ambiguity troubling, buckle up, because systems thinking is full of ambiguity. You won't be careening around blind corners recklessly, though. You are shifting your expectations and enjoying the journey without always needing to know exactly where you are going.

When software systems are changing, software delivery skills like Go or AWS implementation tools or hypermedia API design are valuable and necessary. But they do not predict success. Brilliant software developers, product managers, and strategic leaders are often sincere and hard working, yet making little progress. We are all blocked by two obstacles:

1. We are spectacularly terrible at nonlinear thinking. We are constantly tangled up in our opinions, cognitive biases, fears, assumptions, conditioning, and logical fallacies. It takes practice to skillfully and consistently untangle ourselves.

2. We don't know that we are terrible at it. In fact, the worse we are at nonlinear thinking, the more certain we are that we are good at it!

Therein lies a paradox: we must be good at nonlinear thinking in order to see that we aren't good at nonlinear thinking.

Fortunately, as Carl Jung said:

> Only the paradox comes anywhere near to comprehending the fullness of life.

MAGO's Quandary

Throughout this book, I will describe a fictitious organization with increasingly common, real-world systems challenges. Meet MAGO.

For decades, MAGO published the most popular, internationally distributed magazine in the world. Their state-of-the-art publishing software and distribution system ensured each edition reached millions of people worldwide, on time, every Sunday.

In 2010, MAGO launched a website. Over the next few years, everything in print was also shared digitally, their articles, graphics, ads, and collections highlighting timely topics. Like most organizations, they built their digital presence with a single piece of software and then extended, customized, and scaled it by adding lots of caching. They encouraged the world to come view the information available at a URL. Page views quickly rose to millions per day.

MAGO, like most organizations at the time, translated a printed page into a web page. Their data architecture, delivery workflows, and software choreography revolved around the concept of a "page." HTML was invented to structure digital pages. MAGO didn't realize that the emerging global information system that is the internet would shift the paradigm. Today, what does "page" mean in a world where people share content everywhere?

An entire ecosystem of organizational infrastructure arose during this shift. Decoupling the subscription workflow, tracking and analyzing reader behaviors, monitoring system availability, morphing assets (like images) into varying shapes, sizes, and types. Business processes were digitized, as were payroll, hiring, and events management (something MAGO was known for). Communication tools became inextricable from productivity, enabling distributed teams to meet, plan work, and track progress.

The world around MAGO's website became increasingly interconnected. They needed to also show up on search engine results, social media platforms, news aggregators, and video and audio platforms. The world, not just the website, needed a steady diet of content. Discussions about published articles, which MAGO hoped to track, moved away from comments on a page and happened wherever people chatted.

People accessing information on their desktops wanted different information than people on their phones. MAGO built an app, then another. Soon that wasn't sufficient. People expected information to morph in the browser depending on the device they used to access it or where they were geographically. The demand for information *in context* was quickly becoming the norm.

As bandwidth increased, so did the demand for multimedia content. MAGO expanded staff to create extended video stories, podcasts, and custom interactive graphics to show data trends. Each of these innovations required software systems to support them.

The biggest change was the increase in asynchronous workflows. Publishing no longer fit into a weekly, or even a daily, rhythm. Various content and the software supporting it went through various delivery workflows. More people needed to keep these workflows in sync as the foundational systems structure, delivering pages, was quickly eroding. Information was increasingly ubiquitous, and the shape of information was transmuting. In fact, the shape of everything was changing.

To keep up with the relentless pace of modern technology, the MAGO team built a lot of software. As it became increasingly difficult to continue extending the original, now legacy, digital software, product people went rogue and built separate websites for new content. The software created, over time, an ad hoc collection of mostly dissociated parts. Very few people could name all the parts or knew how they functioned. The system looked like a Rube Goldberg machine (*https://oreil.ly/L92o6*), with production people moving data by hand (see Figure 1-3). It emerged that MAGO was facing a Quandary.

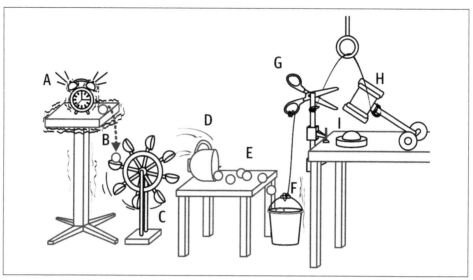

Figure 1-3. MAGO's legacy software works, just barely, most of the time, but it's held together with duct tape and chewing gum

As relational complexity increased, it became clear that continuing to expand the current system was not going to work. How many pieces of software can be duct-taped together? They could effectively ignore this problem—until the pandemic. Six months after lockdown began, the maintainers of their core software went out of business.

MAGO's initial reaction was "replace the software now!" But the company went out of business because organizations no longer buy the 20-year-old software that MAGO relies on. The paradigm had shifted. Rather than keep going the way they'd been going, MAGO's Quandary became: How do we design a system that meets the demands of the modern systems age?

As we explore systems thinking and nonlinear approaches, we will come back to MAGO's Quandary.

> If you happen to know that I've architected systems for organizations like *The Economist* and the Wikimedia Foundation, you might wonder if MAGO is a thinly veiled tell-all. While the fictitious examples you'll read in this book are inspired by real-world experiences, they reflect modern patterns and challenges faced by many, if not most, information systems. Any resemblance to actual people or specific organizations is simply because everyone is trying to figure out how to evolve into the systems age.

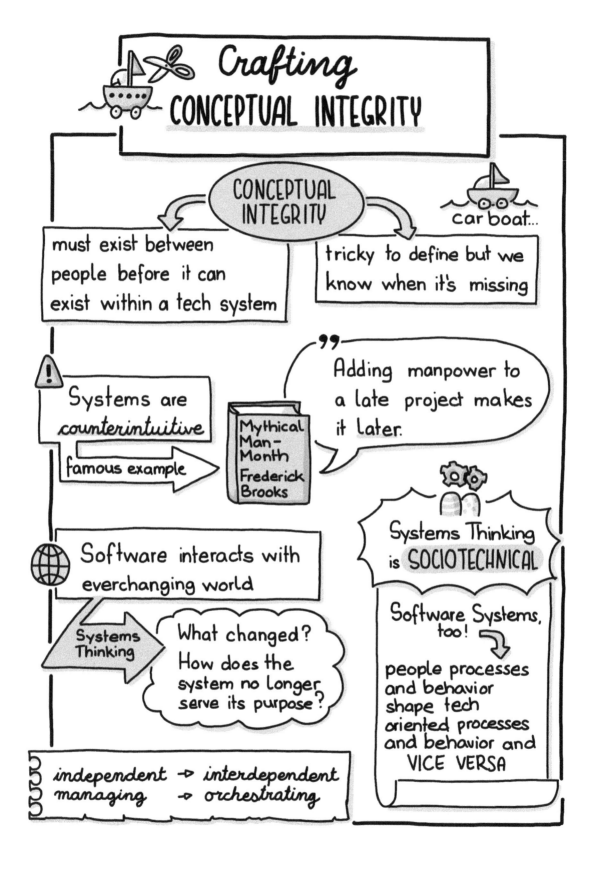

CHAPTER 2

Crafting Conceptual Integrity

Conceptual integrity is the most important consideration in system design.
—Frederick P. Brooks Jr., *The Mythical Man-Month: Essays on Software Engineering*
(Addison-Wesley)

Our ideas design our systems. When an idea floating in our stream of consciousness takes shape, becomes meaningful, matterful, helpful, or relevant, the idea becomes a concept. Whether we recognize it or not, the coherence and interconnectedness of our concepts shape our technological systems.

Concepts are our primary tool in systems design. Everything running in production represents our concepts—the ideas we prioritized, communicated, structured, and adapted with others, then crafted into code. Concepts also structure the way we think about the technology systems we encounter or inherit. If we want to change what is running in production, we need to first change our concepts, the way we think about what is running in production.

When our ideas are cohesive and in good relationship with each other; when they are supported by healthy, shared patterns and principles; when we push code changes that improve the system's ability to serve its purpose, we create conceptual integrity.

Concepts become actionable when people in an organization communicate them. Ideas get into production through a process of structured communication. Sometimes that structure is two engineers whiteboarding; sometimes it's a RACI model. The impact of that structure is massive. As Conway's Law (*https://oreil.ly/rFa1g*) states, "Organizations, who design systems, are constrained to produce designs which are copies of the communication structures of these organizations."

When our concepts can't work together in harmony to serve a purpose, our software systems will reflect that lack of integrity. Integrity is the measure of how well a system operates as a whole. Linear thinking has skewed this measurement toward prioritizing efficiency and profit generation. Efficiency is important, but it causes systemic problems when it's dissociated from the impact. For example, an efficient and profitable system that generates poverty for workers or pollution for the environment *includes* those aspects of the system. Conceptual integrity is understanding the whole system, not just the parts we optimize.

In *The Mythical Man-Month*, Fred Brooks describes the lack of conceptual integrity as a software system with "many good but independent and uncoordinated ideas." Many good but independent and uncoordinated ideas…describes nearly every software system I've encountered.

When conceptual integrity is low (or missing), you might see situations like the following:

- We can't share data across the digital ecosphere because of silos. (In the technology system and the people system.)
- Software is wired directly to other software with that one Python script someone wrote 10 years ago. We can't break that chain, ever.
- We can't work effectively across teams or roles. Teams openly distrust (or even dislike) each other and defend silos. Patronizing communication is considered normal.
- We can't "do DevOps" because the legacy software has become a giant ball of mud with painful weekly (monthly, quarterly, yearly) releases.
- Product teams avoid building things "the right way" because it's too hard. They've built seventeen "side products" that are duct-taped together. Three of them are doing the exact same thing for different teams.
- There is no shared, semantically meaningful data structure among the software. One database talks directly to another database, skipping the logic (software) layer because, well, that was the easiest thing to do.
- It's difficult to tell what the parts are there to *do*; there is no domain language in the software.
- Technical debt is how we describe the lack of cohesion in the system.

Conceptual integrity means that parts of a system are in good relationship to each other. What is a "good" relationship? It depends. On the spectrum between a tightly coupled monolith and decoupled software silos, there exists the land of ambiguity. In that space, there is more than one "right" answer, and it's difficult to know what is "right." Conceptual integrity helps us design interdependence, information sharing, and patterns that shape system dynamics by helping us discern what might work, right here, right now, for this system.

A microservices architecture that solves a problem for one organization might cause a disastrous problem in another organization. You can't do what Netflix does and expect the same results. Information systems that worked brilliantly in 2019 became totally obsolete in 2020 when the pandemic hit. Conceptual integrity helps us discern, to stay open to multiple interpretations, yet still design and build relationships in systems.

Relationship design is systems design.

Relationships Produce Effect

You think that because you understand "one" that you must therefore understand "two" because one and one make two. But you forget that you must also understand "and".

—Donella Meadows, *Thinking in Systems: A Primer* (Chelsea Green Publishing)

Donella Meadows defines systems thinking as how "parts together produce an effect that is different from the effect of each part on its own."

Relationships produce effects. Software becomes a system of software when "parts together" achieve something that could not exist without the "together" part. When "parts together" no longer fit our circumstances, we usually can't simply change a piece of software. We need to change the way software interrelates.

Creating conceptual integrity involves understanding the effect produced by relationships. For example, there may be two pieces of software that each does something valuable, but the relationship between them produces a bottleneck in the system.

When we think about systems, we consider some key things:

- How do the parts interdepend?
- How do they share information?
- What are the patterns that keep the relationships functioning?
- What are the patterns that block the system from evolving?
- Can we improve the relationships and patterns to deliver the highest-value outcomes?

Linear thinking can have a major negative impact on conceptual integrity. Reductionism, breaking down complexity into parts in order to design, build, and control those parts, inherently reduces our understanding of how relationships produce their own effects. Interdependence, information sharing, and patterns shape our system's dynamics as much as the parts themselves.

Let's use a neighborhood as an example. We can map property boundaries and show that they contain structures like houses and X number of people. We can label the spaces providing services, like a police station or elementary school. Will this map help us *understand* the neighborhood? Will it help us predict how the neighborhood will change over time as circumstances change?

In a neighborhood, infrastructure like water and sewer lines are in relationship to the ecosystem (like wildlife). Local agriculture feeds (or not) the people and impacts the system design (where to put grocery stores, for example). Our concepts are in relationships with each other…the demographics of a neighborhood, the groups people form by proximity, will influence the way a neighborhood grows. Shared language, for example, can form a boundary around a neighborhood that won't be visible on a map.

All of these relationships form circumstances, and those circumstances depend on patterns. When events change those patterns in unpredictable ways, the parts of the system are impacted in unpredictable ways. A sudden event, like the closing of a factory, can trigger complex systemic problems that don't have a quick and easy solution. Events that happen more slowly, like decreased demand for local services or gentrification, have a similar impact over time.

Changes can be restrictive, like the loss of water access. Or expansive, like improvements in digital connectivity. A change in traffic patterns turns a quiet area into a noisy one. A global pandemic impacts neighborhoods designed for commuters. Interdependent changes will transform a neighborhood in unique ways. None of these changes are shown on the property model.

Events transform a neighborhood *because of the relationships among elements.*

When our software systems don't behave as we intended, too often we consider that a failure. Yet, in my experience, unexpected results are far more common than "everything worked perfectly on the first try." Why not embrace the fact that systems will surprise us? If we pay attention, the surprises can also teach us. In software systems, relationships are driving the digital revolution. Like all revolutions, danger and opportunity are working together to serve a purpose…conceptual integrity helps us keep our attention on that purpose.

Systems Thinking Is Sociotechnical

So, what is a system? A system is a set of things—people, cells, molecules, or whatever—interconnected in such a way that they produce their own pattern of behavior over time.
—Donella Meadows

For many software professionals, the biggest mindshift when thinking in systems is also the most important one: software systems are sociotechnical. When I say our systems are *sociotechnical*, I mean that our thinking, behaviors, and communication patterns are inextricable from the software systems we produce. I mean that the relationships among our mental models, our ideas about how the world works, powerfully influence how we act. Our software systems reflect what we think we know. And we also have to consider external factors, the world around us and cultural pressures.

 You can't improve the technology system without improving the people system. And vice versa. From a systems perspective, they are one and the same.

Thinking in systems, developing conceptual integrity, includes the whole ball of wax, not just the code running in production. As you'll see in Chapter 3, underneath our decisions about code is a world of patterns, structures, and mental models influencing us. We are also tricked by cognitive biases and logical fallacies, as you'll see in Chapter 7. Our thinking is influenced by code we've already delivered! Patterns of behavior in the software system impact the way people think about the software.

Three microservices running in Google Cloud are not necessarily a system. By themselves, they are a collection of software. A collection becomes a system when there is a relationship among the parts.

A team is a collection of people. A team becomes a thinking system when there are relationships among the team members. The team is also in relationship with other teams and the organizational structure. There is a relationship between the team and the mission they serve in the world. There is a relationship between the team and the software they build (including the languages and tools they use to build it).

Linear thinking doesn't simply describe how we think about code. It shapes what we expect from people too—that is, we expect them to be predictable, rational, repeatable, procedural, dualistic, and concerned with control. People's ideas are rewarded, punished, adopted, or ignored depending on how well those ideas match the organization's ideas about "how we do things."

In a traditional, linear, top-down approach to change, "leadership" thinks about and communicates strategies that are implemented by teams. Reality, though, challenges this approach. For example, without input from the team, how does leadership know how long something will take to build? Deciding that a new feature must be delivered in three days doesn't make it possible. "Agile was invented because reality refuses to bow down to power" (Joe Eaton, systems engineer).

Reality exists in the relationship between the strategy and its real-world implementation. Vertical hierarchies don't leave space for uncertainty, for understanding how strategy and implementation are integrated into an impactful change. Sometimes you change one thing and all hell breaks loose. Sometimes you give users the feature they say they most want and nobody uses it. We can't be certain how a change, in the midst of relational complexity, will play out.

Say a service that returns critical information is too slow. The team adds autoscaling to make the responses faster under load. It works as intended until the third-party software that the service uses to translate time zone data stops responding. The interdependent software's database couldn't return asynchronous results fast enough. The critical information isn't merely slow now—it's dead, until a fix is applied.

Initiatives like "digital transformation" or "modernization" or "monolith to microservices" can't be a (strictly) top-down initiative because they aren't linear changes. If an organization tries to design and deliver a system inside of a linear thinking structure, it will struggle, and likely fail, to deliver lasting change. It'll deliver *something*, but that something will lack conceptual integrity.

Here's a metaphorical example: One group in an organization wants a car. Another group wants a boat. Rather than resolve these different perspectives at the systems level, both groups push their new product. The engineers are told to build a carboat. Everyone hates it; nobody wanted a carboat.

I've seen *so* many carboats. The two groups needed a systems-level change, but there was no process for reconciling their needs into an evolving systems design. Only a battle of wills that, from a systems perspective, everybody lost.

Some groups flip the top-down approach and adopt a strictly bottom-up approach. Individuals and teams should do whatever they want; they are the experts. Bottom-up communication structures, by themselves, aren't a magic bullet. Anarchistic approaches potentially create the antithesis of conceptual integrity, "many good but independent and uncoordinated ideas" (Brooks).

In between top-down and bottom-up is systems design. Empowered teams aren't empowered by total control and independence; they are empowered by the ability to self-organize collaborative work. To share knowledge in ways that enable them to produce a positive impact on the system as a whole. In non-human systems, self-organizing systems develop hierarchy to serve the needs of subsystems. Hierarchy, in systems, is there to improve information sharing. We can learn a lot about sociotechnical systems by studying other systems.

The book *Bad Blood* by John Carreyrou (Vintage) describes the limitations of human hierarchies. In this true story of a billion-dollar fraud perpetrated by a Silicon Valley startup, there are familiar social patterns at scale:

- A disconnect between engineering reality and leadership demands. Communication runs down the hierarchy but not up. Essential feedback loops are missing.
- So many communication silos.

- A disconnect between PowerPoint presentations and reality. Product-driven demands reflect no concern for the system as a whole.
- The inability to solve complex problems together because trust, psychological safety, and effective feedback loops, all necessary for systemic reasoning (which we will explore in Chapter 7), are missing.
- Performance is measured by aggressive monitoring of hours worked rather than actual value produced. Forceful pressure is applied to "inspire" people to work harder or deliver faster.
- Having to defend novel or unwelcome recommendations to near exhaustion is normal.

Most of us have not experienced anything as extreme as Theranos, the company described in *Bad Blood*. Theranos exhibited all the harmful patterns, all the time. But many familiar daily-life norms in technology work, the fact that we think of them as reasonable, masked the harm that these norms can create at scale.

In my experience, successful teams that effectively deliver difficult changes have also been enjoyable teams. The ability to think well together is not only energizing and productive; it's a business-critical skill. "Psychological safety allows for moderate risk-taking, speaking your mind, creativity, and sticking your neck out without fear of having it cut off—just the types of behavior that lead to market breakthroughs" (Laura Delizonna, Stanford University).

Exhausting teams, overfocused on power and control, have been my worst career experiences, not because they were difficult to work on (they were) but because they delivered very little meaningful change.

We inhabit, you could say we embody, the systems we develop. Small changes in the way we think and communicate scale to big changes in the software system.

That's how systems work.

Counterintuitiveness

When we want to change a system, we aren't looking for "fixes," we are looking for leverage points. Leverage points are places in a system "where a small shift in one thing can produce big changes in everything," as Donella Meadows puts it (*https://oreil.ly/4V8f-*). We'll explore leverage points in Chapter 10—there are topics we need to explore before we dive in too deeply. Finding leverage points is the most difficult, and most powerful, practice in systems thinking.

For now, let's imagine that you've discovered that a relationship between two teams, and the services they develop, is blocking an impactful change. For example, the two services share information by directly coupling a relational database. Other services need this information, and more tight coupling is planned. You realize that if you structure the information using semantically sensible keys and then share it via an API, you will enable other services to make use of the information they need. This change will bring new services online quicker, services that meet the system's emerging needs. Plus, as a bonus, you can replace legacy migration scripts with a tidier and more sustainable process long term.

You tell everyone, "Hey! Look! This idea will solve a big problem!" And nobody believes you. They don't believe you because of counterintuitiveness. Donella Meadows says, "And we know from bitter experience that, because of counterintuitiveness, when we do discover the system's leverage points, hardly anybody will believe us."

The most powerful insight of my career was learning about counterintuitiveness. Changes that "make sense" in a system make sense to us because they match what we already think and know. When we discover a leverage point, a change in a system that we previously didn't see, it isn't "intuitive." It doesn't seem right to us because it works against what we know. The common, inevitable, reaction is doubt. We don't believe it; we don't listen; we need to experience a learning process.

The "right" answer to a systems challenge will rarely be the one fix that our linear minds offer. "Right" is in quotes because there is rarely a "right" answer, only the best possible answer under the circumstances. We have developed an intuition for familiar systemic patterns. To solve systems challenges, we usually need to change those patterns. We are blind to, and uncomfortable with, ideas that run counter to our "intuition." When we are thinking in systems, the best answer will often push against what we "know."

Jay Forrester, systems pioneer at MIT, describes how many organizations know exactly where they need to make a change. They recognize the leverage point, but...

> Then I've gone to the company and discovered that there's already a lot of attention to that point. Everyone is trying very hard to push it IN THE WRONG DIRECTION!

In the oft-quoted *Mythical Man-Month*, Brooks expresses what is, perhaps, the most famous example of counterintuitiveness in tech:

> Adding manpower to a late software project makes it later.

Counterintuitiveness isn't a bad thing—it is inescapable. We always have blind spots. Systems thinking is proactively looking for them. Actions we take in a software system are *always* an experiment; we can never be certain we'll get the desired result. We increase our chances when our reasoning about that action is sound, relevant, and cohesive. In Chapter 7, we will practice systemic reasoning, the art and science of creating sound and cohesive recommendations.

As you embrace the practice of systems thinking, you are also embracing this fact: you will go the wrong way, make a bad situation worse, fix a mistake with another mistake. In systems, we aren't trying to do the right thing every time because that is impossible. Systems are always in flux.

A System in Flux

We design software to operate in a particular circumstance, at a particular time, serving a particular purpose. But things change. Software interrelates with an ever-changing world. Which means we are ever-changing our conceptual models. Conceptual integrity isn't a static thing; it's a quality we are constantly creating, in a system and in ourselves.

We learn through experience; both the good stuff and the frustratingly recurring stuff teach us. As we learn, we evolve our concepts. The integrity of those concepts, at any given moment, depends on flux, what is flowing in and what is flowing out.

When we move from a monolith to microservices, for example, we are learning new implementation skills, which are significant. We are also learning new ways to think about the world. The monolith fit the world it was born into. The microservices are needed for a new world. What's changed?

A systems perspective depends on understanding what changed. How does the system no longer serve its purpose? (And if the system *is* serving its purpose just fine, why are you redesigning it?) In the new world, the new paradigm, where microservices improve the system, we don't simply need new technology tools—we need new patterns and relationships, in the tech and in the people building it. What needs to change?

To think about this change, let's use Donella Meadows' simplest drawing of a system (Figure 2-1). The middle box is the state of a system: the information, physical parts, and activities it contains at any given time. In our example, it's the monolith, the one large application. Inflows are what we put into the software, and outflows are what we get as a result.

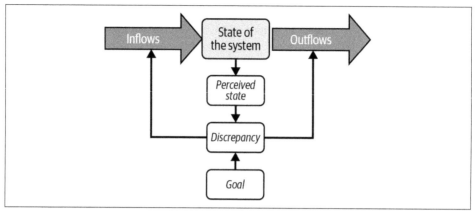

Figure 2-1. Donella Meadows' basic system model

When we want the software to output something different, we are identifying a discrepancy. What we want the software to do is different from what the software currently does. This can be a bug or a way that the software isn't serving the system's purpose. Users increasingly access information on their phones, for example, and the information was designed for a bigger display window. This can be a change that improves the system's ability to serve its purpose. "Users can't see their past purchases, which inhibits our ability to form long-term relationships with our customers." We set a goal, "Enable users to click a button and see their past purchases." We change the inflows by pushing new code or information or both, until users can see their recent purchases.

In a linear thinking process, this is the end. Delivered! But users clicking that button will generate more insight into the discrepancies. Does the data display quickly or does it lag? Does the new code break something elsewhere in the codebase? Was the data we stored about a transaction the same data users want to see? Users ask, "Can I quickly reorder something I've ordered in the past?" "Can I see the status of an order I haven't received?" This system model isn't linear—deliver and done. It's a constant state of learning: observing, analyzing, discerning, designing, and redesigning.

Now imagine that this basic model is a microservice, a single service in relation to other services. The core model is the same. We identify a desired change (a discrepancy between what we want to happen and what is happening). This application has a state, like the monolith.

But where is the state of the system as a whole? When you have software parts in relationship, like in Figure 2-2, you can see that there are asynchronous states in a system.

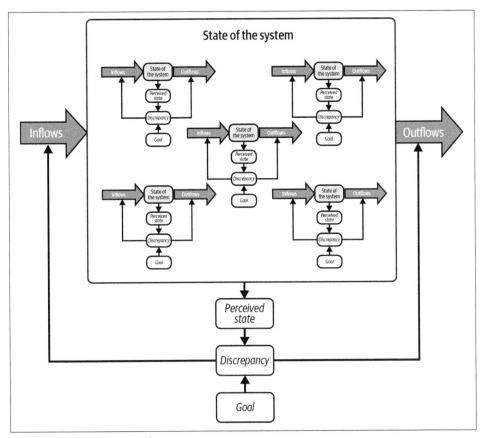

Figure 2-2. A system of software

This demonstrates what I mean by "relational complexity." The state of the system becomes something ubiquitous, inside the software and in the relationships among the software and in the relationship between the system and the world around it. This figure shows one inflow and one outflow for the system as a whole, but often, there are more than one.

If there is a discrepancy, where in the system do you make a change?

The answer to that question is "it depends." Fortunately, systems thinking helps you discern what "it depends on" as you learn how relationships produce effect.

Changes in a system, regardless of the level of relational complexity, happen over time. Over time, the discrepancy in any given area becomes zero. *Time is always a factor* in systems because the state changes over time.

The states change over time nonlinearly. The basic model hides the complexity in most real-life systems because we rarely have one goal at a time. Also, you can't control everything happening outside the state box while the discrepancy diminishes. While you are changing a system, the world is changing around it.

A System of Ideas

The true system, the real system, is our present construction of systematic thought itself, rationality itself, and if a factory is torn down but the rationality which produced it is left standing, then that rationality will simply produce another factory.
—Robert Pirsig

The state box I used earlier to describe software can hold intangible things too, like trust. If you lie about the status of work in progress, the state of trust will lower (over time). If you are transparent, trust increases.

Imagine that the state box is full of ideas. Ideas about how the system works, how it should work, what needs to be changed, and how people should work together. Ideas about top priorities, methods for delivering software, OKRs, and which capabilities are business-critical. The box includes everyone's opinion about which tools are best to use, how to ensure quality, and what defines a good culture.

In Figure 2-3, I've added thinking.

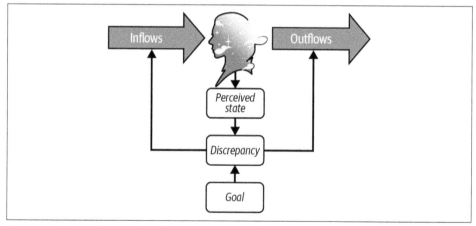

Figure 2-3. Donella Meadows' basic system model plus thinking

Thoughts flow in and actions flow out. In the state box, there are a myriad of attitudes, points of view, opinions, recommendations, knowledge about the technology system (both accurate and inaccurate), and its impact on people...all tumbling around like clothes in a dryer, becoming entangled.

The same thing is happening in our own minds.

When we think in systems, we create cohesion, harmony, a sense of order from that pile of idea laundry. We integrate and synthesize disparate ideas, knowledge, points of view, and activities until we can see and express what matters most to do, under the circumstances. We look at the patterns and relationships, improve our understanding of how things work, until we can see a path toward matterful change.

Time Is Always a Factor

*People assume that time is a strict progression of cause to effect, but **actually** from a non-linear, non-subjective viewpoint—it's more like a big ball of wibbly wobbly...time-y wimey...stuff.*

—Doctor Who

As I said earlier, *time is always a factor* in systems. We like to imagine time as linear and synchronous. We create Gantt charts and set milestones and take "next steps." We manage time with calendars that structure our social attention. We use time-tracking apps to record the time it takes to complete tasks. We are very, very careful about our software's uptime, query and response times, and on-time delivery.

These are all helpful tools, when used with awareness. I write (this book, for example) in regular, structured sessions. I put on my noise-canceling headphones, start my background-music timer, and write for 44 minutes while ignoring (usually, mostly, kinda) mental urges to check email-Slack-Mastodon or do the Wordle.

Yet a lot of "writing" happens in the time between sessions. Insights, thoughts, and mental images arise in my mind at all hours. When I'm deep in a project, other habits stop working for me because my attention has shifted. (I take longer to respond to email, for example.) I get pulled back in randomly.

For example, while writing this book, I get feedback from Shira, my editor, who reveals a blind spot that needs my attention. I drop what I am doing to explore it. No matter how good you are at systems thinking, you will have blind spots. In my case, while writing, I struggle with the curse of expertise. I describe a concept using a concept that you, the reader, might not know yet. But I don't notice because my mind thinks that everyone knows whatever I know. I need people like Shira to have my back. You also need Shiras, because you have and will continue to have blind spots.

Writing is chaotic, and if I hold the chaos at bay, I can't create something novel. If I surrender to the chaos and get swept up in it, I can't create anything at all.

Wibbly wobbly, timey wimey. Linear, synchronous progress exists inside a nonlinear, asynchronous reality that is co-creating something new. That's okay, we don't need to fix that. We just need to recognize that nonlinear time impacts the way we code, the people processes and the patterns we design.

When I'm writing code, I enjoy writing it, running it, and seeing (immediately) what happens. Direct, logical feedback. If it's broke, I fix it.

Nowadays, this feedback loop is increasingly time-delayed. Changing one event in one part of the system might trigger unwanted behavior elsewhere. My IDE can't catch that. Layers of caching, eventual consistency, or explicitly designed time delays make "seeing" what was happening in real time across a system challenging. I need insight, through observability, into what happens over time. And I think about what I'm learning about time as I'm coding.

Similarly, the timing of people processes is changing. When I worked as one of three engineering teams pushing code to a monolith, we did code reviews as if we were one team. We followed the best practices for that software (defining the way we wrote tests, for example), and the syntax rules were shared by everyone.

Now, different parts of the organization build different software that interrelates (or not). Or we are building the same software but because of siloed budgets and very little time or tolerance for designing systemic relationships, we stuff conflicting outflows in simultaneously.

We are also designing relationship patterns, and those are all about timing. Fifteen microservices and/or four teams, working on different software parts, will be inherently asynchronous. Changes are happening asynchronously—the changes we intended and the changes we did not intend.

Questions we consider:

- How do the circumstances change over time?
- What happens in response to a high-impact event?
- What is the root cause of that event? (Why do things happen how they happen and when they happen?)

 Caution: I have heard teams describe asynchronicity as the ability to be "independent." For example, decoupling the frontend software from the backend software so that the two teams can work independently. There is still a *relationship* between those teams, and with the rest of the organization. Those relationships are part of a system.

Even when a team tries to "manage" complexity by building a fortress surrounded by a moat filled with crocodiles to protect the boundaries of their software, that team is still part of a sociotechnical system. A system that includes crocodiles. The software is still part of a system. We still need to understand how the people, and the software, are interdependent. (And understand why we are building fortresses.)

We often use the word "manage" in relation to time. We manage projects and people, complexity and infrastructure. But when projects, people, and patterns act asynchronously, and in unexpected ways, we find ourselves in a muddle.

Systems thinking shifts our attention toward "orchestrating," a more subtle and artful approach. People and activities are viewed as interdependent and interrelated, like a symphony. The whole has cohesion and understandability even though the parts are played in their own time.

Independent and interdependent; manage and orchestration...these are examples of the many conceptual shifts we make when we shift from thinking about software to thinking about systems of software. In the next chapter, we'll explore more conceptual shifts and introduce the Iceberg Model, a core tool for thinking about systems.

Support for Your Practice: Riding on the Front of the Train

Practicing systems thinking and nonlinear approaches has welcome benefits. You can tackle more-complex problems, recommend changes that improve conceptual integrity, grow and learn constantly, build things that matter to the people who use them. With practice, you will be correct more often (in the long run), and, more importantly, you will enjoy thinking with others.

There is one challenge that is, perhaps, not as welcome. Because of counterintuitiveness, you will sometimes be alone, thinking differently, with no one (yet) validating your perspective. In the face of invalidation, sometimes you will change your mind because your thinking is unsound. Sometimes you'll stand your ground because your thinking is sound. Always, it can be challenging to discern the difference.

I have struggled with this challenge, both personally and professionally.

"Nobody thinks like you, Diana." I am standing in the kitchen, leaning on a table edge, across from my partner (at the time) who is sitting on the counter. He is ranting about a work situation, full of pent-up frustration. I've just offered a strategic recommendation for changing his situation. He didn't welcome it.

Fuss, Don't Fix. That's what I call this habit. Blaming our frustration on external circumstances but not changing those circumstances. That's what he's doing. He is certainly not alone, I Fuss but Don't Fix. You probably do too, at least sometimes. There is, as we will see in the next chapter, a lot of blaming circumstances in systems.

"Nobody thinks like you." He was rejecting my thinking because it didn't fit "the norm" in his situation. Ironic, given that the norm in his situation was frustrating him. I was thinking differently.

Perhaps you've had this experience? If you haven't, as you improve your ability to think in systems, you will. Having a perspective that is "outside the norm," feeling alone with a reality denied, is, I'm sorry to tell you so early in our journey together, part of systems design.

My architect colleague, Mark, calls it "the front of the train." He first used that phrase during a meeting in London. We were sitting on uncomfortable chairs in a borrowed office, facing each other. I was jet lagged and Fussing Not Fixing a situation I'd flown over to discuss. "They just don't get it!" I said. "This is important!" I said.

"Diana," he replied gently but firmly, "you are on the front of the train. You look out and see a forest. You say, 'Look at the trees!' People riding in the other cars say, 'What are you talking about? That's a lake!' You don't get to be mad at them. They aren't looking at the trees yet. Riding in the front of the train is your job."

Front of the train thinking is systems thinking and design. Which brings us straight to the hard cheese: there is no technology you can adopt, group you can join, role you can be promoted into, tool you can use, or solution you can recommend that will work universally. This book can't tell you how to "fix" situations using management techniques, using Kubernetes clusters, or hiring more "juniors." People will want you to give them templated solutions, easy answers to complex problems. You can't do that, most of the time.

There is no magic bullet. Even if there was a magic bullet, you'd be standing there holding it, and nobody would believe you. People don't see magic; they see what they expect to see. You need to show people, over time, how the magic works.

You can't know if you are right, but being right is always temporary anyway. Nonlinear approaches value seeing things as they are (and can be). Working with others to get input that strengthens your thinking. Gracefully letting go of wrong views. And being patient, kind, and curious about other people's perspectives while you learn (and learn and learn) to be "right" together.

What works in any circumstance…depends. Depends on the context, depends on the people, depends on how integrous (or not) the communication flow is. Depends on what you say and why people don't want to hear it. Depends on a myriad of factors.

Systems thinking is figuring out what "it depends" on. Then communicating new ways of seeing until people can see it. To become good at communicating, you'll need to practice thinking and communicating your thinking.

Your Practice: Writing as Thinking

A powerful tool for practicing systems thinking is writing. We will dive deeper into using writing as a thinking practice in Chapter 4. Let's begin with an exercise. Grab paper and pen, open a note-taking app, talk to Siri, however you'd like to work. Set a timer for 20 minutes and explore these questions:

Remember a time when you (and your teammates) had a goal, a change that you wanted to make to a system.

- What was the goal? What was the process of resolving the discrepancy, moving from the current state to the goal state?

- How were the ideas being shared? What was the structure or template used? Where were they stored?

- Whose ideas were they? In retrospect, were there ideas that might have been helpful but weren't available or heard?

- What was the output? How well did the output match the goal? How do you know?

- What was the impact of time? Was there a longer-term impact? Did the change(s) trigger changes elsewhere?

- Did counterintuitiveness play a role? Did you discover later that the problem persisted in a different form?

- Do you see any opportunities for improving the process you just described?

Counterintuitive MAGO

When MAGO experienced the loss of their core software, the mandate from the CEO was: Replace the Software, Quick! This makes sense; the organization faced a business-critical crisis, and this pointed directly to the problem.

Except that the problem didn't just happen. It had been creeping up on them for 20 years. And during those decades, they inadvertently made the problem worse by adding complexity to the system that solved the short-term problems (serving digital content in multiple contexts) but made the system's relational patterns difficult, if not impossible, to change.

The concepts that informed the state of the system arose from producing a publication (a magazine, in print and digital). As the system grew, these concepts became blockers. What does it mean to distribute content to many platforms, serving many contexts? How is that different from producing a publication? If MAGO replaces the software with a similar software, they will be making the problem worse, because now they will have spent millions of dollars on something that won't help them maintain competitive advantage.

What should they do instead? Stay tuned!

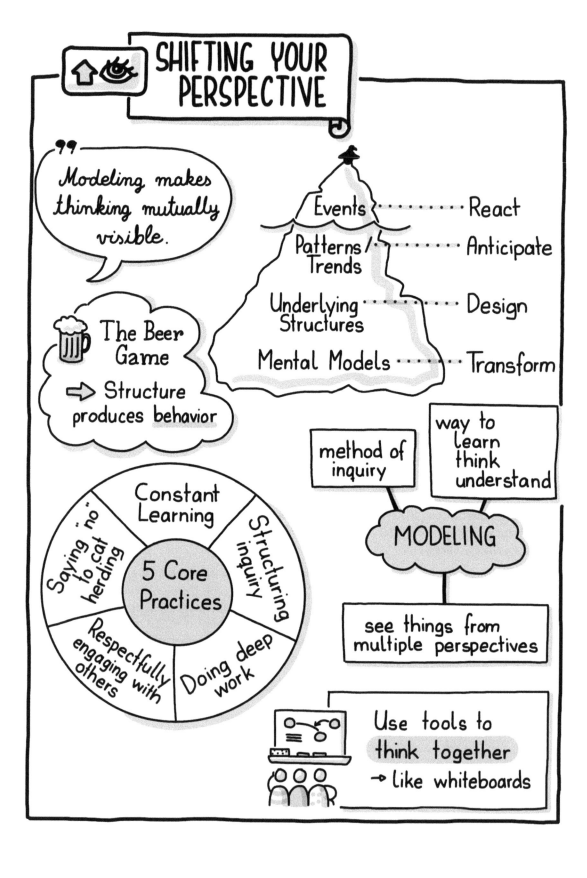

CHAPTER 3

Shifting Your Perspective

Every system is perfectly designed to get the results it gets.
—Donald Berwick

Your perspective, or point of view, is the frame through which you observe the world. You might believe that your perspective is holistic, that you see everything you need to see. In fact, your perspective is a concept, a general notion of what's happening. Creating conceptual integrity requires looking at circumstances through multiple perspectives, seeing it more broadly than our personal framing.

When you identify problems in a particular circumstance, you see them from your own unique experiences, expertise, attitudes, and biases. Someone else might see problems you don't see or solutions you haven't considered. We each take a snapshot that will be different from the snapshots other people will take of the same circumstances. These snapshots filter what we will think, see, focus on, and retain about any circumstance.

In the parable about the blindfolded people and the elephant, people experience one aspect of a whole and believe it represents the whole. We resemble this parable, like Figure 3-1, when faced with a system. We can understand part of it but need to synthesize other people's perspectives in order to think about "the elephant" together.

Figure 3-1. Blindfolded people and the elephant (Source: @GoodStudio/Adobe Stock)

Your perspective is limited by your blind spots. You don't see your blind spots because, blind spot. Thinking with other people can shine light on concepts you haven't yet seen. For example, I look at most sociotechnical problems through a technology system frame. I think about the code, data, tools, patterns, and relationships. My colleagues look at the same problem through frames like user experience, system security, visual design, or business metrics.

 When we think together, we synthesize our perspectives to create a more comprehensive perspective that couldn't exist without the thinking together part.

Shifting perspective is also looking beneath the surface of events. I've heard many people complain that systems thinking is "too abstract." They only want "concrete" thinking and only trust "concrete" answers.

This reaction is a misunderstanding of systems thinking. Systems thinking is going deeper, diving underneath surface-level insights. It encourages us to shift our perspective in order to discover root causes. Without the ability to think below the surface, we can patch systemic challenges but fail to resolve them.

Shifting perspective, like everything in systems thinking, is a practice. Some core practices, like continuous learning and structuring inquiry, inherently train our minds to shift perspective. Modeling, especially with tools like the Iceberg Model, can help make "the elephant" visible.

Perhaps most importantly, developing a shared vocabulary for nonlinear concepts enables groups of people to think together about how to solve their systemic challenges. Words are powerful containers, encapsulating a common point of view. When we reconsider the definition of familiar words and concepts, we discover opportunities for thinking differently.

I'll begin with five core practices that I hope you agree are necessary in our line of work. At least, I hope they don't set your hair on fire.

Five Core Practices

Technology folks are a learning-thirsty bunch, having chosen to do knowledge work in a field of high-speed change. Chances are, these practices are already a part of your life. If you need more practice in any of these areas, this is a great time to begin. Further systems thinking practices depend on these skills.

You Are Constantly Learning

Knowing that there is always more to know, you are a proactive learner. You adopt new approaches and tools when they are helpful and relevant. You value your expertise and also don't mind being a beginner, learning from other people's experiences.

Learning isn't strictly a "consume the curriculum" prospect—you also discern what to learn. When faced with a problem, you ask yourself, "What don't I know that would be good to know?" Then you decide how you'll learn it; sometimes hands-on, sometimes in a course or from a book, sometimes by teaching others, sometimes you mix and match. You apply your learning practice to your life and work.

If you need a learning boost, pick any subject that really interests you. Don't begin with something you are supposed to learn but aren't excited about. Pick something that energizes you. Then find one resource on the subject—an article, a book, a course, a conference talk (or whole event). As you engage with the resource, take notes. (I love Obsidian, acreom, or Notion for this. Though you'll remember more (*https://oreil.ly/mojZD*) if you take notes by hand then transfer them to software.) Want to explore more? Follow one idea to another. Or if you didn't get much from that resource, ask people for recommendations. Keep it light; there's no exam to prepare for, only learning.

You're Comfortable Structuring Inquiry

You figure out how to figure something out. When you are faced with a problem you haven't faced before, you create a strategy for understanding it better. For example, you look up articles or other resources. You speak to people with different but relevant perspectives. You might build a prototype to test ideas. You make a list of questions to answer and then add questions that help you understand from a different perspective.

Systemic reasoning, which we'll practice in Chapter 7, is the art and science of structuring inquiry. To warm up, consider one question you have about your current system. Perhaps you'd like to know why something was decided or how something works. Decide how you'll find out and take proactive steps to discover the answers. Bonus points for sharing the answer with others.

You Do (or Are Willing to Do) Deep Work

By deep work, I mean investing distraction-free time in thinking—becoming aware of, structuring, strengthening, and improving your thinking. Concentration is key. It doesn't matter (too much) what you focus on, code or words or models; the goal is to craft concepts. However you practice—daily, weekly, on regular retreats—focused, generative work happens.

If you've moved into a role that fills your days with meetings, I encourage you to begin now making some space for contemplation. Cal Newport's book *Deep Work: Rules for Focused Success in a Distracted World* (Grand Central Publishing) is a wonderful guide into this practice. If a book is daunting, especially while you are reading this one, begin with a synopsis (*https://oreil.ly/dUAS6*) like this one by Timely.

You Respectfully Engage

When others share their thinking, you engage respectfully. Respect is acknowledging what the other person has said and considering it. Convey understanding and respect for the work they've invested to craft their idea. Find the good. Then, if possible, help to strengthen their reasoning, to make the idea stronger. In Chapter 5, we'll practice this more deeply.

Meanwhile, notice how often your first reaction is, "No." Do you point out when someone is wrong without first ensuring you've understood them? I see a lot of negating, belittling, and dismissing of ideas in requests for comments and other forum-style discussion spaces. The belittler isn't necessarily correct, and even when they are, they are making the communication process harder. As we'll see throughout this book, thinking together is not the same thing as posting your opinion. Relevant and insightful contributions arise when we are open to learning from each other.

You Stop Being Sisyphus

In Greek mythology, Sisyphus was forced by the god Zeus to roll a giant boulder up a hill. Every time the boulder neared the top, it rolled back down. Sisyphus rolled that rock for all eternity.

People with nonlinear skills are often playing "glue roles." They are expected to hold parts together…people, teams, or software parts that don't hold themselves together. Cat herders, we call them.

In nonlinear approaches, nobody gets to be a cat. Cat-like refusal to think well with others doesn't need "gluing"; it needs behavior modification. When we think in systems, our goal is to change patterns, not enable them. With the caveat that occasionally, of course, gluing and cat herding are required. The emphasis is on "occasionally," though.

If you are investing a lot of time overcoming people's resistance to thinking well together, consider ways to shift that pattern. For example, create a single artifact where two people who disagree share their views. Facilitate this discussion with questions like "what convinced you?" and "why does it matter that we do that?" Invite others that engage respectfully to join, setting an example of communication patterns that generate insight into various perspectives on the problem.

Perhaps you agree with these core practices and they represent your approach to most situations. Great! Continue paying attention to these core habits, and see where you might improve your skills. Perhaps you disagree that one, or more than one, of these practices are matterful. If so, experiment. You might be correct. You might also discover that slight shifts in your point of view open doors to opportunities you haven't considered before.

While I call these five practices essential, there is one more to add. Of all the practices I've adopted, the most valuable approach to shifting perspective has been modeling.

Modeling as a Core Practice

> *Remember, always, that everything you know, and everything everyone knows, is only a model. Get your model out there where it can be viewed. Invite others to challenge your assumptions and add their own.*
>
> —Donella Meadows, *Thinking in Systems: A Primer*

Modeling is making relevant concepts in our minds—and the relationship between them—visible. According to Shane Parish, modeling is part of the work we are required to do to have an opinion (*https://oreil.ly/Xa0oq*).

In systems, you do a lot of modeling, but not in a prescriptive way. Modeling is one of those words that means different things from linear and nonlinear perspectives. In an organization, "systems thinking" is rarely happening without collaborative exercises that encourage systems thinking. Yet most organizations confuse modeling with "producing a diagram."

You might be thinking of templates, like C4 and cloud infrastructure examples. You might be thinking of project management charts or documentation describing continuous deployment. You might hope this book gives you a catalog of diagrams that will describe your system.

Diagrams are valuable and necessary, but they are not what I mean by modeling. There is very little focus on diagramming in this book because what you'll need to diagram depends, a lot, on your circumstances. When you want to make a diagram, there are great resources available that show you how.

In this book, modeling is an action verb; it's the process of thinking about a system visually. You can model the same way you write; explore ideas, gain insight, communicate your ideas, synthesize knowledge to understand how a system works. You can just dive in and make models. Yes, recipes help, but you are a knowledge chef. You can create your own recipes and modify them as you learn.

You can choose a modeling starting point—for example, EventStorming (*https:// www.eventstorming.com*)—or you can invent modeling exercises that suit your needs.

Modeling is a method of inquiry, a way to learn, think, understand, and see things from multiple perspectives. You can model with words or pictures or code or all three. You can model alone, and you can model with others. Models make our thinking and understanding visible and explicit.

Models make our thinking visible; they don't represent reality. All models are defeasible. Every model represents what is known at one point in time, framed in a specific way. Our models, like our concepts, become obsolete when we know more or the circumstances change. Models are thinking tools, not reality.

Modeling supports conceptual integrity. Five people solving a problem will arrive at a more-reliable solution faster if they "think out loud" through modeling. Do they understand what is happening and the impact of change? Whenever you are struggling to find common ground or see the "stuck spots," consider modeling the problem. Dive deeper to understand why you see things differently.

Modeling is often dismissed by software teams as a waste of time. "We don't do big up-front design," they say. "The code is my model." This is a misunderstanding of why modeling is valuable. It's not concrete decision making, and it does not replace code. It's creating conceptual integrity, which in turn nourishes and supports our confidence when coding.

 When we think in systems, we are looking for answers by figuring out "What are the right questions to ask?"

Our questions are rarely only about the code. We can use modeling to explore our questions.

Here is an example scenario: the system provides essential information to a user when requested. This activity serves the system's primary purpose. You are told that the delay time between request and return is "too long." What are some modeling activities that can help you?

In Table 3-1, you can see the basic system questions on the left and more detailed questions related to the problem on the right. You can explore these questions using modeling.

Table 3-1. Example conceptual framework for exploring a problem

System concept	What you might model
What is the current state?	What is happening now? How does information flow in and how does it flow out currently? What is happening when the information is at rest and in motion? What is its structure and how does the structure change? What data is available about the timing; what does a chart of response times look like?
What is the goal?	Define "too slow." How fast should the information be received? Why is "faster" valuable—will it enable the system to serve its purpose? How do we know that changing this discrepancy is "better"? Better for whom and in what ways? Are there other goals that supersede this one?
What is the discrepancy?	What is the time difference between the current time and goal time? Under what circumstances does "slow" occur? How do we measure it? Do our measurements actually measure the problem we are solving? What happens during the delay and how is it being reinforced? What is impacted by the delay?
What is the perceived state?	We say "too long," but what benefits do we get from the delay? (For example, failover services are expensive.) What are the tradeoffs involved in making it faster? Does everyone perceive this as a "problem"? If not, why not? If making it faster has impact elsewhere, who will perceive those changes as harmful or helpful?

In Chapter 11, we will dive deeper into modeling as a practice. Here, we'll begin with the Iceberg Model, a tool for diving under the surface of events. We use this modeling approach when we want to discover and enable impactful change in a system.

The Iceberg That Sinks Our Initiatives

> *Rather than reacting to individual problems that arise, a systems thinker will ask about relationships to other activities within the system, look for patterns over time, and seek root causes.*
> —Courage Egbude (*https://oreil.ly/ePvgv*)

In daily life, we are always responding to and impacted by the events we experience. A bug in production, an initiative that's late, a service crashing, catching a cold, or getting a speeding ticket. We focus on the tip of the iceberg. What just happened?

We fix, we patch, we adapt, we plan better features. When an event reoccurs, we take wider action to prevent it, with test coverage, for example. The trouble is, in systems, we can do this endlessly and nothing ever really changes.

Remember the discussion in Chapter 2 about counterintuitiveness? How often are we making the problem worse with our fixes? As long as we stay on the surface, we are likely to reinforce whatever is causing the problem. To look beneath the surface, you can use Figure 3-2, the Iceberg Model.

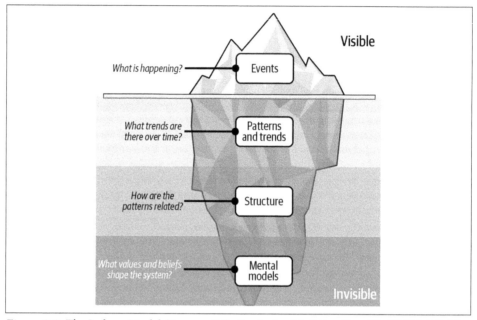

Figure 3-2. The Iceberg Model (Source: @thailerderden10 (https://oreil.ly/Xs7No)/Adobe Stock)

The Iceberg Model guides our thinking down into the underlying patterns, system structures, and mental models involved in the event. We look for the root causes of a challenge. The root causes are almost always our mental models, the things we believe are true that may (or may not) be true. We build our systems to support those beliefs. When we explore a challenge using the Iceberg Model, we discover opportunities for creating lasting change.

Events

What happened? What was visible?

For example, two technology teams are refusing to collaborate on building a better relationship between their software parts. Instead, they are fighting for control. Rather than react by adding more managerial intervention, we can look deeper into the problem.

Patterns and Trends

Has this happened before? When? Under what circumstances? Has resistance blocked other problems from being addressed?

When hiring, the organization prioritized a technology-centric skillset that did not include questions like "How well do you think with others to solve systems challenges?" This pattern has built those teams as well as the organization's culture, and they have never been good at thinking well together.

Structure

What organizational or social structures, rules, rituals, or physical experiences support the pattern(s)?

Whiteboard tests (in some form) are an industry-wide practice; organizations have adopted them as standard. They test for knowledge *stock*, what people know now. But they don't test for knowledge *flow*, how well people learn and adapt as things change. The current teams are made up of people who don't value what they can learn from each other, and learning from others isn't reinforced as being valuable.

Mental Models

What do we believe, or value, that gives rise to those structures and patterns?

Experience with a specific technology tool predicts the quality of knowledge work that will be delivered by the person in the future. People best qualified to develop technology solutions can improvisationally solve coding puzzles, on demand, during interviews. "Soft skills" like communication are not a priority for software engineers (that's what project managers are for).

Some of the best engineers I've worked with have failed whiteboard tests. Three times, I've seen organizations almost pass over a candidate for this, hire them anyway, and six months later, that person was the most valuable engineer on the team.

Conversely, some of the most difficult engineers I've worked with were top experts in their technology stack. They made up the tests others had to pass. They also blocked the adoption of tools or languages they weren't expert at using.

Using the Iceberg Model reveals potential leverage points, places where a change in the system can have lasting impact. We understand that the outcomes we are experiencing arise out of the patterns, structures, and mental models that generate our sociotechnical system.

The mental models that justify hiring practices are not, by themselves, a problem (necessarily). Problems arise when the relationships among events, patterns, and structures arising from our mental models push us in the wrong direction. Then, we need to go deeper and rebuild our thinking from the bottom up.

In our example, the organization did not prioritize communication, cooperation, and systems thinking skills. When it needed those skills to succeed, it floundered. This is a solvable problem. But two things usually happen instead:

- *The organization makes the problem worse* by hiring more project managers to control the situation. The problem was that there was too much noise because the people couldn't think well together, and adding more noise would not improve a situation like that. More project managers may in fact be part of the solution, but by shifting the focus onto a fix, rather than understanding the root cause, the root cause remains and will continue to structure the entire situation.

- *The people in the organization blame the wrong things.* There is a lot of blame in systems. People blame lack of leadership, not enough money, too much focus on the wrong thing, lack of Kubernetes, too much complexity, etc. Tech blames product, product blames tech. We rarely understand correctly how the structure of our thinking has led us to exactly where we end up.

The Blame Game

In *The Fifth Discipline*, Peter Senge describes the Beer Game (*https://oreil.ly/Qydmb*). Invented by Jay Forrester at MIT in the 1960s, the Beer Game teaches systems thinking by demonstrating, through experience, the nonlinear nature of change in a system and how systemic outcomes are largely caused not by external "market pressures" but by the people in the system.

The game is simple to play but difficult to win. Players are split into four groups across the beer distribution chain. On one end is the Retailer team; they own a popular shop selling craft beer and kombucha. On the other end of the chain is the Brewery team, a small group of friends who brew cranberry craft beer. In between, the Distributors order beer from the breweries and sell it to Wholesalers, who keep the retailers supplied.

The teams communicate orders, Retailer → Wholesaler → Supplier → Brewery, using a weekly order form. The game begins with an event: Taylor Swift drinks a cranberry craft beer at the (American football) Super Bowl. Suddenly, everyone wants some. The Beer Game players take turns ordering beer each week, adapting to the change.

Millions of people, from college students to experienced CEOs, have played the Beer Game. Most of those people lose.

They lose because they react to the event without considering the patterns, structures, and mental models underlying the event. In response to increased demand, the Retailer orders more beer. The Brewery needs four weeks to make more beer. (Time is always a factor in systems!) The Retailer doesn't know this; they just know their orders aren't being filled. So they increase their order, hoping to fix their problem. In frustration, each team along the chain, each week, orders more beer than they need. Until midway through, when too much beer starts flowing back downstream.

In the end, the customers have moved on to Taylor's new favorite beer, and the Retailer has a pile of unsold cranberry beer.

Structure produces behavior.

The hierarchical and linear structure of the ordering system encourages teams to play as four siloed parts. Each part operates from its own perspective. (We are out of beer!) The structure offers no dynamic information, shared across the system, in real time. Rather than operate as parts of one system, they operate as dissociated parts.

If the teams redesign their communication structure, they can win. But they don't.

Long-standing mental models about how business works, like perceptions about the competitive, dog-eat-dog world, also influence the teams' behavior. Even when players are given hints, told how to order optimally, they still make decisions based on their trust, or lack thereof, of other teams in the chain.[1]

When the game ends and players are asked "What went wrong?" they don't blame the systemic structures or mental models. (Spoiler alert: that is why the system fails.) Instead, they blame one another.

The profound lesson of the Beer Game is that we blame often, and we blame the wrong things. As John Sterman says, "It just cannot be true that, by chance, all the smart people ended up as retailers and all of the people running the factories were dumb."[2] What even fewer players recognize is that their own actions pushed the system toward collapse.

If your career has been anything like mine, you don't need to play the Beer Game. Blame is all around you, every day. Every systems architect I know who walks into a new situation is walking into the middle of a Beer Game.

---

1 Ignacio J. Martinez-Moyano goes into this from a historical perspective in his article "History of the Beer Game" (*https://oreil.ly/pclDe*), in *System Dynamics Review*, February 2024.

2 John D. Sterman is the Jay W. Forrester professor of management at the MIT Sloan School of Management and a professor in the MIT Institute for Data, Systems, and Society. He is also the director of the MIT System Dynamics Group and the Sustainability Initiative at MIT Sloan.

I'm not blaming blamers. We are terrible at thinking in systems. We believe that we are correct, and many people are sincerely trying to help. I teach this subject and still find myself blaming the wrong things. The Beer Game simulates a common human experience that is extremely difficult to avoid.

But we must try to avoid it if we want to design resilient systems. In the Beer Game, redesigning the feedback loops and the patterns of information sharing and inserting a few patience-promoting constraints would enable everyone to (eventually) succeed.

How do you train yourself to stop reacting and start responding with systems thinking? In Chapter 5, I will answer this question in more detail. If the teams playing the Beer Game had opened a digital whiteboard and quickly modeled their system as a whole, the bottlenecks might have been apparent. First, we'll train ourselves to step back and ask ourselves, "What is happening here?"

Your Practice: The Iceberg Model

Bring to mind a recurring problem in your current system. If you can't think of one, remember an event that triggered a fire drill–style cascade of people reacting. What happened?

Use the Iceberg Model to consider the patterns, structures, and mental models that might give rise to that event. Don't worry about being "right"; there are many right (and wrong) answers. Just play with the idea that structures produce behavior; look for anything that reinforces behaviors and ways of thinking.

One try is usually insufficient. Make a few versions, and look at the circumstances from different perspectives. How do users, for example, experience this situation? You can invite someone else to do this exercise with you and compare your answers.

Before you made your model, what did you blame for the problem? What did other people blame? Did your modeling work suggest other options for solving the problem? How might you respond differently the next time you are faced with the same problem?

MAGO's Quandary: Shifting Perspective

Explaining the difference between a linear and nonlinear approach is tricky—it depends on your mindset. Two teams can be doing the exact same behavior with very different core mental models and reinforcing structures and, thus, experience very different outcomes.

Here are some shifts in perspective that might help the MAGO teams. If you are familiar with information systems like MAGO (or perhaps even if you aren't), you might want to argue against some of these shifts. You might interpret items on this list as "the wrong way" and "the right way." Keep in mind, our "right way" is often making a problem worse.

Here are some alternative approaches to problem solving that MAGO might consider:

What MAGO plans to do ...	What MAGO could do instead ...
Diagram a "north star" target architecture, break it down by teams, and distribute the work.	Model the system's capabilities: write content; publish content. Manage subscriptions. Model the relationships among those activities. Can those relationships be better designed?
Fix the obvious problem (replace the obsolete software).	Model the current system's pain points. Identify the patterns and structures that generate those pain points. Is there a leverage point that will improve the system as a whole?
Build an API that returns information from a source (a web page, for example) that is accessible by other software parts.	Create a data model that structures information understood by other software parts. Enable it to translate a source concept (web page) into a distributable concept (text with context and styling metadata).
Store information by context (say, a blog post published on March 23, 2024).	Store information that is inherently interrelated and queryable (information about beet farming in the American Southwest). Use metadata to describe how the information has been used.
Build services that request information from existing data stores (through APIs or shared databases).	Design an event-based system that supports new services without direct integrations (loose coupling).
Replace old software parts.	Reconsider the context in which those parts operate now. Can better relationships be established among parts?
Plan a lift-and-shift migration to the cloud.	Consider incrementally rebuilding software parts using cloud-native approaches or serverless, when possible. Discern which parts of the system benefit from cloud technologies and which, at the moment, don't.
Build a greenfield system to completely replace the complex legacy system.	Iteratively redesign software parts and bring them online, designing for eventual obsolescence (strangler fig pattern).
Architect the change and ask for everyone's opinion (or make all the decisions without feedback).	Synthesize knowledge across the system to identify where to make impactful change. Restructure the people system to organize teams who can generate the needed changes.
Blame the software, the vendor, "leadership," JavaScript, previous developers, Agile, and/or another team for the current situation.	Identify how current patterns, structures, and mental models are creating the current situation.

Support for Your Practice: Shifting Perspective Is Hard

Before we begin Part II, let's pause....

This is difficult work.

Systems thinking is valuable when paradigms shift, when the purpose of a system is changing. The purposes of many software systems are changing. Before you can design those systems, you have to shift our own internal paradigm. You'll need to see potential changes for yourself. And you'll need to think well with others, some of whom aren't the slightest bit interested in systems thinking.

We aren't simply tweaking our thinking with these practices. We are detangling our thoughts and experiences and conceptual models and feelings and communication patterns and the world around us. Detangling is deep work.

I want you to know that this work matters to do. And you are not alone. We are faced with so many systems challenges nowadays—we need you. We need you to consider alternative approaches and perspectives, even when it would be easier to think and act linearly. I trust that we are up to the challenge. I'm with you, as you move through this, with battle scars and a deep desire to sally forth regardless.

PART II

You Are a System of Thinking

You can't improve your thinking if you aren't aware of your thinking. There are many factors that influence our ability to create conceptual integrity. Self-awareness, also known as metacognition, is the ability to understand and adapt your thinking patterns. Practicing with your own thinking is, perhaps unsurprisingly, the foundation of thinking in systems.

Most of the time, we are reacting to what's happening around us, rather than practicing self-awareness and learning to respond effectively. This is not a bad thing; there is important information in our reactions. They rarely, though, get us what we need to improve our circumstances. Systems thinking shifts us toward observing the reactive patterns, in our selves, in others, and in the technology system, in order to discover ways to improve those reactive patterns.

Systems thinking is an integrative approach to learning. It is learning all the time, structuring inquiry in ways that generate relevant knowledge. In Part II, you'll practice self-awareness, of your thinking and your reactions. And you'll develop a plan for continuous learning that guides you toward knowledge, understanding, and, with any luck, a bit of wisdom.

CHAPTER 4

Self-Awareness as a Foundational Skill

Self-awareness is a trait—or maybe "practice" is the more accurate way to put it—that everyone can always improve at. It is part emotional intelligence, part perceptiveness, part critical thinking. It means knowing your weaknesses, of course, but it also means knowing your strengths and what motivates you.

 —Neil Blumenthal, cofounder of Warby Parker, "Know Yourself" (*https://oreil.ly/ 87KEG*)

You cannot improve your thinking if you aren't aware of your thinking. The best way to begin practicing systems thinking is to practice with your most intimate system: yourself.

Systems thinking is grounded in metacognition: critical awareness of your own thought processes. Critical thinking is the ability to analyze and evaluate situations. Your critical thinking skills depend on the quality and cohesiveness of your own thinking process. The way you objectively interpret thoughts, feelings, and experiences leads directly to your chosen courses of action. Your ability to reach sound conclusions via a path of observation, consideration, and inquiry is a strong measure of your systems thinking skills.

 The difference between having an opinion and reaching a conclusion is…when you reach a conclusion, you know how you got there. And you can map the journey for others.

Metacognition is the process of becoming self-aware. Self-awareness incorporates more than awareness of your thoughts. You are an embodied system of thoughts, cognitive patterns, feelings, physical sensations, core beliefs, mental structures, habitual behaviors, future expectations, and past experiences. You are a thinking system that exists inside of thinking systems that influence and shape your thinking.

Many of your thoughts arise as a result of systemic patterns that you've experienced. Self-awareness is noticing how you react to your experiences and understanding the way you learn best, how you change your mind. If you've participated in Retrospectives, the Agile rituals of evaluating experiences as a team, you have practiced a form of metacognition.

Without self-awareness, you can't create conceptual integrity. If you pay careful attention, you'll see that you are often being mentally dragged around by your unconsidered thoughts and reactions. You'll notice when your thinking is reactive, fallacious, habituated, and lacking conceptual integrity.

Remember our simple system model (Figure 4-1)?

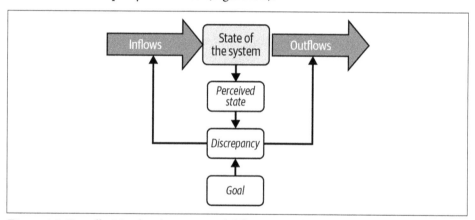

Figure 4-1. Donella Meadows' system model (https://oreil.ly/4V8f-)

You consume information from external and internal sources. Your mind interprets that information and responds based on a myriad of factors—the environment, chemistry, genetics, upbringing, what you ate for breakfast, etc. You have goals, you identify discrepancies. Your thoughts generate your actions, and vice versa, in reinforcing feedback loops.

Your experiences are a feedback loop. For example, when your ideas are heard and helpful, your confidence increases, and you share more ideas. When your ideas are ignored or dismissed, you are more likely to doubt your thinking and keep it to yourself. Self-awareness helps us discern which circumstances nourish our thinking and which inhibit it.

Without self-awareness, you also can't overcome counterintuitiveness, the habituated solutions that feel "right" to you. Counterintuitiveness, if you remember from Chapter 2, is a common systems thinking experience.

The Iceberg Model (Chapter 3) reveals that systems thinking is working with mental models. Metacognition is the skill that enables us to *see* mental models. Our core mental models design our systems. Self-awareness helps you discover the mental models at the bottom of your own icebergs.

For some software professionals, Part II of this book will challenge your definition of "technology skills." We have been taught to focus on *what* we know, rather than *how we think, feel, and learn.* Knowledge work, we've been told, is the measure of our knowledge stock. How much do you know? A truer measure of knowledge work is the flow of knowledge. How much can you learn? The next three chapters help you improve your knowledge flow velocity by removing the common blockers that inhibit this flow. We begin with challenging our desire for concreteness and certainty.

Systems Thinking: The Hard Parts

An architect adds real value to an organization not by chasing silver bullet after silver bullet but rather by honing their skills at analyzing the trade-offs as they appear.
—Neal Ford et al., *Software Architecture: The Hard Parts* (O'Reilly)

Systems thinking expands your capacity to do hard things. Perhaps you imagined that the "hard things" are developing asynchronous, event-driven software systems with increasing layers of abstraction orchestrated by infrastructure as code. Those are hard things! Harder still is developing the tolerance for ambiguity and uncertainty that those systems require.

Ambiguity is the quality of being open to more than one interpretation. When I take my thoughts at face value, I presume they are correct. When I look deeper, I see how interrelated my thoughts are with my point of view. From my point of view, I might be correct. When I consider a different point of view, I discover different, also correct, but sometimes opposing, ideas. The more relationally complex a system is, the more ambiguity there is—there is rarely one right point of view.

"Concrete" thinking seeks exact and singular interpretations, not ambiguity. Mind-shifting, looking at multiple potentially correct ideas, teaches me that everything depends on everything else. There is not One Answer for me to discover. There are only tradeoffs, letting go of three good ideas in favor of one idea that better serves the circumstance. I might need to accept less of something desirable to get more of something valuable. For example, maybe the service I develop isn't as fast as I'd hoped it would be, but it is reliable. I might determine that, in this case, reliability matters more.

Linear thinking processes are designed to construct certainty, to generate as much reliable exactitude as possible, especially when we are making decisions. The problem is, when it comes to systems, you cannot be certain…about anything. Every thought, every decision, is, to some extent, a guess. Everything is an experiment, a learning curve. In software systems, like in life, there is a Grand Canyon–sized gap between what we intend to happen and what actually happens. That's not a bad thing—innovation is born in that gap.

Uncertainty is uncomfortable, in part because we have greedy minds. Our minds want, and sometimes believe that we can accomplish, everything we imagine. Constraints, the limitations that all circumstances place on what's possible, can seem unimportant or irrelevant and, especially, inconvenient.

When we accept that uncertainty is always part of the equation, we leave space for curiosity, learning, and observing what happens when we set our thoughts in motion. We make use of what we discover.

The more comfortable you are with the ambiguity and uncertainty in your own mind, the more comfortable you will be when immersing yourself in complex situations.

In systems thinking, your mind is your instrument. Your ability to hear your own mental music is critical to the work. When you practice thinking, you are also *listening to* thinking. Mastering your own mind is harder than any cloud architecture you will ever encounter.

Decision Making Is a Noisy Process

We tend to run our whole life trying to avoid all that hurts or displeases us, noticing the objects, people, or situations that we think will give us pain or pleasure, avoiding one and pursuing the other.

—Charlotte Joko Beck, *Everyday Zen: Love and Work* (HarperOne)

As you strengthen your metacognition, you'll discover that you are not as "in control" of your thinking as you might imagine. Sometimes, your true goals operate under the radar of your conscious awareness.

For example, when I'm faced with a tricky coding problem that I don't know how to solve, I might think, "I'm hungry. I need to go to the grocery store." Perhaps I am hungry and need food. My goal, on the surface, is to solve my coding problem by helping my brain think better.

Self-awareness has taught me to be wary. My true goal might be (and often is) avoiding the discomfort and uncertainty of facing the problem. My secondary goal is to ease that discomfort with a dopamine rush generated by the chocolate I'll get at the grocery store. The goal of solving the tricky problem is a distant third. Without awareness of my own thinking patterns, I get carried away from what matters.

Conversely, when I am solving a tricky problem, I sometimes ignore hunger. For hours, I tweak and test and Google and fret. No joy.

In desperation, I get up and make a snack. Walk the dogs. Toss a load of laundry in the washing machine. Then sit back down at my desk…and immediately see the solution. In those situations, the thought "I'm hungry, I should go get food" would have been helpful.

Your mind supplies an endless flow of information in the form of ideas. And you are endlessly consuming more ideas and information. All that information flowing through your mind can seem equally important, equally worthy of your attention. Some thoughts, triggered by anxiety, will shout, like "I can't get this done by tomorrow!" Some thoughts, triggered by insight, will whisper "pause and have a snack." You know from experience that the louder thoughts are not necessarily the more helpful thoughts.

We call discerning which thoughts to prioritize distinguishing *signal versus noise*. Noise describes all the information that, despite its seeming importance or "shoutiness," distracts you from what actually matters. Signal is an idea, information, insight, or concept that points your attention in a matterful direction.

Systems thinking is not simply generating new thoughts, or even different thoughts. It is, more often, discerning signal from noise. Noise makes your mind spin in circles, chasing its own tail. Signal is a path through mental clutter, a pointer toward meaningful change, even though you can't be sure you're going in the "right" direction.

If ambiguity and uncertainty are the hard parts, the tall buildings we must leap, discernment is the super power that enables us to leap them. Discernment is the ability to understand situations and make decisions, even when there is no concrete or "right" answer. We do this by discerning signal from noise.

Discerning noise from signal is how we discover leverage points, the most valuable changes in systems. Your own mind is your sandbox, where you can practice discerning signal from noise.

I would love to give you a concrete example, "this is signal and this is noise." Of course, it depends. What is *noise* in one circumstance is *signal* in another. The more complex a situation, the more discernment you'll need to navigate it.

What I can describe is what I call the "Cupholder Dilemma." When I begin architecting a technology system, I focus on the core capabilities. If I were designing a car, I'd be thinking about engine power and the context it serves. "Under what conditions will people drive this car? What does the car need to handle well?" Other capabilities come later.

When I meet with stakeholders, I want to talk about the engine design. Invariably, the stakeholders are more concerned with the cupholders. "Where will drivers put their coffee cups?" In technology cultures, we call this *bikeshedding*. People tend to focus on trivial matters (noise), which are easier to solve and likely at the top of the Iceberg Model, rather than focusing on more complex matters like patterns, structures, and mental models (signal). This would be like designing a co-working space and spending half of your time figuring out where the bike shed should go and what it should look like. It might be easier and more enjoyable to think about that than, say, the plumbing or electrical system, but it'd be a mistake to start there.

The stakeholders are right, though, in a way. Cupholders are not trivial. When driving day to day, most of us care more about cupholders and phone chargers than horsepower. Cupholders matter. From a systems perspective, the key is timing—knowing when to talk about the engine and when to talk about the cupholders.

In Chapter 2, I said that time is always a factor in systems. Alas, our brains' translation of time is unreliable and complex. Our thoughts jump around in time, to a solution that worked in the past or a problem that might arise in the future. Sometimes, past experience and future strategy help us find signal. More often, time jumps derail and confuse us. Discernment involves not simply knowing what to think about but also when to think about it.

Difficulty with discernment is a systemic problem. People have goals operating under their own radar. So do organizations. Groups of people grab hold of ideas that make the situation worse and ignore helpful ideas. When problem solving, people are overly influenced by past experiences or future fears, but they don't share those experiences or fears. Thinking together can be like wandering in a forest (or trying to figure out what an elephant is) with a blindfold on.

The more you understand these patterns in yourself, the easier it will be to navigate them with others. You'll be less likely to follow the drum beat of noise.

I encourage you to model because modeling helps discernment. Visual thinking can help people discern where to focus attention. Opening a Miro board might help people envision where cupholder discussions fit in the overall system design. A group that models together regularly is, in my experience, better at discerning together as well—especially when resolving competing priorities.

There is no avoiding competing priorities. For example, I want short-term pleasure and longer-term health. When deciding whether or not to eat a brownie, my mind tries to prioritize both things, even though they naturally conflict. When faced with a backlog of things to build, I want to build them all, except the ones I don't enjoy. When you pay attention to how you make decisions, you'll see that your mind goes to great lengths to *avoid making tradeoffs*.

Our technology lives are full of brownies. Remember the carboat from Chapter 2? One team wants a car. Another team wants a boat. The engineers build a carboat, which nobody wants. Discernment is the skill involved when designing the system that people actually need.

Noisy, conflicting opinions about what is best to do can feel like walking down the middle of a road during a hurricane. We get blown around by every idea, veering off course and getting lost in the fog. Systemic forces push against some of our choices and encourage others, invoking feedback loops. This entire book is about working inside of those forces, but your ability to do so will be limited by your self-awareness.

We cannot control our thinking, or other people's thinking, but fortunately, systems thinking is not about gaining more control…it is about making better choices. Finding leverage points, places where a change will have a big impact. Like Donella Meadows says, "We can't control systems or figure them out. But we can dance with them!"

Learning this dance begins with becoming aware of how we arrive at conclusions. What information do we pull from the stream? What happens when you make choices? Do you feel confident, uncertain, overwhelmed? What drives you? Is it distraction, fear, logic, interest? You will likely discover that your own process mirrors many choice-making processes around you.

Watching your mind is like watching the weather. *Chaos,* the book by James Gleick, tells the story of how the science of systems thinking began…with a meteorologist literally studying weather patterns. He found patterns in the absence of patterns.

You'll find patterns too, but only if you practice. You will not maintain physical strength while lying on the couch eating brownies and binging Netflix. The same goes for self-awareness—it is a strength developed by exercising it. That is why we need to continuously practice, paying attention to the thinking we consume and the thinking we produce.

Fortunately, the first step is no sweat. Begin by observing your thinking.

Observe Your Thinking

> *We can listen to what the system tells us, and discover how its properties and our values can work together to bring forth something much better than could ever be produced by our will alone.*
>
> *We can't control systems or figure them out. But we can dance with them!*
>
> —Donella Meadows, *Thinking in Systems: A Primer*

There are fascinating books, courses, and other resources describing the neuroscience of self-awareness and metacognition. I don't recommend that you start there. Don't begin by thinking about how your mind should work, could work, might work. Instead, begin by looking at how *your mind actually works*. Become familiar with its patterns and processes. If you are like most people, you find getting swept up in interesting theories easy. Paying attention to your own thoughts, feelings, and experiences—that's hard.

Nonlinear approaches always begin with observation—paying attention to how things work. When I begin learning about a new system, I begin by modeling the current software system, describing the flow of information and the stuck places. I listen to the frustrations people express because those frustrations point me to the stuck places, the leverage points. I ask, learn, see, understand.

 I would not need to do this, to the extent I have, if there was already an insightful description and model of the system and how it serves its purpose. I have yet to engage with a software system that has this systemic view available to peruse. As part of your systems thinking practice, you might want to create one.

We continue to observe throughout the delivery process and the whole lifecycle of the system. Observation never ends. But as we do, we are still looking at what is present now. What is actually happening? How are the patterns reinforcing (or not) our goals? Continuous observation will show you what you need to learn before you act.

We don't begin with trying to "fix" our thinking because if you try to fix something without awareness, you will make a mess. Perhaps you've experienced this in your professional life? The new boss who wants to transform the software without knowing anything about it? The new silver bullet, say Kubernetes or continuous deployment, that fixes some problems but creates more? Without awareness, your fixes are New Year's resolutions that are abandoned before Groundhog Day.

Who is the "you" that wants to control your thinking or fix yourself? That part of your mind is extremely steeped in linear processes. Those are not the processes we want to strengthen. We want to strengthen our ability to notice, understand, listen, and see clearly. We want to spot patterns, blind spots, and habitual processes.

Without self-awareness, when we dance with systems, our unexamined thinking and emotional reactions will color, block, or reconstruct what we see and hear. We will jump on bandwagons that lead us nowhere. Our thinking impacts everything we build, every team we join, every meeting we are in, everyone who works with us. It is the stuff that knowledge work, and doing hard things together, is made of.

Your Practice: Flow with Your Thinking

I think self-awareness is probably the most important thing toward being a champion.
—Billie Jean King, one of the greatest tennis players of all time

Cal Newport, bestselling author and CompSci professor at Georgetown, argues that daily solitude is essential for knowledge workers. He defines solitude as "isolated from input from other minds." I'd add that we don't just need to be isolated from input, we also need to train ourselves to pay attention to our thinking.

There are many ways to do this, but one practice has been, by far, the most valuable to my work. You might love it and, like me, do it every day for the rest of your life. You might discover it's not for you and try something else. I encourage you, though, to *try* it. See what happens. Let the experience reveal (or not) its value.

The practice is: just write.

For one week, wake up every morning, pick up a pen and paper, set a timer for 10–20 minutes, and write whatever comes to mind.

Now, maybe you're thinking, "No way, Diana, that is never happening." Cool, you can skip this and still practice systems thinking. Or you can try writing at a different time of day. Mornings really are ideal for thinking…but here's an alternative….

For one week, every day after a meeting or focused work session, pick up a pen and paper, set a timer for 10–20 minutes, and write whatever comes to mind.

Write whatever comes to mind. If you get stuck, write "I don't know what to write" until more thoughts come to you. If you think "this is a dumb exercise," list all the ways it's a dumb exercise. *The only rule is: keep your hand moving.*

Sounds simple, yes? Perhaps, but you will come up with 17,659 reasons not to do this practice. If you can't do 20 minutes, do 10. If you can't do 10, do 5. Notice, and write about, all the things you think you should be doing instead. Why you hate it, why you resist it. Or why you love and need it and find the practice worthwhile.

There are great journal apps available that include daily prompts. If you feel stuck, try one of those. Or write down a thought that occurred to you during the day and explore it during your session.

Write notes to your cat. It doesn't matter what you write about, only that you create space to observe your thinking. Of course, you can write about systems! I encourage that—practice using the Iceberg Model. But don't worry if your brain wanders into "what will I have for lunch" territory; you're learning about your thinking system.

When the week is up, if you see a benefit, commit to 30 days.

Here's an example of a situation where my free writing practice had a major career impact.

At one organization, I was buried under a pile of chaos: leadership changes, circuitous and endless disagreements, maddening and unworkable "new" strategies, derisive words being said in meetings…it was a mess.

There were also good strategies, helpful supportive colleagues, and matterful work to be done. I could no longer tell the difference between what mattered to do and what was a waste of energy. Thoughts, opinions, and emotional reactions (like feeling powerless) were tumbling around in my mind. I felt paralyzed and powerless.

During my morning writing practice, a question occurred to me. "What if I were in charge?" What if I were the incoming CTO, someone who could say or do whatever was strategically sensical? I wrote out exactly what I would do, including what I would say to the people when I made the changes.

In other words, I listened to myself.

Through this exercise, I discovered a path to insight. I didn't show anyone what I wrote; I didn't need to—I knew what to do. Eventually, I moved on from that organization, but not as a blameful reaction, as a solid choice to navigate in a different direction.

Alternative Practices

A morning writing practice is helpful for many people. Are you one of them? I've been teaching workshops, using writing as a thinking practice, and attendees have found this practice surprisingly beneficial.

If you want to try something else or you'd like more than one practice, here are more recommendations.

Walking
> This is the practice Cal Newport, like many before him, has adopted and recommends. Want to ponder? Take a walk.

Rhythmic movement
> Running, yoga, hiking, dance, rowing, or cycling are examples of meditation in motion. As you engage in them, notice when your thinking drags you elsewhere and return your attention to your physical experience.

Meditation
> You can practice meditation while sitting still, moving, doing breathing exercises, listening to music, drumming, chanting, following words spoken by a guide, or some combination of these.

Discourse

Talking to trusted people about your experiences helps you become more aware of your experiences. Discussion can be used as a deep self-awareness practice.

Making art

When we get immersed in a creative process, we are usually, also, listening closely to ourselves. We practice both acting on our impulses and deciding when not to act on them. When art is used as a self-awareness practice (rather than strictly a crafting exercise), it can be a powerful tool. We can make models and code as we would make art.

There is no right way to cultivate self-awareness. Trust yourself to discover the ones that work for you. There are many teachers whose purpose is to support self-awareness practices; you might find that having one helps you.

When done with the right mindset, *reading* can be a foundational and valuable practice for understanding your own thinking. When Joseph Campbell, who co-wrote *The Power of Myth (Doubleday)*, was asked what form of meditation he practiced, he said "I underline sentences."

> I believe that reading and writing are the most nourishing forms of meditation anyone has so far found. By reading the writings of the most interesting minds in history, we meditate with our own minds and theirs as well. This to me is a miracle.
>
> —Kurt Vonnegut, *Palm Sunday* (Delacorte Press)

The practice that you choose is not what matters most. What matters most is that you show up for it.

MAGO: Everything Is in Our Blind Spots

> *You don't see something until you have the right metaphor to let you perceive it.*
> —James Gleick, *Chaos: Making a New Science*

Even in the increasingly interconnected world of today, we all live in binary mental models. Manager/contributor. Architect/engineer. Frontend/backend. Product/tech. OO/functional. Systems thinking, however, is nonbinary. Exploring nuance, all the subtleties that happen between, beneath, and around our binary views, is how we understand a system. We will reinforce those constructed dualities and limited worldviews unless we proactively practice seeing beyond them. It's easier to get stuck between two opposing views than it is to explore the nuanced, often unconscious biases that narrow our vision.

We all have blind spots, realities we don't perceive because we are limited by our current mental models, structures, and experiences. This is not a problem. Even if it was a problem, we can't fix it. We can't know everything about everything, and our concepts are constructed by the world around us. To some extent, we see what we've been shown.

We get stuck when we forget that *everything we've been conditioned to think may not be true*. In any given moment, our fundamental mental models are flawed, not because they are a lie but because they are limiting. Insufficient. Ideas that were correct (enough) in one context are not correct in another. Nevertheless, we try to apply them.

Paradigms shift. The rules we followed, the structures we built, the patterns we learned to trust through hard times…become our limitations. Growth is evolving as paradigms shift. We struggle with this. And so do organizations.

MAGO's system developed over decades. The roles people play, the way they do their work, the software systems they rely on—all arose to serve their evolving needs. Remember from Part I of this book that MAGO's thinking and communication structures have led them to a crisis: they're in a quandary; their current software system is inadequate for the contemporary media landscape, but fixing it seems impossibly disruptive. They will benefit from becoming aware of those structures.

Simultaneously, the paradigm has shifted around MAGO, and still is shifting. Their system is being shaped by pressures from the outside, as well. The world of print magazines and static content and subscription websites is fading. The world of digital information systems is arising. What will help MAGO see the world they don't yet see?

Five activities can help people at MAGO to become aware of their own thinking patterns and proactively seek out what they don't know they don't know.

Model the Current System

The people at MAGO understand the system from their point of view. But they probably don't understand how the parts work together. They probably also don't understand how their work impacts other people's work. By modeling how the current system works, not just the tech but also the people processes, MAGO can uncover blind spots in their thinking about their system.

Research Similar Systems

Chances are, MAGO is trying to solve the same problem as other organizations. There are three benefits to researching how other similar systems work:

1. *Uncover the landmines.*
   The wicked problems that nobody knows how to solve yet might not be worth investing in. MAGO can adapt their strategy to avoid those problems, if they know what they are.

2. Highlight the opportunities.

MAGO is held back by its current system. As a result, they might not have envisioned strategic opportunities that would be relatively easy to accomplish. Other organizations might be seeing these benefits already.

3. Define technological constraints.

Most organizations, including MAGO, dream of doing things that our current technology tools can't yet do. Systems that share MAGO's purpose will have qualities and constraints in common. By understanding the technological landscape, MAGO can decide where to invest in innovation and where to accept the trade-offs that come with their software options.

Listen to the Pain

As a systems architect, one of the most impactful things I do is watch people use the system. I'm astounded by how differently people experience software. The experience is impactful because it helps me discern what matters. What works now? Why does it work? What sucks now? Why does it suck? Listening to engineers and product people answer these questions is the quickest way to uncover leverage points in a system. And, of course, listening to feedback from customers is crucial.

MAGO is solving a problem—do they understand what their problem really is? Will their "replace the software" solution solve their pain points?

Make Some Prototypes

When we face the unknown, we are full of doubt. Thinking doesn't relieve our doubt. Experience does. Before MAGO takes a leap of faith, they could experiment. If MAGO was brand new, today, how would we design the system? How would we organize the people? What tools would we try first? Choose a capability that could be built in the "brand new MAGO" way and give it a try. You are guaranteed to discover at least one unknown in the process.

What If We Do Nothing?

Proactively seeking out what you don't know you don't know sounds like a paradox, doesn't it? How does MAGO know what MAGO doesn't know? One way to uncover blind spots is to ask, "What if we do nothing?" Stay with the line of thinking, even if it gets weird. The things organizations most fear are not usually the things that they should fear. (Just like people.) Explore the pathway of "we take no action" and the pathway of "we take one action like replacing the software" and follow it to the end. What does this reveal?

MAGO faces the same challenges we all face: how to adapt to changing circumstances. There are a myriad of ways to develop awareness and discover blind spots. In systems, most solutions will be waiting for us there.

Support for Your Practice: 12 Things Self-Awareness Taught Me

To encourage your practice, here are 12 insights that self-awareness practices have revealed to me over the years. Perhaps you'll make a list of your own, to help encourage your practices?

- The quality of my deliverables is equivalent to how well I can discern between good thinking and habituated thinking.
- The level of psychological safety in my environment is directly correlated to the quality of work I can deliver.
- I overcomplicate things until I can see the elegant simplicity.
- Fighting other people's thinking is usually a waste of energy. Demonstrating sound thinking more often gets me what I need.
- The mental models that shape how I think are often contradictory and sometimes nonsensical. Discerning which models to rely on and which to discard is challenging.
- My thoughts are not always truthful, reasonable, intelligent, or have my best interest at heart.
- My first instinct about whether or not to trust my own thinking, before objectively considering it, is unreliable.
- The quality of my thinking improves when I'm focused. It degrades when I get busy.
- Complexity is a nourishing pool that I can dive into. Generally, I've preferred to stand on the edge and shout at it.
- I am more swayed by other people's opinions, and more often, than I want to admit.
- I often make bad decisions when my emotions are leading the way. I make even worse decisions when my emotions are ignored.
- What I perceive as my own needs are often manufactured needs. For example, "relaxing" activities, like binge-watching Netflix, aren't necessarily relaxing. The streaming media experience is designed to create a "need" for more.

Understanding my own mental and emotional patterns has made me a more nuanced systems designer. When I'm caught up in the noise, I recognize that sooner. I've been burned out and angry after investing myself in a situation that didn't change. I wasn't wrong, but my frustration, blame, and negative reactions eclipsed new thinking. Through self-awareness, I slowly but surely have learned (and am still learning) to be the change I want to see in the world.

REPLACE Reacting WITH *Responding*

Reations often block ability to think systematically

⬇

Focus on noticing reactions

Reactions are usually defensive

⟹ makes them unreliable

EMPATHY *core systems thinking skill*

Breathe in 4 sec

BOX BREATHING

Hold 4 sec

Repeat ≥ 5 min

Breathe out 4 sec

" *Leadership is developing a wise relationship with our own reactions.*

---

visible reactive

invisible proactive

Events

Trends / Patterns

Systems

Structures

Mental Models - Culture

🖊 BREATHE.

✏ WRITE.

🚶 WALK.

⏱ WAIT.

CHAPTER 5

Replace Reacting with Responding

The difference between Action and Re-action is originality and timing.
—Aniekee Tochukwu Ezekiel

Systems thinking is the ability to shift from *reacting to events* to *responsive patterns of behavior* to *generating (improved) systemic structures*. This book is organized to reflect this migration of skills. For most of us, getting past reacting to events is challenging.

As you practice self-awareness (Chapter 4), you'll notice that you are constantly reacting. Something happens in the software. Someone says something in a meeting. Someone does something that impacts you. As a result of that stimuli, you have experiences: thoughts, emotions, physical sensations, attitudes, impulses, or a combination of all those things.

Some of your reactions are benign, like gritting your teeth during a meeting. Some are explosive, like screaming at a driver who cuts you off. Most of your reactions exist somewhere in between, a constant shifting of your mental and emotional state, depending on inputs.

You might not realize how often your thinking is controlled by your reactions.

Figure 5-1 is a slightly different version of the Iceberg Model, where the top levels show visible events and trends. The iceberg process is happening all around us, but also inside of us. We react to situations in ways that are informed by our mental models and reinforcing structures. We may or may not be aware of those underlying layers. But they will inform the things we think, say, and do.

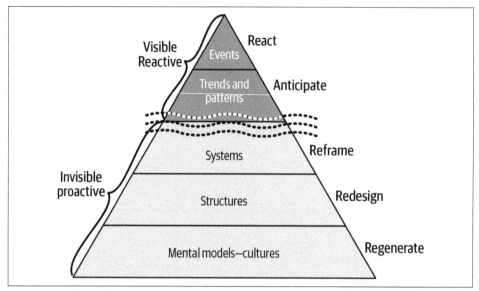

Figure 5-1. The Iceberg Model, with visible and invisible elements delineated, by Jaap Schaveling, Bill Bryan, and Michael Goodman

A reactive mind is antithetical to a proactive mind, which is systems thinking. Just like in the Beer Game (Chapter 3), we believe our reactions are caused by circumstances outside of us, rather than our underlying system. (Which is only sometimes true.) We are, like Beer Game players, blaming the wrong things.

We are *always* in the midst of reactions, our own and everyone's around us. Reactions are unavoidable and often informative. They also add more noise to a noisy situation. Reactions shift us out of systems thinking and into a binary "yes it is, no it isn't" mindstate. Yet our reactions give us information about systemic patterns—ignoring them is ineffectual.

Ideally, you will *experience* a reaction and *contribute* a response.

In Part III, we will develop responses in the form of systemic reasoning. In this chapter, I will recommend ways to recognize and work with reactions.

Noticing Your Reactions

We're such a reactive culture.... It takes a certain strength to be patient and have a plan.
—Greg Berlanti[1]

I'd like us to begin by pausing for a moment. Remember a meeting, or other discussion, where someone said something you didn't like. Remember how it felt, the thoughts that went through your mind, what you experienced afterwards. What do you remember?

Here's an example from my own experience. During a problem-solving Slack discussion, I said something that I hoped was respectful and encouraging. The original poster did not interpret my post as intended and responded with some upsetting and confusing words.

I did not respond; instead, I wrote down my reactions. Here they are, in quick succession:

- I was sorry for inadvertently hurting their feelings.
- I wanted to push back and justify what I'd said.
- I was embarrassed, angry, and frustrated about not being given the benefit of the doubt.
- I quit Slack, then reopened it. Multiple times.
- I sat there doing nothing, confused about what to say or do.
- I remembered a difficult exchange I'd had with this person in the past and decided this was "what they always do."
- I wanted to quickly resolve the problem.
- I decided to practice all the things you will read in this chapter. Because this happened *while I was writing it.*

I had to practice the recommendations you'll read in this chapter because, in the heat of things, we all do.

I took a break and when I came back, the situation had resolved itself. The outcome also demonstrated three key points that are so essential to good systems thinking that I encourage you to read them twice:

---

1 Quoted by Jace Lacob in "'Political Animals': Greg Berlanti on the Clintons, Fiction, and More Clinton Nostalgia," the *Daily Beast*, published July 2012, updated July 2017.

1. *I would have made the* actual problem *worse by reacting.*

   Notice that none of my reactions had anything to do with the actual problem we were trying to solve. You don't even know, reading my reactions, what the actual problem was. By the time I responded, that problem was resolved, and everyone was happy.

2. *Had I reacted, I would have done more damage to the relationship.*

   The next day, we had a friendly, respectful, quick, and clarifying exchange that resolved our miscommunication. I understood how I contributed, and we built trust.

3. *My reactive patterns are so predictable, half the items on the previous list would be there in every example I shared.*

   Even though my reactive patterns rarely get me what I actually need, I always believe they are trustworthy in the heat of the moment.

There are as many reactive patterns as there are people. Some reactive patterns are, perhaps, more common in technology cultures. For example, see Figure 5-2, xkcd's fifth most popular comic, Duty Calls (*https://xkcd.com/386*):

Figure 5-2. From xkcd (https://xkcd.com/386), a webcomic by Randall Munroe

Our habit of only responding to the thing we hear that is "wrong" is so pervasive, I'm surprised when someone doesn't do it. This reactive pattern, coupled with saying "No!" until persuaded otherwise, is perhaps the biggest barrier to systems thinking.

Another one is acting on the impulse to say, do, or fix something immediately—creating endless fire drills with little time for considering root causes. Personally, I've needed to practice not taking an action before I know what might help. I still don't find that easy.

When people don't tend their own reactions or practice self-care (like eating when hungry), they shift a lot of emotional labor onto the people around them. When someone is reactive and lacking self-awareness, they become the cats that need herding. Remember, in systems thinking, nobody gets to be a cat.

The most challenging reactive patterns are the ones that happen over and over again. Death by a Thousand Papercuts. One instance, by itself, maybe isn't a big deal. Someone said something that wasn't particularly friendly in a Request for Comments. But the pattern in which nobody ever says anything friendly or respectful can trigger reactions that are valid but difficult to recognize.

Reactions are recursive. We have a reaction, and we react to our reaction and react to our reaction to the reaction…this is a highly combustible process. When you feel upset by something someone said in a meeting and then judge yourself for feeling upset ("I'm too sensitive"), now you have two reactions to deal with. Now you not only have the original thing bugging you, you also have the desire to fix yourself, or someone else, like the person who upset you.

With self-awareness, we notice the heat generated by our reactions. And practice experiencing them without setting the situation on fire…

…unless or until setting the situation on fire is how we choose to respond.

There are two patterns that often block our ability to transform reacting into responding. The first is the pervasive normalization of opinion giving as knowledge work. The second is the missing skill that too often disables organizations from thinking in systems.

Opinion-Driven as Normal

Opinions are quick ways to share our views and judgments about something, whether or not we have sound reasoning to support our thinking. Whenever two or more are gathered, opinions about technology proliferate. We form tribes with those who share them.

I love our opinions. I'm not a big socializer. At 9 p.m., I'm not heading out to dinner, a bar, or a party. I'm heading to bed, carrying my Kobo.

Except at tech conferences. There, I'm wide awake, long past my toddler bedtime. I once left a conference after-party in Bucharest just in time to catch my early-morning flight. At most conferences, I'm among my tribe, endlessly discussing ideas.

While it can be fun to debate opinions, when it comes to systems thinking, being opinion-driven has its downsides:

We debate dualities.

Our opinions are usually structured as "for or against," "yes or no," "right or wrong," "option A versus option B." Nuanced, intersectional thinking styles are uncommon and sometimes unwelcome. I've rarely heard "for or against Agile" discussed as "it depends on the circumstances and how it's implemented."

We want to be right.

We love our opinions, and we fight to defend them. We want to be right, and we want people to agree that we are right. This is antithetical to systems thinking, where we want to learn and grow.

We ignore context.

Very few things in life, and in tech, are Always Right or Always Wrong. Most things depend on the context. What worked for Netflix or Spotify might be a disaster somewhere else. Opinion-driven discussions don't usually focus on understanding the complexity inherent in each context. Figuring out what "it depends" on would serve us better than debating a universal truth.

We focus on "wrong."

> When someone is accused of being wrong, even the most emotionally intelligent people will get defensive.
>
> —Karen Kwong in *Fast Company* (*https://oreil.ly/dumRN*)

When I share an idea with a group of people who don't work in tech and their responses are kind, respectful, and curious, it surprises me. I've learned to anticipate reactions that immediately point out what I said wrong. Changing this habit is the single most impactful practice I've adopted.

We are emotional.

For a culture that prides itself on Spock-like science logic, people sure do get incensed about a lot of things. I hear endless disdain for other people's thinking, especially people who don't code. I've seen grudges endure and backchanneling run rampant.

I'm fairly sure Spock wouldn't be gossiping in Slack about ideas he doesn't like.

Generally speaking, there is no avoiding forming opinions. When practicing systems thinking, it helps to remember that the definition of an opinion is "a view or judgment formed about something, not necessarily based on fact or knowledge." There is more work you still need to do.

As knowledge workers, our expertise is not demonstrated by our "correct" opinions. Our expertise is demonstrated by our ability to change, drop, and transform our opinions as we learn and grow.

Empathy as a Core Skill

To deeply assess contexts, to truly read undercurrents as well as surface activity, to not miss emerging correspondences between seemingly disparate things, we need to talk about empathy as a skill.

—Ann M. Pendleton-Jullian and John Seely Brown, *Design Unbound* (MIT)

Even when you are responding respectfully and productively to someone else's opinions, you are (usually) missing a key element of systems thinking. Empathy. Your mind might be reacting to that word right now. (Mine does.) Before you reach a conclusion, though, let me describe what I mean (and don't mean) by empathy.

Reaching conclusions objectively, as an observing neutral party of sound judgment, is our usual, linear approach. We analyze (examine methodically), assess (evaluate value), and gently criticize (identify faults). Many of our opinions are formed through this process. As always with linear thinking skills, these are necessary skills.

To think in systems, we shift perspective. We reach conclusions through "feeling, thinking, and perceiving things from an internal frame of reference rather than from an external or objective one" (Pendleton-Jullian). We don't need to (or want to) rely strictly on our own perceptions, but instead, proactively integrate thinking and experiences that are not our own.

Systems thinking is an embodied practice. We are not simply "participating in a complex environment of interdependent relationships and exchanges" (Pendleton-Jullian). We are designing that environment.

We reach conclusions by identifying with other points of view, knowing that we are closely linked to that point of view because we are part of the same system. We are exercising our capacity to understand things from different points of view. You understand (as best you can) what other people are experiencing and how those experiences are interrelated with their thinking. You express both your analysis and your understanding.

This shift is internal and can be very subtle. I do a code review by analyzing the quality of the code, making sure the tests pass and asking for changes in the inefficient parts. I do a code review by understanding what the developer is trying to do and recommending changes that will improve her ability to accomplish it. In both cases, I've left the same code-change comments. But in the second case, I've also left an additional, matterful element: understanding.

Understanding is expressing favorable awareness of other people's experiences. It is thinking and behaving as if you are cognitively and emotionally embedded in the systems you are designing.

Empathy is thinking and acting as part of a system rather than as someone "working on" the system.

When you do a code review, you are part of the communication structure and patterns in the organization that generate events. If your core belief is "I provide leadership by judging code quality," that will scale to "how we do things." If your core belief is "I provide leadership by improving everyone's capacity to write effective code," that will also scale.

Understanding someone's thinking and experience doesn't mean you have to agree with or go along with their conclusions. You can empathize with someone who leaves nasty comments in a code review and still ask them to change their behavior. Empathizing is not the same as condoning.

In my experience, organizations confuse empathy and understanding with avoiding accountability and get stuck. Understanding a systemic issue from someone else's point of view does not mean enabling or empowering (or even agreeing with) that point of view. Respect is acknowledgment, not necessarily tolerance.

We are looking for leverage points in the sociotechnical system. We will inevitably discover them in behavior, especially communication and thinking behavior, that needs to change. If organizational culture is causing many of its own systemic problems, developing tolerance for that culture without changing it won't change anything.

Empathy is a complex topic. I'm going to refocus your attention now back on your own reactions and recommend practices that help you practice empathy toward yourself.

Create Space for Your Reactions

Our reactions are messy and raw. When we create inner space for them to arrive and be a little rowdy, we can help them settle down and become orderly. If conceptual integrity and cohesion are the most important considerations in systems design, then reacting is the storm that is constantly pulling those qualities apart.

Our goal is to increase our capacity for holding reactive thoughts in our state box, while we construct more-cohesive output.

Our reactions to other people's thinking or our circumstances, like all systemic phenomena, depend on many factors. Understanding the root cause takes time and consideration. Our goal is to give ourselves that time. There are four ways we are practicing when working with reactions:

- Notice them without judging them.
- Look for systemic information in our reactions.
- Don't suppress them.
- Manage your own reactions and let others do the same.

We all experience table-flip moments, an urge to push back on the person disagreeing with us in a meeting, our partner, our boss. When we do push back, we might feel better in the moment, but we rarely say something that improves the situation. When a group of people are stuck in reactions, they create momentum that moves them further and further away from a cohesive conclusion.

An important caveat: sometimes, your urge to push back is the correct response. "No, stop, back off, this is not okay." How do you discern? There is, alas, no rulebook to follow. It depends. We learn through experience. Linear thinking sorts behaviors into "right" and "wrong"—reacting is not (necessarily) either.

Reacting is, when it comes to systems thinking, potentially unskillful. You are being derailed by other people's thinking. When we practice, we create more options for ourselves, including the option to react in the moment.

Here's an example: a new architect is meeting with an engineering team for the first time. An engineer is sharing his screen to demonstrate a problem. A Slack notification pops up, sent by the team's boss, who is also in the meeting. The notification says "I don't think we should trust what she [the architect] says, she's not technical enough." The architect, of course, sees this. So many reactions arise!

A month later, that same boss is quite happy with the architect. But that's not the point of the story. The point of the story is that the actual problem being shown by the engineer would not have been solved if the architect had been derailed by reactions. The boss was wrong. The architect's technical skill became apparent over time. I'm sure you can imagine, though, how challenging it was for the architect to continue focusing on the problem.

In this situation, the architect did not respond to the comment. In a different situation, she might have paused the meeting and dealt with it. There wasn't a "right" decision here. But there was a reactive option available.

Our reactions are usually defensive, which makes them unreliable. They derail productive insight because the focus shifts to resolving the inner discomfort. Our reactive thoughts are filled with emotional baggage, cognitive biases, conditioned responses, misunderstandings, and false narratives. Logical fallacies, which we explore in Part III, thrive in our reactive minds.

That's okay! Our reactions are still worthy of our attention. The architect felt insulted, and that's a fair response. This wasn't the first time strangers had presumed that the architect isn't technically skillful or capable of leadership. When we are reacting to a pattern, that pattern probably exists as a systemic feedback loop.

Your reactions contain information, insights that are as-yet unformed, that might help you construct a response. The salient point isn't that our reactions are bad, it is that they might be a tangled mess that lacks cohesion.

After the meeting, the architect still had all her reactive thoughts, feelings, and an adrenaline rush, like boxes of stuff piled up in her garage. She needed to tidy up, sort out which thoughts to keep, and recycle the rest. In systems thinking, we are tidying all the time. Decluttering and prioritizing communication.

Organizational thinking is more likely to set things on fire than build something. But when we speak for the system, we try to create elegant simplicity from the mess.

We don't necessarily act on our reactions…we also don't suppress them.

I have a chronic habit of suppressing what I think and feel when I'm in upsetting situations. I clamp down, hold my breath, and put on my most reasonable "adulting" face. I *manage* these situations. Managing reactions is sometimes a good trait to have professionally. It helps us avoid devolving into unproductive squabbling. But it isn't authentic.

When I stuff down my feelings, controlling my body language and tone of voice, silencing my reactive thoughts…they all come out later. Except later, they come out in the form of resentment, confusion, exhaustion, fighting about nothing with my family, pervasive frustration with my job, and eventual burnout. My reactions pile up until I perpetually feel unheard and unacknowledged.

Those feelings have been an accurate assessment of some situations. But they also indicate that I am not listening to and acknowledging my authentic experiences.

The flip side of this habit is managing other people's feelings. I have seen this trend accelerate in technology groups, putting managers in the role of "cat herder." Their unacknowledged job is to keep people happy by sorting out all their reactions, trying to keep their thinking on track.

Managing other people's reactions is the work we do with toddlers. Leadership is the practice of creating psychological safety, not by managing people's reactions but by expecting everyone to develop self-awareness, do their own emotional labor, and pay attention to their impact on others.

More importantly, systems leadership is developing a wise relationship with your own reactions.

The practices I will recommend are decidedly non-technical. Breathe. Write. Walk. Wait. That doesn't mean they aren't critical to quality technical design. In your experience, do groups embroiled in drama, in need of cat herding, deliver quality code?

In my experience, teams that pay attention to their reactions without getting swept up in them also deliver great work. The more we practice, the more impactful we can make our (eventual) responses.

Your Practice: Options When Reacting

How do we minimize the amount of reaction we contribute? What do we do when reactions get triggered? How do we create space?

First, and most importantly, we notice when we are reacting! We watch our thinking and feelings, noticing the warning signs of a reactive pattern. You'll see that your reactive patterns are predictable, and maybe even tedious.

Here are some practices that might help. The first one, when thinking in systems, is essential.

"Yes, and…"

This practice is the easiest and most impactful way to generate the right mindset for thinking together. "Yes, and…" is a rule followed by improvisational comedy actors. These actors get up on stage in front of a live audience and make up scenes in real time. This is daunting work. The television show *Whose Line Is It Anyway?* is an example of improv. Figure 5-3 is an image of actors using the "Yes, and…" technique, to think well together in real time.

Figure 5-3. Swedish improv actors from the Stockholm City Theatre (Source: Frankie Fouganthin (https://oreil.ly/_aEg0))

"Yes, and…" is critical to their work because it trains them to cooperate, to think well together and create a flow of ideas, rather than shut down contributions before they have a chance to flourish. Improv teams warm up playing "Yes, and…" the way runners stretch before a run.

The practice is simple: when someone expresses an idea, you acknowledge it and add something to it. In your body and mind, you accept what is happening, you mentally say "yes." When you respond, you add to the idea, flow with it, strengthen it.

To be clear, this does not mean agreeing! Acknowledging has nothing to do with agreeing. Here are two examples:

> Hollis: We need the API response times to be faster because too many client connections are dropping after three seconds.
> Briar: The response times are fast enough. That's not the problem.

OR

> Hollis: We need the API response times to be faster because too many client connections are dropping after three seconds.
> Briar: Thanks, Hollis, for describing the impact of response times. I wasn't aware of slow response experiences. What alerted you to this problem?

You are always listening critically. You are working together to generate momentum. As soon as someone contracts into "No," the whole scene crashes. I've experienced this as an actor—it is nearly impossible to recover from, and the audience can't help but notice. I've experienced it in countless tech meetings too.

Perhaps you can already see why changing this one habit would improve most technology discussions?

"Yes, and…" is a respectful approach to discussing ideas: acknowledging what the previous person said and adding to it.

"Yes, and…" isn't about everybody agreeing or pretending to get along. It is about breaking the powerful mental habit of contracting, demanding that others "change my mind." It is an agreement to do the necessary systems thinking work by leaning in and thinking critically, together.

When thinking in systems, knowledge workers are technology's improv teams.

The 24-Hour Rule

This practice changed my life. I was caught up in a situation that was full of demanding drama. In the midst, I was given this advice: wait 24 hours to respond. When I received the next emotional email demanding an answer, I did not respond for 24 hours.

This practice didn't (at first) change the emails I received. It changed the answers I sent (when and if I sent them). I realized that I wasn't giving myself space, and 24 hours made my responses wiser.

Professionally, I've been surprised by this rule. When I waited 24 hours and then read the email again, at least half the time…I'd simply misunderstood.

Breathe

The first time I taught breathing exercises to a group of software engineers, I feared they'd rage quit the workshop. Instead, they asked me for more. Stress is a constant part of our work, and breathing exercises actually help.

I asked the group to remember a stressful situation and notice what they thought and how they felt. Then we did five minutes of breathing practice. I asked them to notice again how they felt. Most people said they felt much better. One person asked for exercises that energize them during boring meetings.

Breathing techniques calm the flight-or-fight reactions in our mind and body. As the adrenaline stops pumping, we can think more reasonably.

The instructions are easy and flexible:

1. Make yourself comfortable.
2. Set a timer for at least five minutes.
3. Breathe in while counting.
4. Breathe out while counting.

Count to one, count to five, or count any number in between. Choose a number that is comfortable but a stretch for you.

When your exhales are longer than your inhales and you slow down the number of breaths you take per minute, the practice has a calming effect. Faster inhales and exhales, with more rounds per minute, will be energizing.

My favorite variation is box breathing.

1. Breathe in for four.
2. Hold for four.
3. Breathe out for four.
4. Continue this for at least five minutes.

There are apps that guide you through these exercises. You can add soothing music or white noise in the background. For some people, breath lacks sufficient sensation to keep their attention. You can squeeze a ball, squeeze and release, to help keep your focus.

Whatever method you choose, experiment with breathing before you send an email or take an action. Experiment whenever you are reacting. See what happens.

Go for a Walk

Have you ever worked for six hours trying to find a bug, gave up, went to bed, and in the morning, you knew how to fix it? Given up when stuck, gone out for pizza, then knew exactly what to do when you got back? The same magic works when you are stuck in a reaction. Go for a walk. Stretch, move, dance, ride your bike, play with the dog or cat or hacky sack…move your mind off the problem and into a physical experience. You'll think better afterwards.

Make a Snack or Take a Nap

There is a handy acronym to consider in moments of reaction: HALT. It means hungry, angry, lonely, or tired. You are more likely to overreact to input from others when any of these qualities are present.

You will struggle to construct a sound response if you are overtired or haven't eaten since yesterday. Take time to eat or cat nap and you'll improve your mental balance. Eat healthy food, take a nap, or connect with a loved one.

If you must act under HALT circumstances, try to do the smallest possible thing. For example, create space by saying "I'll be back in 30 minutes and will respond then."

Write

Set a timer and write out, by hand, everything happening in your mind. Don't edit, just go. This practice is best paired with a physical follow-up, like going for a walk. The writing will help you gain insight; the walk will help you relax.

Writing is a method of inquiry. The writing can take any form or no form at all. Letters you never intend to send, modeling or documenting a problem, trying to see it more clearly. The goal isn't to write for sharing; it is to sort out your reactions from your more trustworthy perspectives.

Notice Your Triggers: They Are Clues

A logical fallacy is a flaw in reasoning. For example, "if we adopt cloud technologies, eventually we will get massive bills that will bankrupt us, so we should stick to on-prem hosting." This is called the "slippery slope," which equates a single step with inevitable catastrophe. There are many steps in between those two extremes.

The further we move away from linear, incremental reasoning toward systems thinking, the more space is created for logical fallacies to flourish. They are a form of reactive reasoning.

Erroneous leaps of logic trigger a spiral of reactive, fallacious thinking. Rather than constructing sound recommendations, when we share them, we trigger a maelstrom of reactions. In the previous example, everyone will be distracted by the assertion that cloud adoption leads to bankruptcy, rather than focusing on the problem at hand. Also, when there are gaps in our reasoning, people might lose faith in our thinking, so being knowledge workers, it's very important to notice them.

Advertising and politics depend on the use of logical fallacies; we are exposed to them constantly. They appeal to our baser instincts. We are trained to use logical fallacies rather than to spot them.

We need to spot them. Bugs in our reasoning will inevitably lead to buggy systems design.

In Part III, we go into specific examples of logical fallacies. For now, notice when your reaction is triggered by an error in logic. No doubt, this is happening more often than you realize.

MAGO's Reactions

While this chapter might seem the furthest away from "technology skills" so far, it actually describes the challenge for MAGO better than all other chapters. MAGO is reacting to an event: the maintainers of their core software have gone out of business.

This reaction potentially blocks, or at least makes difficult, responding to the change as a systemic challenge.

Paying closer attention to reactivity gives them three opportunities:

Re-evaluate the binary thinking
Binary thinking like print versus digital has defined how people and technology are currently organized. Understand the nuance that is inherent in their current circumstances. (For example, the *New York Times* trained their journalists (*https://oreil.ly/En-hA*) to develop a wider range of digital artifacts.)

Change the decision-making structure
The obsolete software isn't an unexpected crisis; it's the logical outcome of decisions over 20 years. If the MAGO team can step back from their reaction and retrospect, they might discover a leverage point—a place to change their communication structure to serve the system's emerging needs. (Team Topology case studies (*https://oreil.ly/emZJR*) illustrate an approach to these types of changes.)

Explore the reaction
Organizations, like people, are (usually) reacting to a valid, frightening possibility. If MAGO's core software fails, they will lose millions of dollars a day and disrupt business-critical operations. To avoid this crisis, they dove into finding a solution. What if they stayed with their reaction longer, gave it space to inform them? For example, they might model "what happens if a quick solution isn't available?" Shifting their perception might uncover multiple paths forward. (The pandemic gives us many examples of organizational reactions to a crisis—from Amazon's strike-inducing response to employee's health concerns to Zoom's focus on their competitive advantage: making the video quality better.)

MAGO's situation is common during a paradigm shift. They need to keep their current system running while simultaneously bringing their future system online. This nuance is challenging for many organizations. In MAGO's case, embracing the complexity of their circumstances is a crucial step forward.

Support for Your Practice: The Stories Don't Have to Be the Same

Here is a story to illustrate how complex, and intersectional, reactions are in real life. The motto is: Don't ignore them and don't take them too personally.

I'm standing on a street corner, waiting for my husband to pick me up at our agreed-upon time. Cool spring rain is pouring down, and I don't have an umbrella. My light jacket is soaking through as the minutes pass beyond the pickup time.

I scowl at every car that isn't our car. I've called and texted him multiple times. "Where are you?!" "I'll be late for my meeting." "My laptop might be ruined." "Where are you? My lunch is getting cold." This sucks. I'm growing increasingly angry as the chill sets in.

Then fear takes over. He hasn't answered. What's happening? Maybe he's dead?!?!

Fourteen minutes later, my husband pulls up. When I see the car, my fear evaporates. Okay, he's not dead. Now I'm angry again, the words already forming on my lips as I open the door.

Earlier in our relationship, an escalating Reaction Fest would begin. He'd react to my anger because, from his point of view, it was unfair or unwarranted. He'd react to my reaction. I'd react to his reaction and we'd spiral all afternoon.

Today, he says, "Oh my goodness sweetie, you're so wet, I'm so sorry, that must have sucked." He listens to my frustration. He digs around the backseat for a towel to dry my hair. He asks me if I still have time to make it to my meeting. "This is awful and sucky, you must have been so worried."

Then, as I take a breath, he tells me his story.

He'd stopped at the grocery story on his way to meet me, as agreed. When he arrived, he reached into his pocket to check the shopping list on his phone. His phone wasn't there. We'd visited three shops that day. He'll need to retrace his steps. He decides to quickly run in and buy groceries, pick me up for my meeting, then go find his phone.

Twelve minutes later, groceries paid for, he rushes out to our car with just enough time to get me. Another car is stopped behind ours, blocking him in. The driver's side door is open; there is no driver inside.

My husband stomps around the parking lot, looking for the offending wanderer. He yells, "Hey!" but no one is around. He goes back into the store and waits impatiently in line at the customer service desk, behind someone returning apples. When the apple person moves off, he asks the service representative to page the driver.

"Oh!" she says, "he was having chest pains. He came staggering in, asking us to call an ambulance. The EMTs are on their way. I'll get someone to move the car for you, if the keys are in it."

He goes back outside and discovers that the car parked in the opposing spot has left. He pulls through and drives as quickly as he can, while still being safe, worrying about me standing in the rain.

In the past, when I discovered that my feelings of anger, frustration, or confusion were unwarranted, I'd feel guilty for having those feelings. I'd suppress them. Why couldn't I stay all Zen while waiting in the rain with my ruined lunch and no ability to get in touch with him? Why wasn't I more worried about the poor man having a heart attack than my meeting?

What changed our dynamics was one little mantra: the stories don't have to be the same.

We learned to empathize with the experience the other person actually had…not the experience they would have had if they'd known things they didn't know. Not the experience we think they should be having. I don't have to make him wrong or make myself wrong. The whole situation created frustration for everyone. Even though nobody, including the driver of the blocking car, is to blame.

When we are reacting, we are almost always blaming. We are always projecting our story onto other people. When we don't understand what's going on, blame tries to fill the gaps. Sometimes, blame is accurate. But it will rarely help us *solve* the problem.

Systems thinking is integrating the story of standing in the rain with the story of being stuck at the grocery store with no phone. It is integrating the business point of view with the technological reality. It is understanding the pain other teams experience when we make upstream systems changes. It is recognizing that your point of view, real and matterful as it is, is not the whole story.

A confluence of events happened that day, not a recurring systemic issue that needed addressing. My husband is rarely late. Blame will push you to fix fix fix. Sometimes you do need to change a systemic pattern. Sometimes there's a problem to fix.

Sometimes, the right move is to simply dry off and go home.

A SYSTEM OF *Learning*

> " Systems Thinking is, above all else, an integrated approach to learning.

ⓘ **Metacognition**

Ability to reflect on how we think and learn

Life-long Learning

Learning never ends until you do

Improve how you think, not what you think

Knowledge Worker

uses mind to originate and craft knowledge

Learning = Inquiry in a nonlinear way

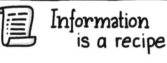 Information is a recipe

 Knowledge is a cook

 Wisdom is a chef

Non-linear learning process

DATA ⟷ KNOWLEDGE

UNDERSTANDING

INFORMATION ⟷ WISDOM

CHAPTER 6

A System of Learning

A firm's competitive advantage depends more than anything on its knowledge. Or, to be slightly more specific, on what it knows—how it uses what it knows—and how fast it can know something new.

    —Larry Prusak

This book is titled *Learning Systems Thinking*. So far, we've talked about systems, and we've talked about thinking. Now, we'll talk about the most important word: learning.

You might be imagining classrooms and chalkboards, workbooks and homework, AWS certification exams, and whiteboard tests. Maybe you are excited to read this chapter; maybe you want to skip it. Our learning experiences have a profound impact on whether or not we enjoy learning. Whatever you imagine will probably be different from what I mean by "learning." As systems thinkers, our focus is on generative learning—increasing our capacity for synthesizing knowledge and experience.

This chapter encourages you to design your own learning practice, a lifelong endeavor that improves your capacity for systems thinking. Learning outcomes, from this point of view, include goals like the following:

- Improve your ability to shift perspective
- Increase your tolerance for ambiguity
- Understand context and relational impact
- Identify patterns and structures
- Create groupings and boundaries without reductionism
- Think critically and apply sound judgment
- Develop effective interpersonal skills

If wisdom is the goal of learning—and in systems, it is—we can envision learning along a continuum of increasing contextual and relational complexity (Figure 6-1).

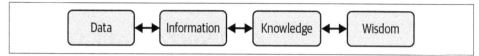

Figure 6-1. Data, information, knowledge, and wisdom

Data is raw materials, facts. I was born on April 22nd.

Information gives the data shape and meaning. It has more conceptual relevance than data. My mother was young when she gave birth to me, in the middle of a late April snowstorm, on what would later become Earth Day in the US.

Information is, to some extent, conceptual. Imagining my birth requires you to make inferences, reach conclusions without explicit data. You don't have a photograph of my mother or the inches of snow outside the hospital window. (You didn't know I was born in a hospital.) When you imagine my mother and the snow, you will draw on your own experiences. The images in your mind will be slightly different from reality but sufficiently similar for us to understand each other.

There is nuance in information, subtle shades of meaning. Nuance increases as we move toward knowledge and wisdom.

Knowledge is trickier to define, in part because experts are endlessly debating the definition. We don't agree on what it is because knowledge is a slippery, fluid thing. The following is a commonly used definition of knowledge, favored by knowledge strategy professor Larry Prusak:

> *Knowledge is a fluid mix of framed experience, values, contextual information, expert insight and grounded intuition that provides an environment and framework for evaluating and incorporating new experiences and information. It originates and is applied in the minds of knowers. In organizations it often becomes embedded not only in documents and repositories but also in organizational routines, processes, practices and norms.*
>
> —Davenport and Prusak, *Working Knowledge* (Harvard Business Review Press)

Knowledge is a sophisticated integration of data, information, and experience. It is the conceptual material we use to create laws and theorems; best practices and heuristics (mental shortcuts for solving a problem); strategies and predictions based on patterns (like during a pandemic).

Knowledge relies on conceptual integrity (Chapter 2), the glue that holds context (a unique situation) and knowledge (insight about that system) together. It requires a bigger conceptual leap of faith because it depends on justifiable inference. Inference is reaching a conclusion based on reasoning and evidence. In systems thinking, the quality of our knowledge depends on the quality of our systemic reasoning. That is why the next chapter—Chapter 7—is all about practicing that skill.

An example of a concept we accept as knowledge is $E=mc^2$. You probably have faith in Einstein's theory of special relativity even if you don't know all the data that justifies it. We accept concepts as knowledge when we know they are integrated with experience, observation, and sound reasoning.

Nothing escapes "it depends," not even $E=mc^2$. Knowledge depends on the context. This equation is only true for objects (mass) *at rest* and is not true for photons, which are massless.

Data, information, knowledge, and wisdom. What is the difference between knowledge and wisdom? Russell Ackoff, systems thinking pioneer, says that wisdom "is the ability to increase effectiveness."[1] Wisdom is applying knowledge in ways that generate growth in a meaningful, impactful direction. What is a "meaningful direction?" How do we discern what "meaningful" means in a particular context? Therein lies a paradox (systems thinking includes self-contradictory statements that are nonetheless true). We need wisdom in order to recognize wisdom when we see it.

We are cultivating wisdom when we are aware of how much knowledge we are missing: how much we don't know. Systems thinking begins here—with the understanding that we can't know everything about everything. We don't need to. We can learn how to operate in circumstances we can't fully understand.

Understanding is the effort that binds data, information, knowledge, and wisdom together. Ackoff adds a layer between knowledge and wisdom called "understanding." Understanding is knowing why the knowledge matters. Understanding is the process of discerning how knowledge enables growth in a particular context.

Figure 6-1 showed data, information, and knowledge along a continuum, which is helpful to envision. The actual relationship is nonlinear and looks more like Figure 6-2.

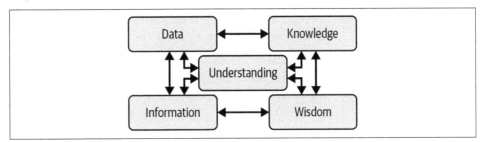

Figure 6-2. Nonlinear learning process

---

1 A short article by Russell Ackoff worth reading! From *Ackoff's Best: His Classic Writings on Management* (*https://oreil.ly/et4H-*) (Wiley, 1999), pp. 170–172.

I've used the word "knowledge" many times in this book. This chapter is about learning. And I call us knowledge workers. Given the ambiguity, the inexactness of definitions, what do I mean when I say these words?

Using Larry's definition, Ackoff's description, and my own knowledge experience, here are the definitions we'll rely on when practicing systems thinking:

Knowledge
> Our ability to generate artifacts (models, documents, code, software), routines, processes, practices, and cultural norms that are insightful and valuable in a particular context.

Learning
> The ability to craft knowledge.

Understanding
> Our ability to discern which knowledge will be most effective in a particular context.

Wisdom
> Our ability to discover true leverage points in the systems we inhabit and push them in a valuable direction.

Therefore:

Knowledge work is understanding and applying knowledge (experience, values, contextual information, expert insight, and grounded intuition) in ways that enable organizations to evaluate and incorporate new experiences and information.

A *knowledge worker* is someone who generates and applies knowledge in ways that create more knowledge.

Two more important words are needed: *stock* and *flow*. Knowledge stock is the store of knowledge you have developed or can access. Generally speaking, your knowledge stock increases your *efficiency*. Your knowledge flow is your ability to transfer knowledge between people (or between people and technology) in ways that change and shift the system. Knowledge flow increases your *effectiveness*.

In technology cultures, we tend to value knowledge stock over knowledge flow. Knowledge stock is knowing a lot about JavaScript frameworks and how to apply that knowledge. A 10x developer is a prime example of knowledge stock.

Knowledge flow is the measure of how much knowledge you cultivate in the world around you. It is also your ability to evolve your knowledge as paradigms (as well as tools, practices, and processes) change. Can you synthesize knowledge and experience (yours and other people's) in ways that generate impactful and valuable changes? Can you use knowledge to help others generate valuable impact?

The better your knowledge flow, the more likely you are to discover (at least some) wisdom.

On his list of 11 common mistakes organizations make, Prusak includes "Emphasizing knowledge stock to the detriment of knowledge flow." Learning is increasing your capacity for knowledge flow.

Let's make our definitions even simpler. Here is my favorite metaphor for understanding the difference between information, knowledge, and wisdom:

> Information is a recipe.
>
> Knowledge is a cook.
>
> Wisdom is a chef.

 As a chef, you might learn how to flambé, but your goal is not to become a flambé developer, hired to flambé, after demonstrating your flambé skills in an interview. Your goal is to do appetizing things with food, sometimes by setting it on fire.

Learning, as we'll explore in this chapter, is becoming a knowledge chef.

A Learning-Driven Career

The illiterate of the 21st Century will not be those who cannot read and write, but those who cannot learn, unlearn, and relearn.

—Alvin Toffler

Twenty years ago, while learning PHP, I downloaded an open source CMS for the first time (Drupal) and got curious about it. I found a client with a problem I could solve using that application. I continued learning necessary technical and social competencies as challenges arose. How do I manage clients? Where do I go for support when a bug won't fix? How do I set up good deployment processes? How do I push data from my dev instance to production without committing mortal sins? Competency is the ability to do something successfully or efficiently.

A few years later, I was engineering lead at one of the top Drupal consultancies, building enterprise sites and teaching core competencies at conferences. My career has always depended on constant learning, alone and with everyone around me. Fortunately, when you put learning at the center of your career, you scale.

Lately, I've heard a lot of discussions about whether or not software development attracts people who love to learn. Some experts say that my passion for learning isn't common among technologists anymore. This may be true. Most of us are shaped by an educational system that trains us to meet external expectations as preparation for a career meeting organizational expectations. Our actual interests, our deep curiosity and desire for knowledge, might be relegated to after-hours hobbies.

 Thinking of learning as meeting expectations can be a tough mental habit to break.

Systems thinking arises from an internal motivation, a desire to understand and contribute knowledge to the world around you. Developing a systems mind requires constantly learning—about yourself and the reality in which you exist.

There is no way, that I'm aware of, to think in systems without developing personal mastery—a deep understanding of your learning process and how to improve it. While I appreciate that not everyone wants to be a systems thinker (and that's totally fine), I remain convinced that systems thinking depends on a strong impulse to learn.

The practices in this chapter help you create a framework for thinking about yourself as a knowledge worker. I hope you will be inspired to embrace lifelong, generative learning—and as a result, experience both deeper satisfaction and increasing professional value while you navigate the complex world of technology systems.

Let's begin by understanding what drives you.

Practice 1: What Motivates You?

Set aside 20 minutes (or so) to write answers to these questions. You can use the prompts or you can simply write about your motivations as a knowledge worker.

- What drives you?
- Why did you choose this career path?
- What motivates you to keep learning? Why do you learn new things when you could be binge-watching Netflix or playing video games?

If nothing comes to mind, ask yourself: If I could spend a week learning anything, what would I learn? Why is it matterful to me? What do I enjoy about it?

Next, consider the value. Why do I care about this subject? What value does my knowledge generate? For myself? For others? Why does that value matter to me?

Here are some examples:

From a chef
> Nourishment is the most intrinsically valuable human experience. It influences our health, sense of belonging, personal satisfaction, and the ecosystem that supports us. I want to be part of that nourishment and improve the impact food has on people and the planet.

From a systems architect
> Reality refuses to bow down to power. Many of our concepts, mental models, tools, social structures, and ways of doing things limit, rather than enhance, our ability to thrive in the world. I want to transform the systems that hold us back into systems that generate wisdom.

From a JavaScript developer
> Software tools enable people to do important things, generate knowledge, and live more efficient lives. I want to create tools that empower people.

Designing Your Learning Activities

You've already learned a lot about learning in this book, though you might not have realized it. Nonlinear thinking, crafting conceptual integrity, shifting your perspective, improving self-awareness, and finding signal amidst the noise all depend on continuous learning.

You've also done practices like writing, modeling, and contemplating that are core learning practices. As you continue, there are four types of activities that I encourage you to integrate into any subject, skill, concept, or theme you are exploring; generate artifacts, observe and inquire, synthesize knowledge, and gain experience.

Generate Artifacts

As technologists, we use language, symbols, and reasoning to create software. We use spoken languages like English to talk about problems and solutions. We use symbolic languages like shapes and icons to create models. We encode our ideas using, well, code. Code is a language (like Python).

Knowledge work is inextricable from language and the structure of communication.

When we construct concepts (ideas), we share them using language. This connection, moving ideas from our minds into a language construct, is our most impactful learning practice. It is the way we give form and shape to concepts. It's also how we generate knowledge flow.

Artifacts can be made of other stuff, like music or, in the case of our chef example, food. The point is less about "write something" than it is about "make something" with your thoughts.

Examples of artifact activities that increase knowledge stock:

- For the chef: Dinner
- For the systems architect: A model
- For the JavaScript developer: Code

Examples of artifact activities that increase knowledge flow:

- For the chef: Making dinner with other people
- For the systems architect: Getting feedback on an artifact
- For the JavaScript developer: Documentation

Observe and Inquire

In systems, the questions you generate are more valuable than the answers you discover. You can't discover answers unless you are asking the right questions. When learning, incorporate observing and letting your curiosity generate questions. Good questions will occur to you as you observe. If not, you can always rely on the tried and true "why, what, how, who, and when" to structure further inquiry.

Examples of observe and inquire activities that increase knowledge stock:

- For the chef: Eat meals made by others; ask questions
- For the systems architect: Observe how a system works; ask questions
- For the JavaScript developer: Read and run code made by others; ask questions

Examples of observe and inquire activities that increase knowledge flow:

- For the chef: Share your observations about vegetable ripeness and quality
- For the systems architect: Do EventStorming with a group
- For the JavaScript developer: Pair with another developer

Synthesize

This is where the familiar learning activities happen: reading books, watching talks, listening to podcasts, or taking a course, working with others. Your goal is to synthesize other people's knowledge and experience with your own. For best results, do the other three practices along with this one. For example, reading this book gives you information. Practicing systems thinking generates knowledge.

Synthesizing is different from accumulating information. Your aim is to identify and understand the patterns and core concepts that matter. You are looking for relationships in your subject of interest, the themes that recur, and the ideas that are trusted. You are thinking critically about the knowledge you are synthesizing, not simply storing it in your mind.

Examples of synthesize activities that increase knowledge stock:

- For the chef: Reading J. Kenji López-Alt's books
- For the systems architect: Attending a software architecture conference
- For the JavaScript developer: Taking courses in various frameworks

Examples of synthesize activities that increase knowledge flow:

- For the chef: Writing a book
- For the systems architect: Teaching a hands-on workshop
- For the JavaScript developer: Publishing code samples that solve a tricky problem

Experience

Experience is our greatest teacher. Applying what you are learning to real-world challenges will teach you how to adapt your learning practice to solve real-world problems. When I teach courses for software professionals, the most asked questions are about challenges I rarely read about in books. The questions are about "How do I develop this skill I didn't know I needed?"

In the real world, we are experiencing everything, all at once. Our chef isn't (just) making a dish; they are making a menu or building a team of chefs or running a restaurant. Our systems architect isn't (just) implementing Kafka streams; they are discovering a leverage point or building a learning organization or inventing an information system. Our JavaScript developer isn't (just) writing JavaScript; they are selecting frameworks or building component libraries or enabling an organization to better serve their customers.

The hardest part of learning is understanding the relationship between your knowledge and the entire framework of knowledge that you inhabit.

Experience, if you engage with self-awareness, will also reveal your strengths and weaknesses. You'll discover your super powers, the things you do whenever you need to do it. And the things that you can't do, even when you practice harder. Focusing on your strengths and partnering with people who have skills you don't is a dynamic way to learn.

Examples of experience-building activities that increase knowledge stock:

- For the chef: Create a multi-course meal
- For the systems architect: Build a software system
- For the JavaScript developer: Build software

Examples of experience-building activities that increase knowledge flow:

- For the chef: Design the relationships between the courses
- For the systems architect: Design relationships between the software and people parts
- For the JavaScript developer: Design relationships between the components

Practice 2: Describe Your Activities

Before you start this practice, reread your learning motivations and values. Select an area of focus that will help you embody what you value. For example, our chef might choose local food options and how to rely on them. Our systems architect might choose a systemic challenge like knowledge management. Our JavaScript developer might choose developing expertise in multiple frameworks.

Describe ways you can apply the learning activities to your area of focus.

- What artifacts can you create?
- What can you observe?
- What questions do you want to explore?
- What learning resources will help you understand?
- Who are people with the expertise you need?
- What can you build?
- What other opportunities for experience do you want to explore?

Now that you have a plan, let's expand it to include the systems thinking skills you most need.

Designing Your Learning Outcomes

Learning objectives for systems thinkers are different from traditional learning outcomes. Our goal is to increase systems thinking skills and knowledge flow, which are impossible to measure with traditional knowledge stock measurements like exams. A Python course, for example, might measure your learning by giving you a graded assignment. As a systems thinker, the real measure will be "Can you discern when to use Python to help solve real-world problems and, then, deliver that solution? What other tools, skills, and practices do you need to accomplish this?"

When you are improving your ability to think in systems, your goals are to:

- Improve your ability to shift perspective
- Increase your tolerance for ambiguity
- Understand context and relational impact
- Identify patterns and structures
- Create groupings and boundaries without reductionism
- Think critically and apply sound judgment
- Develop your interpersonal skills

You are learning to build concepts. Concepts are the building blocks we use to construct knowledge. Imagine that every new idea or insight you experience is a Lego brick. As you learn, you expand the number of bricks available to you. You increase your ability to build new shapes with bricks. And you improve your ability to discern what missing bricks are needed to form a meaningful, solid shape.

You also improve your reshaping skills. You can look at a process constructed by concepts (like a CI/CD pipeline) and figure out which bricks to remove. Or which bricks to move so you can form more effective relationship patterns. Learning is pattern thinking as well as information gathering.

Software depends on structuring concepts more often than you might realize. A function call, for example, is a conceptual structure used to organize code for the human mind. The code itself, generally speaking, doesn't care. We use functions to form conceptual relationships and categorize activities. Our concepts are so interwoven with working software, there is no potential (or reason) to pull them apart. We think, therefore we build. Our conceptual processes are the code and vice versa.

In the next practice, you'll identify learning outcomes and how you might measure them. You don't need to achieve all of them! And you might come up with a few that aren't included.

Practice 3: Learning Outcomes

Select a few skills on this list that you'd like to develop as part of your learning plan. I've given you a few questions to consider and examples from our chef, systems architect, and JavaScript developer. Even if you choose only one of these outcomes, you will be shifting your perspective away from knowledge stock toward improving your knowledge flow capabilities.

Improve Your Ability to Shift Perspective

Linear thinking directs us to look at things from one perspective. Systems thinking always involves multiple perspectives. Training ourselves to shift perspective is a core practice.

- Can you think about this subject from multiple points of view?
- Can you look beneath the surface of events to discern the patterns, structures, and mental models?
- Can you identify the impact of a systemic change on everyone that might be impacted?

Examples:

- Chef: Describe the impact of a meal on the land and farmers who produce the ingredients.
- Systems architect: Describe a systems change from five different perspectives.
- JavaScript developer: How will this interface be experienced by a blind person?

Increase Your Tolerance for Ambiguity

In systems, there is rarely one right answer, magic bullet, or right way to do anything. Even if there is a right answer, things change. Soon enough, your answer is no longer right. We are always holding multiple mental representations simultaneously in our minds, like the code, the software architecture, and what the code is meant to do. We are also creating new mental representations by integrating our previous experience and knowledge with the novel challenges we face.

Developing cognitive flexibility means changing your own mind as you consider new perspectives or reconsider old ones. Cognitive dissonance, the sometimes uncomfortable experience of holding two (or more) contradictory ideas in your mind without rationalizing them away, is part of that process.

- Does my learning increase my comfort with complexity?
- Does it strengthen my conceptual flexibility?
- Does it put tools in my toolbox that help me continue working in changing situations?

Examples:

- Chef: How do you decide what to create?
- Systems architect: How do you begin working on a complex challenge?
- JavaScript developer: Why is my approach a good fit for this circumstance?

Understand Context and Relational Impact

In systems, we are forming and reforming conceptual relationships between ideas and experiences, whether or not those relationships are explicitly communicated. We are designing solutions to challenges that are directly related to the context that is experiencing the challenge. And we are trying to predict the impact of a change, even though we can't know for sure what it will be.

- How is my subject dependent on context?
- How is it related to other subjects?
- Does my learning improve my ability to predict patterns of change?

Examples:

- Chef: How do different cuisines interrelate? How do they relate to the cultures they originate in? What other factors (like economy or industry) impact them?
- Systems architect: What is this system's purpose? What are the activities that make up this system's purpose? What is the relationship between those activities; how do they rely (and not) on each other?
- JavaScript developer: Why does this software matter? What is the relationship between this application and other software, tools, and contexts (like phone versus desktop)?

Identify Patterns and Structures

Pattern recognition is understanding how events over time form patterns that then inform choices and behaviors. Structures arise to reinforce those patterns. For example, the organizational hiring process is a series of steps designed to generate "good hires" through a structure that enforces ideas about what "good hire" means.

- What patterns and structures influence this subject?
- What patterns or structures need to be improved?
- What patterns are essential?

Examples:

- Chef: How is a kitchen set up to enable preparation? What trends are influencing tastes? What are eaters' expectations when they are served my meals?
- Systems architect: What are the enterprise integration patterns? How does organizational decision making and culture impact systems design? What are the most-impactful events in the system and what downstream processes do they trigger?
- JavaScript developer: What impacts performance? What are the limitations of JavaScript and why do they exist?

Create Groupings and Boundaries Without Reductionism

How do you create conceptual boundaries and categories that help people engage with complexity? For example, the Dewey Decimal System turns a giant pile of books into a library. Domain-driven design envisions software that matches its context. Services and classes delineate boundaries in software systems.

- What are the key concepts that help break down this subject into parts?
- What are the different ways of grouping that help people engage with and understand this subject?

Examples:

- Chef: Salt, fat, acid, heat. Breakfast, lunch and dinner. Cuisine types like Italian and French.
- Systems architect: Domain boundaries, microservice architectures, system performance measures.
- JavaScript developer: Design systems and libraries, components, modules and other ways of structuring code.

Think Critically and Apply Sound Judgment

Sound judgment is the ability to critically discern which information matters to consider and which to set aside. Critical thinking enables you to recognize inaccurate assumptions and logical fallacies. Together, they create conceptual integrity between ideas and actions.

- What are the guiding principles, the most important things to understand, about this subject?
- What are the biases, fallacies, and other commonplace mistakes?

- Can I find an example of counterintuitiveness? A problem that people are likely making worse?

Examples:

- Chef: Every single decision requires discernment.
- Systems architect: Systemic reasoning (Chapter 7) and discovering leverage points.
- JavaScript developer: Recognizing quality code and delivery processes that serve their purpose. Making tradeoffs between speed and functionality. Recommending improvements in the frameworks.

Develop Your Interpersonal Skills

All of these skills will invariably involve other people. Thinking well together is a top priority for systems thinkers and one that learning can help us improve.

- Who can help me learn this? Who is thinking deeply about this subject?
- Am I engaging in dialogue about this subject with others? Does that dialogue help me to understand and perhaps even improve the guiding principles?
- Am I developing the communication skills I need to be effective?

Examples:

- Chef has relationships with cooks, farmers, other chefs, and eaters.
- Systems architect has relationships with everyone involved.
- JavaScript developer has relationships with other coders, stakeholders, other teams, and users.

Design Feedback Loops

When you are learning something new, it's helpful to get feedback on your progress. Andrew Harmel-Law, who was also writing a book, read these chapters before I shared them more widely. He pointed out sticky spots, asked questions, and made recommendations. His feedback made the writing stronger. Stepan Protsak never fails to make my code better with his feedback or to help me get out of a stuck spot. Learning partners are our greatest support.

Sadly, the majority of people we interact with can hinder, rather than help, our learning process. We might share our nascent attempts and get aggressive or demeaning criticism, unhelpful opinions about what we should do instead, or impatient judgment of our learning process or, and this has happened to me more than once—someone is just plain mean.

You can't avoid the negative attention sharing your work will inevitably attract. You aren't contributing much value if you only share ideas that everyone else likes and agrees with! But unhelpful feedback should not be integrated too early into your learning process. We need people who can help us do hard things, not knock us down. You want critical feedback but only when it helps you develop personal mastery, not personal shame.

When you ask for feedback, be specific. "Reading this, did you trip over anything or feel confused anywhere?" "What about this idea is really strong?" "What about this is not quite strong enough yet?" "Can I tighten up this code?"

If you don't ask for specific feedback, you are likely to get "This is good!" That won't help you make it gooder.

Practice 4: Who Can Help Me?

Think about who can help you learn. Reach out to at least one person, someone you can trust to give you good feedback, and ask them to partner with you on your journey.

One Day at a Time, Forever

In higher education, there's a strong bias toward people under 35. (This bias also exists in many tech cultures.) We think of learning as something people do in their 20s. Then they apply that learning for 40 years and then retire. A linear line from kindergarten to daily golfing.

Learning, like breathing, is something we continue doing, in various forms, regardless of age or circumstance. If you carry this age bias, I suggest you drop it. When you are 50, 35 will seem still young. People who are 70 look at 50 as young. Learning later in life is, in some ways, even more rewarding. I've pivoted three times in my adult life. Who knows where the next pivot will lead?

Learn before you have kids, learn while they grow, learn after they move out. Learn things that you aren't supposed to learn because of your gender or circumstance. Ask the hard questions. Do the thinking you think you can't do. Don't put any restrictions on how much you can learn or what you can learn to do. Enjoy the journey, all of it, while it lasts.

Learning never ends until you do.

MAGO: Boundless Learning Opportunities

MAGO, as a learning organization, will need the same skills we are developing as knowledge workers. Here are some examples of how systems thinking approaches can help MAGO approach their quandary.

- *Improve MAGO's ability to shift perspective* by modeling the system from different perspectives. Make the impact of decisions transparent so that people thinking about the business, for example, can see how the technology supports (or doesn't) their goals.

- *Increase MAGO's tolerance for ambiguity* by focusing on a leverage point, a place to begin pushing the system toward its future state. Don't try to figure everything out—figure out what needs to be figured out first.

- *Understand context and relational impact* by defining the highest-value goals of the system. What is MAGO's core purpose, its reason for being? What are the activities that support that purpose? Do the relationships in the software system (and the teams) make those activities easy to evolve? What is MAGO's competitive advantage; what does this system do better than any other? How can the system be designed to do that thing even better?

- *Identify patterns and structures* by using the Iceberg Model to understand how MAGO designed the current challenge and how they will need to change patterns, structures, and mental models to design a system that fits their current situation.

- *Create groupings and boundaries without reductionism* by mapping the current systems software boundaries to the most valuable activities in the system. For example, does it matter where content will be shared when it's created? Most content will be shared in multiple contexts; how does the system make that easy? What needs to change?

- *Think critically and apply sound judgment* by working toward understanding what changes will generate the most value for MAGO and what changes are Band-Aids.

- *Develop your interpersonal skills* by accepting that the solution to MAGO's problems lies in their ability to improve knowledge flow. Focus on that when deciding what to do next.

Support for Your Practice: It's All Interrelated

Not interested in learning JavaScript or technology architecture? Want to learn to knit mithril instead? No worries, it's all interrelated.

If your experience is anything like mine, your learning interests are convergent. Communication skills interact with programming skills; technical implementation skills interact with organizational leadership skills; learning from others interacts with deconstructing your own mental models.

From the day I was born until I was 30 years old, my primary focus was theater. It was my college major, where I invested my creative energy—I even taught classes. I never moved to LA, got a part on Broadway, or, for that matter, made a living acting. You could say that I failed, and in some ways, I did. In other ways, I benefit every day from the skills I developed.

When I began my science career, I thought I was quitting acting and writing and other creative pursuits. But of course, there is more overlap than difference. Five skills in particular have been instrumental in my career:

I'm comfortable with public speaking.

I can get up in front of a group and impactfully present ideas. While I'm not Ryan Reynolds, I'm not tedious and boring either. I can usually get people on board with a recommendation if I have the chance to present to them.

I'm very self-aware.

People think acting is being fake when it's actually being deeply real. You must be aware of what your body is doing, what you're feeling, and how you are interacting with others. When I'm able to tap into that authenticity, people experience my presence and sincerity. This makes trust building and team forming more effective.

I'm good at improvisation.

I can stay cognitively flexible, listening to what others are saying and interacting in ways that, I hope, evolves the ideas.

I think a lot about backstory.

What you see onstage is the tip of the iceberg—actors are conveying the complexity of the situation even though it's not explicit. When a "scene" or circumstance is playing out around me, I consider what is unsaid and unseen, too. This skill is especially valuable as a systems architect.

I will risk making a fool of myself.

Like most people, I'm afraid of public speaking and being authentic and asking for help when I don't know something. Those things aren't easy for me, even after years of practice. I do know, though, in my bones, that they are worthwhile. Even if I totally flop or ask the stupidest question ever asked, I'll grow.

What are the non-tech disciplines that help you in your technology career?

PART III

We Are a System of Thinking

Systemic reasoning is the art and science of supporting ideas, concepts, recommendations, or theories with sound reasons. We need systemic reasoning when conditions are uncertain…and the vast majority of the time, in software systems, there is no One Right Way of doing things. There is only the best possible solution, under the circumstances, based on what we currently know. When people strengthen their reasoning together, they build conceptual integrity (and, therefore, more impactful systems).

Reasoning together depends on building conceptual bridges between different points of view. It also depends on learning from people with expertise you don't have. We generate the flow of knowledge that improves systems thinking with feedback loops. Most of the time, this means we need to rethink the way "feedback" currently happens.

Systems thinking, reasoning, and discovering root causes of systemic challenges are all forms of pattern thinking. In many ways, pattern thinking is synonymous with systems thinking. In Part III, you will practice systemic reasoning, design feedback loops that improve your reasoning skills, and identify the types of patterns that, when thinking in systems, will usually demand our attention.

COLLECTIVE SYSTEMIC REASONING

(i) Systemic Reasoning

🖌 Art and Science 🧪 of reasoning systematically in support of an idea, action, or theory

Difficult to do well

Engage people who disagree with you *explicitly* & *purposefully*

(!) ARGUMENTATION ≠ (!) ARGUING

99 "The point isn't only to support your claim... It's to test it."

STRENGTHEN REASONS
make them more...

- ⟷ understandable
- ⟷ reliable
- ⟷ relevant
- ⟷ cohesive
- ⟷ cogent

TOP DOWN ELABORATION

= Summary =
= Why =
= What =
= Who =
= How =
= When =

CHAPTER 7

Collective Systemic Reasoning

Ambiguity…presents a puzzle. It challenges one to grasp something from multiple perspectives, each of which demands equal attention. One never solves an ambiguous situation, but puzzles through it, searching for the unity of multiple perspectives, for the sense of the thing this, which is illusive and shifting.

—Ann M. Pendleton-Jullian and John Seely Brown, *Design Unbound: Designing for Emergence in a White Water World*

In Chapter 5, I encouraged you to notice your reactions and stop allowing them to drive your thinking. Later, I said, we would learn how to respond. Here, in this chapter, we'll build a response.

As knowledge workers, we are proposing ideas, actions, or theories, formally or informally, all the time. We do this through structured communication. Making artifacts like documents, models, working code. Sending an email or Slack post. Joining a meeting discussion, or modeling session, skywriting…the form doesn't matter. What matters is the quality of the thinking we contribute, and how well our process supports knowledge flow.

We will frame the practice of responding as "creating a proposition." Creating a proposition is systemic reasoning because it includes *the reasons that support your proposition*. The process is deceptively simple but diabolically difficult.

A proposition includes three key components:

- The idea, action, or theory you are proposing (your premise)
- Three to five reliable, relevant, sound, and cogent reasons that justify your premise
- Why this idea is highly impactful and matters right now

Easy, yes? Try it! Pick an idea you want to share and try to create a proposition. You'll likely discover that the practice is anything but easy, even for expert practitioners. Remember, we are (generally speaking) terrible at nonlinear thinking. Our ideas aren't as well integrated and sound as they feel. Your early drafts will reflect this.

The ideas in your mind seem quite strong...until you write them down along with the reasons that convinced you. I'm constantly surprised by how challenging it is to come up with strong reasons. Describing how I "know" something can be tricky. I don't always know how I know!

Sometimes I haven't developed the vocabulary and conceptual understanding to describe my thinking. I just kinda know, or I think I do, until I examine my knowing more closely. Sometimes I have an experience that taught me a lesson and that lesson stuck.

Other times, I am applying a lesson that doesn't apply in a new context. I'm putting a square idea in a round situation. Or I discover I am wrong or misguided. The inevitable fallacies and weak links in our thinking are interwoven with the quality of our thinking, like tangles in hair.

When you create a proposition, you are detangling your thinking.

 As a practice and a process done with other people, collective systemic reasoning is a driver of systems thinking.

What Is Systemic Reasoning?

The aim of argument, or of discussion, should not be victory, but progress.
—Joseph Joubert, French moralist and essayist

Systemic reasoning is the art and science of reasoning systematically in support of an idea, action, or theory. When you practice systemic reasoning, you move beyond sharing your opinion. You construct ideas by integrating the reasons that convinced you that the idea is sound, relevant, and matterful. You synthesize your own thinking with the thinking of others, arriving at *the best possible conclusion, under the circumstances, when conditions are uncertain.*

In systems, conditions are always uncertain.

We create propositions, ideas supported by reasons, when we can't know what is "right" to do. This is common in systems; there is rarely one right answer. As knowledge workers, we are usually making an educated guess. The "rightness" of our guess will depend on our point of view. Right for whom? Right for what?

Systemic reasoning increases the likelihood that you'll have a positive impact because your propositions are more cohesive, trustworthy, and holistic than an opinion. This practice also increases the likelihood that when you recommend an action, you will learn from the results, so you can iterate and improve. You'll want to know if your reasons stood the test of experience.

Systemic reasoning has several characteristics:

- *It is a tool, a practice, and a mindshift*, a tool for constructing ideas, a practice of reasoning skills, and a mindshift toward looking at change more holistically.
- *It provides reasons.* The core of systemic reasoning is providing rationales—supporting and justifying our ideas with reasons that others can evaluate and help to strengthen.
- *It involves strengthening the reasons that justify our claims*, weaving ideas together until they have conceptual integrity.
- *It is proactive*; we synthesize diverse knowledge and experience, using sound judgment, into ideas based on valid reasons.
- *It is a method of inquiry* that involves exploring, analyzing, discerning, deliberating, testing, and expanding our knowledge.
- *It's difficult to do well*: practicing is essential.

Technology systems are a tapestry of ideas, actions, and theories (concepts) that we have woven together. Systemic reasoning strengthens the bonds (integrity) between the ideas that support our actions or theories. When we strengthen conceptual bonds, we are more likely to make the system itself stronger.

Imagine a knitted sweater that keeps you snuggly warm on a chilly day. A well-reasoned proposition has similar strength and integrity. Now imagine a sloppily knitted scarf that unravels at the slightest tug. When the ideas pushed to production lack conceptual integrity, they make a system rickety and frail.

Systemic reasoning enables us to construct ideas, actions, or theories supported by as much conceptual integrity as we can muster, despite uncertainty. It takes us beyond our usual understanding of problems (and potential solutions), aiming toward seeing what is true about a system.

As software professionals, when we look at a problem in a linear (mechanistic) way, we tend to ask a few questions:

- What just happened? (We react to the "top of the iceberg" event.)
- Does it work as expected, or is it broken?

- How do I fix it or make it do something else?
- How long will it take to fix?

When we look at a problem systematically (nonlinearly), we also make a few more inquiries:

- How do we know, first of all, that it's a "problem"? What is the impact, now and in the future?
- A problem for whom?
- How does this problem compare to the other challenges we are currently facing? Is it core to the system's purpose?
- What has been happening over time?
- What are the structures or processes that make it keep happening?
- Is there a shift in our mental models required to alleviate this problem, rather than patch it?

What I discovered, as I learned systems thinking, is that whenever five people are discussing a problem, they are often solving different problems, even as they use the same words to describe it. Too often, I presumed that others already see the world from my perspective. But they can't possibly see my perspective unless I make it visible.

Systemic reasoning, done together, uncovers disparities and makes use of them to generate a more trustworthy solution.

How Systemic Reasoning Is Collective

Your propositions will always be limited by your own point of view. By themselves, your ideas and your reasons aren't very systemic. What transforms a proposition into systems thinking is working with other people to strengthen the reasons, broaden your point of view, and deepen the understanding underlying your reasoning.

In systems, everything is interdependent. No piece of software lives in a vacuum, isolated in space-time from all other pieces of software. Even this statement depends on how you define "a piece of software" and "isolated." We can rarely think about the system without the support of people familiar with other parts of the system.

Unless you are coding alone on a desert island, you aren't making every decision about what gets pushed to production by yourself. Your thinking interrelates with other people's thinking.

Software lives in a changing world. Users won't do the same thing, in the same way, forever. We can't always predict how changes in the "real world" will impact our technology systems. The better we understand diverse experiences, the more likely we are to see holistic solutions.

When we reason systematically, we integrate and synthesize diverse points of view. The user experience, tech reality, business needs, real-world constraints, *and systemic patterns*. The relationship between, for example, my view and a product person's view creates a richer understanding than my view alone.

Thinking collectively, acting cooperatively, does not mean "kumbaya, everybody agrees and lives happily ever after!" In systemic reasoning, we engage with people who disagree with us—explicitly and purposefully. That's an essential part of the practice. We do this so we can grow our understanding and increase our knowledge.

For example, let's say that I propose a knowledge graph to help MAGO achieve their goals, and a knowledgeable person raises a legitimate concern about the scalability of knowledge graphs. My reasons, then, should describe why a knowledge graph is still the best possible solution despite potential scalability issues.

Systemic reasoning is not changing hearts and minds. You cannot change other people's minds. Everyone must change their own mind. All you can do is offer a sound, well-reasoned point of view. Systemic reasoning relies on consent. Other people choose whether or not to agree.

When we consent, we learn. We change and adapt our own thinking as we synthesize it with other people's thinking. We grow as we engage with other people's insight, experience, and expertise. When we are open to changing our minds, we listen critically and respectfully. We practice discernment and good judgment when we decide what to accept and what to question. We increase knowledge flow by helping others to strengthen their systemic reasoning.

The "winner" in this approach is the system itself. The prize is the benefits we share when our systems are vibrant, healthy, well-directed, and purposeful.

Discovering leverage points, systemic patterns, and the structures influencing those patterns will inevitably require subject matter expertise you don't possess. For example, I learn the most about a system by watching people use it and asking them questions. When I ask people who are building different parts of the system "What is holding you back?" I learn about patterns I can't know from experience.

Modeling with other people is a great support for developing a proposition. In order to create new mental models, I need to understand the current ones. Thinking and modeling with others, diving deeper into *why* they think what they think, is a fast train to mental-model land. When discussions only focus on events, you can't get there.

Systemic reasoning alone isn't sufficient if you want to truly understand a system. It is one of the tools in your toolbox. But this practice, done together, is a giant step toward nonlinear thinking and generates a shared understanding of shared circumstances.

Propositions are interrelated, forming a matrix that describes our current system's conceptual architecture. When we share ideas, we usually do so in a linear way. "This feature will do X and be delivered on Friday." We get feedback in a RACI structure (with people categorized as responsible, accountable, consulted, or informed), or we gather other people's opinions.

Collective reasoning is a different approach. A proposition interlinks information, weaving our ideas with ideas already shared by others or in the code itself. We proactively create this interlinking by synthesizing other people's thinking with our own to support our ideas, actions, or theories.

Systemic Reasoning Has Other Names

In school, you might have learned argumentation and recognize its use here. If you've ever written an essay, taking a position on a hot cultural topic like abortion, civil rights, animal welfare, or wearing a mask during a pandemic, you've been introduced to argumentation. Argumentation is also called informal logic, a practice we often engage in as software designers, whenever there is no clear "right" way to do something.

Argumentation is not arguing. It is not fighting about who is right and who is wrong. Some practices, like debate, frame it as a "for or against" approach, but the practice does not need to be binary. I would argue that binary arguing is a major blocker for most technology teams.

Argumentation is a social process but it is not persuasion, though we hope people will agree with us. It is not negotiation, finding the most palatable option among people who want different things. (That's a carboat.) Argumentation is supporting claims with strong, sound, and cohesive reasoning. We use this approach to strengthen our systems thinking and communication.

Like "systems thinking," systemic reasoning is a practice that is applied differently in different contexts. Here, we are applying it to software systems, so I am highlighting some aspects and setting aside others. In this chapter, we structure a proposition because, as knowledge workers, we rely on that skill. If we were lawyers, biologists, or climate scientists, we would take a slightly different approach.

Law and science both draw heavily on argumentation skills. In science, we use evidence-based justifications to support our knowledge claims. Lawyers use adversarial argumentation, where the goal is to win. This "winning-focused" approach doesn't help us in systems approaches. The pursuit of truth is better served by cooperative argumentation, or as I call it, collective reasoning, where people practice argumentation with, rather than against, others.

To some extent, I am designing a system (of thinking) that fits our context and serves our purpose. In other words, I'm using systems thinking to structure systems thinking so I can do systems thinking. Systems are meta like that.

In workshops, I called these practices "nonlinear thinking." Systemic reasoning is one of the many ways to explore nonlinear thinking. Here are some similar concepts:

- Informal logic
- Critical thinking
- Pattern thinking
- Deductive, inductive, and abductive reasoning
- Abstract thinking
- New rhetoric
- Lateral thinking
- Design thinking
- Strategic thinking
- Working with mental models
- The decision-making process
- Analytical thinking
- Creative problem solving
- Learning-driven teams (like in the book *The Fifth Discipline*)

You can use any nonlinear thinking approach that will generate insight and build sound, well-crafted ideas. They all help to create a systemic understanding of the software and the systems around you.

Systemic Reasoning Is Building an Idea

The practice of building a proposition is deceptively simple:

1. Write down your idea, action, recommendation, or theory.

2. Write three to five reasons that support it. What convinced you?

   Include a direct connection to the system's purpose (why does this matter now?).

3. Strengthen your reasons and their relationships until they are cogent—clear, logical, and convincing. Work with others to do this.

4. Describe any known negative consequences, valid disagreements, or challenges to current thinking (especially in ways that might be unpopular).

Figure 7-1 shows a simple template you can use to model your proposition.

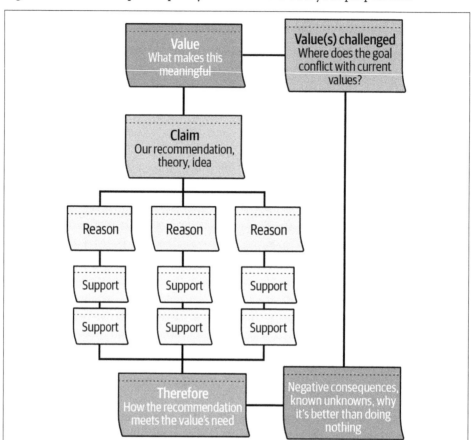

Figure 7-1. A simple model to structure your thinking

I have said "building an idea," but like all thinking processes, you'll do more rebuilding than building. Your first attempt will rarely be your final attempt. Trust the revision process more than the origination process. It takes time to get clear.

> If it is to be a minute speech I shall need four weeks in which to prepare, if a half hour speech, then two weeks, but if I am to talk all day I'm ready now.
> —Rufus Choate, Senator from Massachusetts, US, 1859

Your Practice: Create a Proposition

Let's try it! Grab a pen, open a document editor or digital whiteboard, and get ready to capture your thinking and make it stronger.

Identify Your Idea, Action, or Theory

If you woke up tomorrow and knew that everyone would listen to you and trust what you say…what would you say? What is the idea, action, or theory you most want to express?

Your core conclusion, idea, recommended action, or theory is also called your *premise*. To identify your premise, imagine someone reading your proposition, nodding, and saying, "Yes, I agree"…what are they agreeing with?

Write your premise as clearly as you can.

For example, "I recommend semantically structuring the information we publish to consumers via the API."

You can improve this claim by including an example. "I recommend semantically structuring the information we publish to consumers via the API, similarly to this example [link]."

Later, you can remove the "I recommend" part and make your claim directly. First, you'll need the reasons.

When you begin, don't get too attached to your premise. As you do the work to justify it, your premise will likely change. As you build the relationships between your idea and the reasons that support it, you will probably edit your premise and your reasons, multiple times.

Right now, your only goal is to clarify to yourself what you think and why you think it.

Identify Your Reasons

What convinced you that your claim is the best possible conclusion? Using the previous example, what convinced you that semantically structuring information was a good idea and valuable to do now?

Your reasons describe why your claim matters. Why does it matter right now? Why is it a good idea in this context? Your reasons should describe how your proposition improves the system's ability to serve its purpose.

If I had a dollar for every time I heard someone say "we should do [something]" or "that won't work" without any reasoning to justify it, I'd be sitting on a beach reading novels instead of working for a living. If you haven't seen this pattern at work, you've likely seen it on social media—posting as if the speaker having a strong opinion sufficiently justifies their claim. The problem with these types of assertions is they put everyone else on the defensive. You must change their mind, topple their "rightness"— and who wants to do that?

Expanding on our example: "I recommend semantically structuring the information we publish to consumers via the API, similarly to this example [link]. Here are reasons:"

- *Consumers need the information structured to serve their purposes.* They don't need or want to know how the software structures information to store in the database. They want the information in an understandable-to-them format.

  A few examples: We use four different labels to mean "the title of a piece of information," because different software teams structured that data differently over time. There are two different date formats. Internally understood labels for metadata, like zmby-o, don't describe the information to consumers.

  Adding a story can add emphasis: "Recently, when a customer saw 'rtsd-io: Critical,' they asked, 'Does this mean a zombie apocalypse is imminent?'"

- *Using a data model is an industry best practice.* We want to follow best practices when they are relevant to our circumstances. Best practices support software parts communicating more effectively and efficiently when separate teams build them.

- *The CTO recently said that our biggest blocker is "localized, duplicated, and hard-to-get data" in our system. Consistency in our data model and information flow will help resolve this blocker.* Our organization's goal is "to become the go-to information source for anyone who benefits from our services." Reaching that goal depends on our ability to resolve this issue quickly.

There are three practices that help you discover your reasons:

- Bringing together any knowledge or experience that led you to your conclusion
- Integrating what other people have said that is relevant to your claim
- Remembering that your goal is to structure a sound proposition, not convince people through power or overt persuasion

When building your reasons, let go of the belief that hierarchies raise up the best thinkers. Perhaps this is true, but the CEO can be misguided or incorrect. The intern might see an ideal solution. If you are contradicting what the CEO, or anyone else, has said...try to first understand the reasons that support their conclusions. Then show how other reasons can support a (different) conclusion.

Too many knowledge workers stay at the surface of ideas. The only way to know a sound (reliable and sensible) and relevant (impactful to the system's goal) idea is to dive deeper into it. As we learned from the Iceberg Model, systems challenges arise from foundational mental models, and systemic patterns keep them in place. If you go through the process of identifying reasons, you are more likely to see some of those patterns and uncover mental models.

Sound ideas are sound because knowledge, experience, and valid reasons justify them. Sharing those reasons makes ideas useful—others can understand *why* a proposition is (or is not) a sound idea. Then they can help you strengthen your reasons.

Strengthen the Reasons

The most critical step in systemic reasoning is strengthening the reasons that support your claim. You can't be certain—time will tell whether or not your proposition will have a positive impact. But if you focus on the reasons rather than getting stuck in "right versus wrong, yes or no" dualities, you improve the odds that your proposition will prove valuable.

When you look deeper into the reasons that support your claim, you might discover that you were wrong, or wrongish. That's good! The point isn't only to support your claim...it's to test it. Talk to others, do some research, consider the relationship between your reasons and your circumstances. Carefully consider opposing points of view, and battle-test your ideas.

There are many ways to strengthen the reasons, including improving your grammar, adding data, and including lively, relevant examples. We'll focus on four qualities:

- *Reliable*: are the reasons true?
- *Relevant*: are the reasons relevant to the circumstances?
- *Cohesive*: do the reasons work together to form a convincing whole?
- *Cogent*: can you make your thinking more clear and convincing?

Reliable

Do you need to do some research or hands-on experimentation to ensure that your assertions are true? For example, if you say "We can use Kafka to solve this problem by doing X," ensure that the current version of Kafka does X.

Are other people justified in believing your reason? If you say, for example, that the software stops running for 4.36 seconds at noon EST on Tuesdays when the moon is in Virgo, your fellow technologists aren't going to take your word for it. You'll want some hard data to back you up.

Relevant

My favorite example of a not-relevant reason justifying a technology decision is "Netflix does it." Unless you are a streaming service whose system has evolved in the exact same way to face the exact same challenge, you'd need to show why this proposition is relevant to your system and circumstances. Even a Netflix developer should not simply say "because this is how we do things." *Why* do you do things that way? More importantly, why is that relevant *now*?

Relevance changes over time. Perhaps something was relevant before and now you are demonstrating why it no longer applies. Or perhaps something has become relevant and you are illuminating it.

Context matters. The value of every decision we make depends on the context in which we make it. In *The Lord of the Rings*, Frodo's journey to destroy the ring is meaningful inside the context of Middle Earth. In a different situation, he'd be a short, hairy guy with apocalyptic hallucinations.

Cohesive

In systems thinking, relationships matter most. Are your reasons well-connected to your proposition and to each other? When you read them out loud, do they flow, one into the next, leading you to a sound and logical conclusion?

A more subtle way to improve cohesion is to use the same term to describe the same thing throughout your proposition. And define the critical words you use to ensure that other people will understand exactly what *you* mean. This is advice I struggle to remember. While writing this chapter, for example, my editor pointed out that I interchange the words practice, approach, tool, and other words that all mean "this is a thinking-in systems-activity." Declutter your thinking by making a glossary of key words and ensure you're using them consistently.

Cogent

Cogent means that if your reasons are all true, your claim is probably also true. You can test this by reading your reasons and then, "therefore..." your claim. Does it follow? Given the context and your reasons, does it make sense to act on your proposition?

Cogency isn't a hard science; it's more of an art form. It's a blend of reliability, relevance, cohesiveness, connection to context, and strong communication skills. The more you practice, the better you'll get at generating cogent propositions.

A key focus is sufficiency: have you considered your proposition from multiple points of view? Systemic understanding depends on conveying an integrated view of the situation. Have you looked at this from multiple points of view? Have you made a strong connection between the circumstances and the proposition? For example, if you are proposing a technology tool (like Kubernetes), have you described how it will benefit the system as a whole, not simply how it will solve a tech problem?

As you can see, when you strengthen the reasons, you generate essential questions and then seek to answer them. The process of figuring out what questions need to be asked is a critical part of systems thinking.

Be Honest About Potential Pitfalls

When you make a proposition, there are (almost) always other options. Why didn't you choose them? There are (almost) always people who disagree with you. What good reason do they give and why do you think differently? There are (almost) always potential pitfalls…things might go horribly wrong. What are the blockers that threaten to derail your proposition?

Be honest about all of those things. You don't have to dive in too deeply and create a whole drama, but you do need to acknowledge potential pitfalls and unknowns. What are you most unsure about? How will you monitor these risks as you move forward with this idea?

Systemic Reasoning Is a Method of Inquiry

> When we study a system, we usually learn where leverage points are. But a new system we've never encountered? Well, our counterintuitions aren't that well developed. Give us a few months or years and we'll figure it out.
>
> —Donella Meadows

In systems, very few conclusions are Globally and Constantly True. Everything "good" to do depends on the circumstances, the timing, the goals and values of the people involved, and the forces acting on the system. "It depends" is the most common answer to any systems question. How do you discover what "it depends" on?

Systemic reasoning is a method of inquiry—a process through which we explore, analyze, discern, deliberate, test, and expand our knowledge. Strengthening our reasons involves proactively understanding and gaining knowledge that better supports our proposition. We are continuously learning, and as we explored in Chapter 6, continuous learning is inextricable from systems thinking.

Coming back to our example proposition: "I recommend semantically structuring the information we publish to consumers via the API, similarly to this example [link]." Here are some potentially relevant inquiries:

- What will consumers do with this information if they get what they want? What do they want?
- What is the current structure of the information?
- Do I know what the system's purpose is? Do the parts of the organization agree?
- Do I understand what each piece is? Can I describe it at a high level?
- What is the industry's thinking on structuring data for consumption?
- What tools and processes are in use now?

- Are there reasons for this structure I can learn from other teams or documentation?
- Do these best practices fit our use case?
- What tools and processes are available, and have we considered them?
- What do consumers do with this information?
- Is this activity highly valuable? How is it related to the system's purpose?
- What do the people closest to this challenge say about challenges and priorities?
- Are there considerations that matter in this circumstance, like speed of response or trustworthiness of data?
- Who is impacted by this change?
- Does this change improve patterns and relationships in the system (as opposed to Band-Aiding a wound)?

A technical problem, like sharing data between software parts, is also a product, business, user, industry, systems, and sociotechnical problem. While our role isn't to develop expertise in every area, we can understand the knowledge and experience shared with us by people who play other roles. When we synthesize that information, we craft a proposition that reflects this integrated understanding.

Systemic Reasoning Is a Worthwhile Investment

Inquiry is an investment of time. When faced with complex situations, it takes time to discover an impactful way to intervene. We need to distill the factors involved until they become clear enough to understand. When our propositions demonstrate an understanding of the factors involved and a reasonable, well-structured conclusion, we increase the likelihood that others will also understand. Thus, we increase knowledge flow.

You might be wondering, "Why bother?" That's a fair question; you are busy enough already. The answer is this: you are significantly more likely to convincingly propose an impactful change. Not because you are politically powerful or charmingly persuasive, but because you truly understand the problem and have arrived (with the help of others) at a cohesive proposition that is likely to have more impact than applying a patch.

You may feel impatient and want to skip inquiry, favoring a strict focus on working code. You might not enjoy the uncertainty of not knowing; you might even dislike the world outside of your role. Many of us feel caught up in organizational civil wars where people who need to think together are, instead, sabotaging and disrespecting each other. Your attempts at inquiry might raise suspicion and "stay in your lane" feedback in organizations that do not foster a learning-driven process. You might feel that, even as I acknowledge you are busy, I don't really understand how much work you are already doing. Who has time for that?!

When I've asked others to help me with inquiry, I've heard: "We don't do big upfront design." I agree with this sentiment. Systems thinking is antithetical to big upfront. Systems thinking accepts uncertainty rather than attempts to make everything concrete. But if we skip design thinking altogether, we will plant the seeds of problems that will later grow into the issues that keep us too busy to think.

It's a vicious cycle.

Weak, unsound, or overly simplified solutions are expensive (in the long run). They are tricky to spot because they feel exactly right in the moment. Investing in systemic reasoning saves us significantly more time later. Your iterations will be more "inching toward a solution" and less "throwing darts at a wall."

 The quality of what we build is equal to the quality of our reasoning—think of it like test coverage for ideas.

When we leave gaps in our thinking and push them to production, we must later identify those gaps and clean up the weedy tech debt that has filled them.

Systemic Reasoning Structures (and Frames) Ambiguity

We are constantly structuring ambiguity, making choices, and taking action when there is no single, clear option. Whether we are aware of it or not, we couldn't function without this skill. As a knowledge worker especially, our success depends not simply on what we already know but on how we navigate a world full of possibilities.

Here is an example of structuring ambiguity in daily life. Three friends are gathered in a living room on a Saturday night, deciding which movie to watch. They can't be certain which movie they will enjoy because they haven't seen them yet.

They decide on *Bridesmaids* because:

- none of them have seen it,
- everyone is in the mood for a comedy, and
- *Bridesmaids* has a 90% Rotten Tomatoes rating.

Out of all the possible criteria, they framed the decision with "Let's watch a movie that is new, fun, and well reviewed." They could have prioritized watching a classic film respected by film professors, with more-complex human relationships. In that case, *Casablanca* might have been the right movie for them.

The "rightness" of a decision depends on how you frame it.

The focus of systemic reasoning is not perfection—it is acting on reasons that are sound, cohesive, and trustworthy.

Perhaps the friends enjoy *Bridesmaids*. Perhaps they are disappointed. Perhaps one friend enjoys it and two are disappointed. Perhaps the power goes out halfway through and they play cards instead. Regardless, they feel the movie was worth a try.

In systems, identifying something "worth a try" is a good outcome. Generally speaking, we feel better about negative outcomes when our reasoning was sound. We know what to try differently next time. The friends might realize they don't enjoy comedies. Next time, they won't frame the choice with "comedy" as a structure. They might choose a whole different approach to framing—say, take turns choosing a movie and watch whatever a designated person recommends. When we practice the art of framing ambiguity, our conclusions might not be right, but they can improve our understanding of what works (or doesn't).

In systems, we aren't simply living the experiences; we are simultaneously and explicitly architecting them. Conceptual architecture is the art of framing inquiry.

Structuring ambiguity isn't all Saturday night popcorn. When faced with ambiguity, the human mind reacts with fear and anxiety. When we are stuck in reacting, like we explored in Chapter 5, we negotiate with reality, try to avoid discomfort and ignore what we don't want to face. Our knee-jerk reaction is to create order from perceived chaos by trying to exert control. Structuring and framing ambiguity gives us a less reactive option and helps us structure a response rather than react.

Many of us learned that software development is making things concrete, nailing things down, moving fast, and breaking things. We like knowing, for certain, what to do. We act on the pernicious fallacy that we can somehow outrun uncertainty…control the future, bend technology systems (and other people) to our will.

Uncertainty is a constant. In systems, we don't try to make it disappear. We act while resting comfortably in the midst of not knowing for sure. And we act again, differently, when we understand things better down the road.

We do this by framing—organizing certain possibilities from the realm of all possibilities. We use systemic reasoning to structure relationships among possible ways of perceiving a situation. We integrate information available to us about how the system operates. We are choosing to tell one story among many.

When done well, we can frame an understanding that magnifies and illuminates the truest, most relevant, and most impactful aspects so we can take reasonable action. There is no right answer, but there are answers that are sound.

The Top-Down Elaboration

Here is a simple framing exercise I recommend for nearly all discussions about systemic issues. I've witnessed teams significantly reduce the "noise" that arises during decision making by introducing a single-page top-down elaboration (TDE) as part of their process. Using a TDE, they became more efficient at making decisions and increased the trustworthiness of their outcomes. More trust meant they gained more control over their day-to-day decisions and more voice in bigger-picture discussions.

A TDE consists of six sections: Summary, WHY, WHAT, WHO, HOW, and WHEN. Reasonable people disagree on what belongs in each section. It depends! That's okay, this artifact can evolve to fit your circumstances. The more you practice this approach, the quicker you'll adapt and improve it.

Here, I describe how I structure a TDE.

Summary

The organization's stated mission is to share information with anyone who will benefit from it. To better serve that mission, we will semantically structure the information we publish so it is understandable to consumers.

The summary can set the context, if there is a need to give background. It can also summarize the sections that follow.

When possible, make this a single paragraph. If you are like me, this will be difficult to write succinctly. But writing it will help you distill the essential points.

WHY

The organization's stated mission is to share information with anyone who will benefit from it. Consumers have reported difficulty discovering and understanding the information we currently publish because it is poorly structured. This is limiting our ability to meet our mission.

Why does this idea, action, or theory (proposition) matter to the system as a whole? Describing why an idea is valuable can be difficult. You might not aim high enough and instead focus on a subgoal like saving money. Saving money doesn't explain why you're proposing something, unless saving money is the system's, and the organization's, primary purpose.

You might substitute WHAT reasons for your WHY. "A world-class solution for our customers," for example, is a WHAT. *Why* does "world-class" matter, and how would you measure it?

A general rule is that everyone who reads your WHY should clearly understand the value. Don't make it up! Why does the system exist? What purpose does it serve? In later sections, you will connect the WHAT and HOW to the WHY.

WHY matters. Imagine Frodo throwing the Ring into the river of molten lava. Imagine a woman standing beside a river on a spring day, taking off her wedding ring and throwing it in. Imagine a man in the midnight shadows walking along a river, sirens and police lights in the distance, taking a ring and other trinkets from his pocket and throwing them into the water.

Same WHAT—entirely different WHYs.

WHAT

The information published via the API is currently unstructured, making it difficult to consume; we will make it easier to programmatically consume by semantically structuring the information we publish via the API.

WHAT—*exactly*—will we do? This isn't "install Kubernetes." This is "decrease downtime by 20% by rearchitecting the infrastructure to be more resilient."

WHO

While this will impact all customers over time, we will work with a small group of volunteer consumers who will help us iterate and improve. The XYZ team will do the work and coordinate with stakeholders.

WHO is impacted, and how do they benefit from the WHAT? How will you measure it?

WHO is doing the work?

HOW

We will write a service that consumes information from our software's API and structure it to match our emerging consumer data model. We will serve this version via an abstraction layer to our test consumers.

HOW will we do, build, design or continue to explore the WHAT? If there are alternative options, describe them. Make a strong conceptual bridge between the WHAT and the HOW. You don't have to get into too much detail here; that's for the team to flesh out just enough detail to support the idea.

WHEN

The XYZ team has not sized the work, but they estimate it will take them approximately three months to deliver the first iteration.

Technologists are often asked, before they have a trustworthy answer, WHEN will this be delivered?" In reality (especially in systems), knowing WHEN can't happen before you really dive in. Usually, though, it helps to say something about time.

Everyone, regardless of role, can practice with TDEs. The next time there is conflict and confusion about what is being delivered, try testing your understanding with a TDE. See if everyone agrees that your TDE describes the work. I have done this with teams that are in conflict and it revealed that they were using the same WHAT to solve different WHYs. I've used this with teams that had a tendency to break up into silos. You can write a TDE and then put a link to it in the tasks, so whenever questions arise later, everyone can stay on the same page.

Strengthening the Reasons

> *Miscommunication is the number one cause of all problems; communication is your bridge to other people. Without it, there's nothing.*
> —Earl Sweatshirt, American rapper

When you describe the reasons that support your proposition, chances are, at first, they'll be the following:

Wrong
Some of your assertions might not be entirely true or accurate. "The most recent update fixed this bug." (When it didn't.)

Weakly connected
Your reasons aren't interrelated. "We need to fix the data structure. It's a mess. Our users prefer more white space."

Disconnected from the context

You've described what you think but not why it matters. "Kubernetes will make failover faster." (Without describing why failover needs to be faster.)

Biased

You've included ideas you like and none that you don't like. "Companies with a heart and soul only use open source tools."

Opinionated

Your own ideas about how the world should be come through in emotionally loaded overtones (this is a form of bias). "Agile is a steaming pile of garbage dumped into JIRA."

Disrespectful or condescending

Anytime you are, directly or indirectly, calling something stupid, this is happening. "This workflow is a mess because marketing people got involved."

Insufficient

The reasoning represents a limited point of view (yours). "Kafka is what we need." (Without describing its need from a non-tech point of view.)

Vague

The reasons aren't well connected and don't follow in a natural order. "We need to make API responses faster. The users are leaving the interface before they finish engaging. The CPO wants more developers focused on JavaScript."

Bad first attempts are perfectly normal and likely unavoidable. You feel sure and solid in your thinking until you articulate it and discover…your ideas need work. Systems thinking requires work. I suspect that some technologists reject "abstraction" (condescendingly) not because it's unnecessary but because it's difficult and time-consuming. Crafting and constructing concepts means climbing over the mountains of your own conditioned ideas and experiences to discover a path beyond them.

Remember from our introduction to systems thinking that systems are counterintuitive. We rarely look at a systemic issue and think "Okay! I see! The challenge is X, and we should do Y. Mic drop!" Instead, because of counterintuitiveness, we do exactly the wrong thing and make the situation worse. Our changes have unexpected and unwelcome impacts.

Strengthening our reasoning is a valuable and humbling practice. Fortunately, once you experience how quickly your outcomes improve, you'll become more patient with the process. You'll know it really is worth the investment.

When your first attempts are less than stellar, you learn! When you practice systemic reasoning, nothing is lost. Even if you discard your first 10 propositions or you act on one and the outcome is disappointing, you are honing essential and powerful skills. When you notice gaps, flaws, or weaknesses in your reasoning, you are improving your self-awareness, a key skill discussed in Chapter 4. When you don't fully understand something, you will figure out how to figure it out, another key skill discussed in Chapter 6. The more you improve your own thinking, the more you improve the sociotechnical systems around by demonstrating conceptual integrity.

You will (probably) do better next time. As long as you stay open to learning—seeing, clarifying, understanding, and discovering as you go—you will improve. I've learned more from failure than from success. We are choosing from nearly infinite potential ideas. The process of sorting and prioritizing them is our knowledge work.

 How do you strengthen your reasons? You make them reliable, sound, relevant, and cohesive. Doing this, alone and with others, improves the reliability, strength, relevance, soundness, and cohesiveness of our software systems.

When you strengthen your reasons, you make them more:

- *Understandable:* well written
- *Reliable:* true and justified
- *Relevant:* well connected to each other and the context
- *Cohesive:* flows as a united whole
- *Cogent:* convincing

Understandable

Good writing will be more impactful than bad or sloppy writing. The tips that apply to all types of nonfiction writing apply here, so any reading you do about writing well (like *On Writing Well* by Zissner (Turtleback Books) or *Dreyer's English* by, well, Dreyer, Random House) will improve your thinking.

- Avoid jargon. Define any words that don't have a specific or easily understood meaning.
- Edit edit edit. Partner with someone good at giving editorial feedback.
- Check your grammar.
- Model your proposition. Put the first sentence of each paragraph on sticky notes, in order. Does it still work?

Reliable

Anything that is untrue, or kinda-but-not-really true, will sink your proposition. True, many of us are living in a "facts don't matter" information era, but if you want to discover systemic improvements, you'll ensure your facts do matter.

- Do sufficient research to ensure what you are saying is true.
- Unless everyone involved has the same subject matter expertise, justify anything you assert. (If you say "graphs don't scale," you need to justify it.)
- Give relevant examples. Whenever you say that something critical to the proposition is true, you probably want to give an example.
- Quotes are valuable; use them to support your reasoning.

Relevant

Whenever the connection between your reasons and your proposition isn't clear, make it clear. Add descriptions to show that your thinking is relevant to the challenge you are addressing. The following components should be considered:

- Include the reason that your proposition has a high-value impact on the system as a whole and matters to pay attention to...now.
- Describe the situation from a cross-functional point of view. If it's a tech proposition, what is the business value?
- Eliminate reasons that don't have substance. "Nobody likes that idea" is irrelevant unless your proposition is "only trust ideas that everyone likes."
- Eliminate generalizations. Phrases like "Everyone knows that…" are cheats.

Cohesive

Like every system, you are working on the parts, but when they come together, the parts should form something larger than their sum. The relationships among your ideas is what makes your proposition cohesive. It should "hang together" as a whole. The following areas of inquiry will guide you:

- Does each reason or explanation add to and extend the previous one?
- Are there clear bridges between the proposition and each of the reasons?
- Get feedback from others who understand the circumstances from a different point of view. Your reasons may be valid but pale in comparison to other forces impacting the situation.
- Look for logical fallacies (see next section) and cognitive biases. They are often hidden in the bridges with your reasons.

Cogent

When all is said and done, is your proposition convincing? This isn't something you can tweak directly, like fixing a carburetor, but there are some things you can try:

- Put your reasons in a natural order. When you read them, in order, does your conclusion make sense?
- Ask yourself, "If all of my reasons are true, how likely is it that my proposition is wrong?" Ideally, the answer is "unlikely."
- Put the idea away for a couple of days. When you come back, read it out loud to yourself. Still work?
- Read it to someone outside of the circumstances. Does it still make sense?

Your Practice: Strengthen Your Reasons

Consider the proposition you created earlier in this chapter. Can you strengthen the reasons? Is there inquiry that might help you create stronger reasons? Here are some suggestions:

Strengthen the reasons

- Edit the writing to make it clearer. Define key words you use.
- Examine your reasons—are they true? Do others know they are true, or will they need more data to believe you?
- Improve the connection between your proposition and the system's purpose.
- Improve the connections and flow among the reasons.
- Read the proposition out loud. Does it "hang together" as one convincing unit of thinking? Can you improve the flow?

Inquire

- What else do you need to understand, and how can you find out about those things? Who else can you engage?
- Have you looked at the situation from multiple perspectives?
- What are the potential pitfalls? Have you tried to illuminate them?
- What happens if you ask different questions? Would you come to the same conclusion?

MAGO's Proposition

Here is an example of a proposition that might be made at MAGO:

> To begin evolving the MAGO system away from dependance on the obsolete core software, I recommend we do EventStorming. MAGO's top goal, as stated by the CEO, is to extend our reach and share valuable content with everyone, in any context in which the reader engages. The current system severely limits this capability. Over 20 years, the system evolved to push content to specific destinations (like the app). it was not designed to publish content, when it's available, to our expanding digital audience.
>
> EventStorming is a cross-functional system modeling process that will reveal key events happening in the current system and guide us toward designing a system that will meet our "create and publish" goal.

Support for Your Practice: The Iceberg Model

Remember the Iceberg Model from Chapter 3 (see Figure 7-2)? You can use it to help you improve your reasoning.

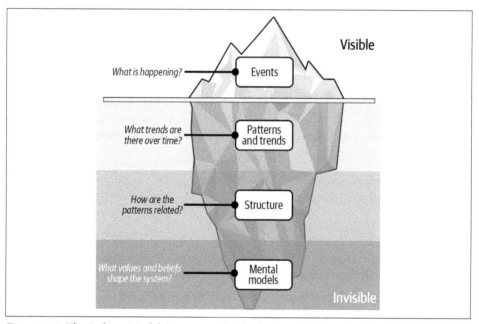

Figure 7-2. The Iceberg Model (Source: @thailerderden10 (https://oreil.ly/Xs7No)/Adobe Stock)

By going deeper into the circumstances, you might see interconnections that you missed. Include them in your reasons. Use the following questions to do this:

- How do you know something is happening? What are the signs that an idea, action, or theory is needed?
- Is this a unique circumstance or part of a pattern over time?
- If so, what keeps this pattern in place? What are the relationships that encourage or discourage it?
- What are the assumptions, beliefs, or values that support or contribute to this pattern? What values or beliefs does your recommendation challenge?

Generally speaking, propositions that change fundamental beliefs, our core mental models, will have more positive impact than the ones that react to an event. If you can move your reasoning down the Iceberg Model, you will contribute more value.

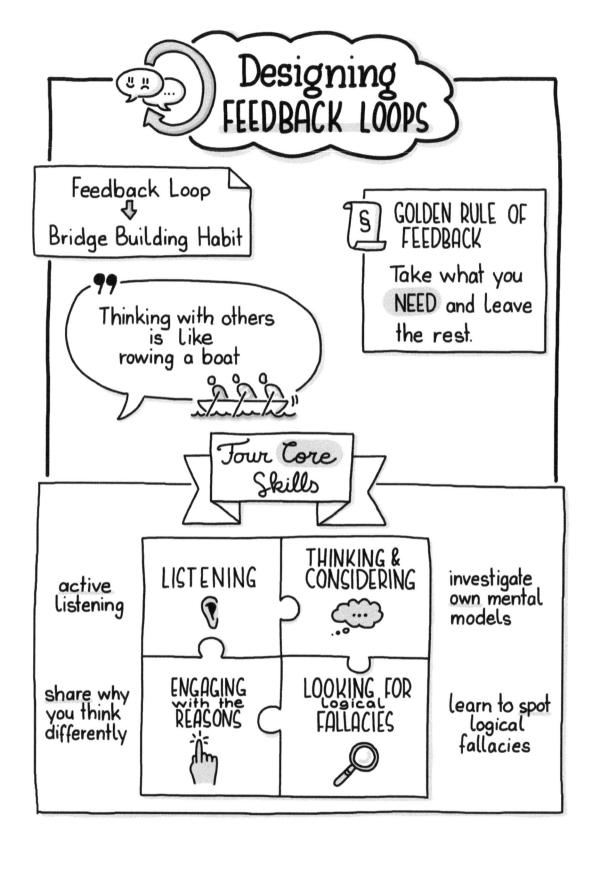

CHAPTER 8

Designing Feedback Loops

Our society lacks a feedback loop for controlling technology: a way to gauge intended effects from actual effects later on.

—Kevin Kelly, founding editor of *Wired*

In Chapter 7, we practiced developing a proposition. We wove knowledge and experience, yours and other people's, into strong recommendations and insights supported by valid reasons. We also strengthened those reasons. To reason collectively, people work together to strengthen the reasons that support their propositions.

This is important. Self-organizing and empowered teams reach sound and trustworthy conclusions without having to be told what to do. They can think, understand, and act in ways that don't rely on persuasion, power, or politics. When there is complexity, they can proactively take a systems view and learn from other people's experience and expertise.

Without the ability to self-organize, very little collective reasoning can happen. You need the friction that arises when your point of view bumps up against other points of view; that's where you'll discover conflicting mental models and positive opportunities for change. You need the support of collective practices that illuminate, rather than reinforce, your blind spots and biases.

To support collective reasoning, and therefore systems thinking, we design feedback loops.

The process of thinking together is a feedback loop. When you hear "feedback loop," you might imagine, for example, software monitoring; notifications sent when part of your system is under duress. You might think of autoscaling. These are visible feedback loops that you can design. When you measure user satisfaction, you are creating a feedback loop.

When I talk about getting feedback, I don't mean the familiar linear processes like the RACI model, a hierarchical structure for getting buy-in, including people deemed responsible, accountable, and consulted, along with people who need to be informed. While this process might, in some organizations, also generate good feedback loops, by itself it is simply a management sign-off process. The RACI model presumes that people on a hierarchical ladder are inherently good at giving valuable feedback on systemic reasoning. This has not always been my experience.

I don't (necessarily) mean an RFC, request for comments, process. Comments are, in my experience, more likely to be opinions than propositions with reasons. If you are taking an opinion poll, the RFC process works. But for deeper work, without clear guidance on giving meaningful feedback, seeking comments doesn't generate systemic reasoning; it is a survey (which might be a helpful step!).

When we think of "giving feedback," we think of a manager describing how an employee can improve. Managers are often taught that "giving feedback" means criticizing performance or improving compliance. While there are circumstances wherein this type of feedback might be helpful, it is not systemic reasoning. Does the manager always think better about the system than people on a lower tier? This has also not been my experience.

You need feedback that makes your recommendation, your systems thinking, stronger. You want to strengthen the reasons that support (or strengthen) your propositions. You want to know if you are about to hit an iceberg, if the reasons are truthful, if you forgot something, if other priorities compete, etc. Which means you'll need to design different feedback loops, depending on what you are thinking about.

As we discussed in Chapter 7, your goal is to make your propositions understandable, reliable, relevant, cohesive, and cogent. Pause for a moment and remember the last time you got feedback. Did it accomplish this goal?

In this chapter, we're concerned with designing a system of thinking. Our goal is to increase knowledge flow in the people system so we can improve the technology systems. We're focusing here on thinking feedback loops that improve systemic reasoning.

Healthy thinking feedback loops accomplish important things:

- They give you the feedback you need to improve systemic reasoning.
- They provide *useful* feedback.
- They proactively engage people with relevant expertise, insight, or experience.
- They always involve consent…not telling people what they *should* think, but instead showing them thinking supported by sound reasoning and sufficient evidence.
- They enable learning and knowledge flow.

We also want feedback loops that enable us to pay attention to impact. How do you know that a systemic change accomplished what you intended? How will you discern whether or not your reasoning was sound? How will you discover what thinking needs adapting?

Four core skills will improve your ability to give feedback on other people's thinking: proactive listening, willingly considering, engaging with the reasons, and looking for logical fallacies. Logical fallacies are the bugs in our thinking.

As we explored in Chapter 2, crafting conceptual integrity between people pushes that integrity to production. When people can't think well together (especially when they are divisive), they build weak and rickety conceptual bridges. They push changes that, over time, architect equally weak and unsound software systems. Gaps in our collective reasoning create unbridgeable canyons in our systems design.

We need to build conceptual bridges over those gaps. Together. In this chapter, we will explore how to design feedback processes and conceptual bridges that will improve your ability to think in systems.

Building Conceptual Bridges

Feedback loops reinforce our mental models. Whenever we are frustrated with our current circumstances, it's important to remember that they arose from our mental models. Our legacy software systems reflect the values and beliefs that we prioritized.

That's not wrong; that's how everything works. To change our circumstances, we can't simply change our toolset, we need to collectively discover and change those mental models. We need to change how we think together so we can reinforce new mental models together.

Reinforcing feedback loops are the patterns and processes that reinforce core mental models. How are the structures and patterns we rely on reinforcing the mental model we are trying to change? The way an organization structures problem solving will usually reflect its core mental models.

In systems thinking workshops, I introduce people to MAGO. Using the Iceberg Model, I ask them to dive down into the mental models that might have given rise to current events. Here are some examples of their answers:

- We have to keep up with trends as fast as we can, as cheaply as we can.
- Don't touch what is working!
- We are not an IT company. (We don't need to invest in software development.)
- Our pre-digital processes and organization structure will work for digital product delivery.

- Using modern tools will modernize our system.
- My group's goals and incentives matter most. I need to get everyone else to do what I want them to do.

Systems thinking is looking at the way we design feedback loops, thinking about our thinking together, and becoming aware of reinforcing feedback loops, rather than reinforcing them. If we try to change a system without bridging the gaps between our old and new mental models, changes won't have lasting impact.

Sometimes knowledge and communication gaps are purposefully reinforced—knowledge is power, after all. Leadership might want to keep people apart, or in the dark, so they are easier to control. Most of the time, conceptual gaps reflect our inability to change linear thinking processes so we can communicate about a system.

When people in an organization can't communicate well, they build software parts that don't communicate well. They constantly try to change the system but without changing the way they communicate. That is a recipe for disaster.

 Building conceptual bridges is creating a thinking feedback process that enables people to understand and learn from each other's point of view. The process supports working together to create a new point of view.

MAGO needs conceptual bridges that generate a resilient system designed to meet their future needs. How would they change their thinking and communication process if these were their core mental models?

- We build a resilient system that can adapt to change.
- Our teams can work together to create knowledge flow, in the organization and the software.
- Our delivery process meets our emerging needs.
- A software system that serves our high-value goals generates a return on our investment.

Thinking with others is like rowing a boat. You won't get anywhere if everyone is rowing in different directions or paddling with different rhythms. Collective systemic reasoning is systemic reasoning that flows through well-designed feedback loops. This process enables and empowers everyone to row together without over-reliance on the captain's orders to provide direction. That is why it's a skill that everyone, regardless of role, needs to cultivate.

Mind the Gaps

Building conceptual bridges among people who are thinking about a systemic challenge is difficult. Really difficult. Even when we want to do it, we are blocked by some inherent challenges. We don't understand other people's points of view; we use language that impedes shared understanding; we resist change; and we impede knowledge flow.

Point of view blindness

When people can't agree on a solution they are usually, unbeknownst to them, solving different problems. People with differing points of view conceptualize ecosystems differently. We can experience the same circumstances and use the same words but mean very different things when we use them. When deciding what is valuable to do, for example, accountants and engineers rely on disparate conceptual models when thinking about whether or not to buy cloud technology.

Before diving into solving a problem, it's helpful to ensure that everyone is solving the same problem. When you begin a discussion with a proposition—systemic reasoning that includes why something matters to consider—you can quickly uncover disagreements about why something matters.

Specialized language barriers

> *A necessity for effective collaboration is a common language. If we use words that have different meanings to different people, or words that others don't understand, then we hinder our ability to work as an effective group.*
> —Simon Wardley

The software world depends on specialized language, often across multiple domains. Product doesn't speak tech, tech doesn't speak business, business doesn't speak systems architecture, architects don't speak accounting. Integrating languages across a domain requires developing a shared conceptual vocabulary. Many times, I've used a word that had a clear meaning for me (like "performance")—only to discover that I was completely misunderstood. The word had a different, antithetical meaning for others.

Generate propositions that define essential words. If systemic reasoning relies on understanding the meaning of "performance," ensure you've defined that word. Create a glossary of unambiguous vocabulary that is shared by everyone involved. Be consistent. Do you use the words user, customer, client, subscriber, and people to describe the same person? This causes unnecessary confusion.

Resistance

Frustratingly, in my experience, resistance is the most pernicious barrier in many tech cultures to thinking well together. People don't want to interrelate and interdepend. They resist or reject communication work as "soft" unless they are assessing the correctness of someone else's thinking. The reality is, some people prefer command-and-control structures. They prefer isolating themselves or their team, building a conceptual moat to keep out "non-technical" roles or other engineers rather than partnering proactively.

I've read books and attended talks that suggest everyone would be truly delightful to interact with, if only they were understood and empowered. This is, sadly, not the case with any human groups I've encountered. Sometimes, people are purposefully harmful or difficult. I've seen a flood of derisive condescension blocking collective reasoning more than once. This can be overt or passive, like meetings where participants don't contribute if the discussion isn't personally relevant.

Organizations sometimes reinforce these behaviors, even reward them. In cultures I've experienced that I would call toxic, I rarely saw anyone held accountable for condescending or resistant communication. Backchanneling—secret conversations that disagree, disparage, or foment resistance—replaced transparent goodwill. Backchanneling became necessary; anyone trying to get things done had to be subversive, at least sometimes.

We can each personally represent and demonstrate the value of interrelation. But we also need to discourage harmful behavior from becoming the norm. When we encounter "won't fix" toxicity, more communication doesn't fix it; accountability does. As knowledge workers, it is fair to expect each one of us to be excellent at sharing and structuring knowledge cross-functionally. Systems thinking depends on it.

Lack of structured transparency

The smallest patterns (which are visible to a team) scale to become the biggest and most impactful patterns (which are visible to the organization). The big and the small are in relationship, shaping each other. The way people interact on teams sets the tone for the whole organization. The whole organization sets the tone for the way people interact on teams.

When closed-door leadership decisions "trickle down" as tasks, true change is unlikely. If "leadership" has come up with a solution but has never interacted with the people who will implement the solution, the solution is more fiction than truth. When parts of an organization, like product and tech, are divorced from each other's thinking process, conceptual integrity in the code is impossible. If recommendations can't be modeled by a cross-functional group of people, they can't represent systems thinking.

What an organization knows is not simply the sum of what individuals in an organization know. What an organization knows, and can learn, arises from interactions between people up and down the macro-micro scale. Systems thinking happens among parts of the organization, which means communication needs to happen there. When information is siloed or controlled, the organization limits its own growth. Knowledge flow is critical to systems success.

In order to understand how to do something, we need to understand why it matters to do that thing. Decoupling the "why" from the "how" is a common organizational habit and, from a systems point of view, counterproductive. Success depends on transparency across the sociotechnical system because it depends on a shared definition of success.

We are all building technology systems that act out a story. We are making that story up together, every time we decide what to do and how to do it. The more we understand the story, and know how to evolve it, the more impactful our role can be in its unfolding.

Transparency isn't simply a culture-building value; it's a business imperative. People who understand the thinking behind a technology system's strategic purpose can contribute more valuable work. They can recommend changes to the sociotechnical system that will lead to impactful and meaningful change.

Without informational transparency, making recommendations is like throwing darts at a wall blindfolded.

The Bridges

In the face of greater complexity today (…) intuition, intellect, and charisma are no longer enough. Leaders need tools and approaches to guide their firms through less familiar waters.
　—David J. Snowden

Command-and-control approaches, like "do what we say when we tell you to do it," work only when teams are inherently directionless and need to be commanded. Most teams are, or could be, strong if the communication process supports their strength. We encourage systems thinking to flourish with approaches that strengthen everyone's ability to contribute strong thinking.

Here are examples of bridge-building approaches to thinking together:

- Before diving into solutionizing, *define the problem* and why it's valuable to solve. When a discussion gets lost in circular email threads, go back to this step. Does everyone agree on the problem and why it's valuable?

- Avoid the curse of knowledge and *define the words you use,* especially if they seem obvious to you. Even better, use common language to describe domain-specific concepts or geekspeak. People don't need to know the words "Agile," "EC2," "JSON," or "value flow" to understand what they are and why they matter.

- *Gather others' expertise* because it is an essential part of decision making.[1] Critically listen to others' ideas and reflect on how well (or not) they solve the problem. Understand and articulate why they view the circumstance differently.

- Decide that *your goal is not to be right; your goal is to be correct under the circumstances.* We can get overly concerned with getting what we want or proving that our solution was right. We need to balance that impulse with the desire to figure out what is right for the system as a whole.

- *Share thinking and discussions* by making artifacts. A quick document, model, or photo of the whiteboard are deliverables. Make sharing information a habit.

- *Structure a digital space* for those artifacts. Whenever possible, create a transparent view of the system and the strategies evolving within it. Make it easy to connect smaller discussions to the big picture. Evolve a digital space that can interconnect groups of spaces, backlogs, or repositories. Use content-sharing tools to make transparency easy.

Systems Thinking Needs Feedback Loops

Chances are, the feedback loops you need to support systems thinking don't already exist. Perhaps they do exist but can be improved. Whatever your circumstances, your feedback experience will improve if *what you ask for* improves. You don't (simply) want other people's opinions. You don't (simply) want agreement and approval (at this point in the process anyway). You don't want admiration and validation, lovely as those things are, especially when you have a genuinely good idea and a strong, matterful proposition.

You want to strengthen the reasons. You accomplish that by asking for the feedback you need, from the people who can give it, following the Golden Rule of Feedback (take what you need and leave the rest) and learning along the way.

Ask for the Feedback You Need

There are a few people in my life who are great at giving feedback on my thinking. They rarely fail to suggest some improvement. With those people, I can simply share a link. "What do you think?" They know what to do.

---

1 Read Andrew Harmel-Law's upcoming book, *Facilitating Software Architecture* (O'Reilly).

With everyone else, or when I need something novel, I need to ask for what I want. If you change nothing else in your current situation, change this. Clearly communicate the type of response you want when you share your thinking.

When you share your proposition with someone, don't simply ask for feedback. Ask specific questions. Here are some questions you can ask the person giving feedback:

- Have I sufficiently understood the circumstances? What am I missing?
- Is what I'm saying factually correct?
- Did anything confuse you? Did you trip on anything?
- What is the point, as you understood it? (Asking someone to repeat your conclusions back to you is an enlightening and humbling experience. This feedback loop will help you shape your thinking by revealing conceptual gaps.)
- Does the conclusion make sense to you? (Notice that this is different from "do you agree?" Your higher-value goal is to ensure the thinking is coherent before you begin to unpack it with others.)

Once you craft the feedback you need, you can identify the people who might give it to you.

Get Feedback from People You Need

Systems thinking is a communication skill that, as we explored in Part I, is not commonly practiced. Nearly everyone can benefit from improved systems thinking feedback skills. And nearly everyone, regardless of their role, is sometimes biased or blind. Designing a feedback group with divergent points of view is a powerful way to strengthen your reasoning.

Who do you ask for feedback? Imagine that you have written down your idea, action, or theory (proposition), and now you want to strengthen it. You might consider asking the following types of people:

People who can edit the writing
When you are communicating in writing, find *people who can edit the writing* itself. You might be surprised by how impactful a little copyediting can be when you don't feel understood. If there are models, ask for design feedback.

Subject matter experts
Even if you are certain that you've thought of everything, getting feedback is like getting a good code review. Seek out a subject matter expert—preferably someone who has your back and looks for gaps you might not have seen.

Other points of view

> People who experience the situation from other points of view are valuable. As software professionals, we look at most challenges from a limited point of view, one that over-emphasizes the technology challenges. Getting feedback from people who are impacted, but not coding the solution, generates a more holistic understanding.

People who are impacted

> If you are recommending a systemic change that will impact how other teams work, ask them to describe that impact rather than presume you know.

Your intended audience

> If you will, at some point, need people to agree with your assessment, ask them up front for feedback. Ask them "How can I make this stronger?" rather than "Are you ready to agree?" You will find the path toward agreement, down the road, smoother if you get early feedback.

People who will pay for it.

> Very few things I recommend are free…they will require a budget discussion. Getting early feedback from people who will get me the money helps to structure the reasons so that they include financial viability.

When you create a proposition, also create a list of people who can give you relevant feedback. Ask them to think with you. List two or three specific questions you will ask them. Notice any relevant patterns in their responses.

Follow the Golden Rule of Feedback

As an actor, writer, speaker, software engineer, and systems architect, I've received a lot of feedback. Some of it has been instrumental in developing my ability to deliver good work. A lot of it has been…let's go with "unhelpful."

Not everyone has the skills, temperament, insight, or relevant experience to give you good feedback. An excellent coder, for example, might be a terrible code reviewer. That's okay; our goal is not to judge other people's feedback skills (necessarily). Our goal is to discern which feedback to prioritize.

 The Golden Rule of Feedback is *take what you need and leave the rest.*

After I give a talk or training at a tech conference, I am sent feedback. This can (and has) helped me give better talks and workshops. Inevitably, though, someone says "this sucked, I didn't like it" but gives me no reasons. Perhaps the talk was not their cup of tea. Perhaps they prefer workshops with more coding. Perhaps they didn't like my style or personality or…I don't know. I don't know because their feedback didn't tell me.

This doesn't do me (or the feedback giver) any good.

Conversely, I often get "I loved this talk!" responses. While I enjoy those more, they also don't help me. What did you love? How did it help you work better?

The feedback I need, the feedback I take, is the feedback that helps me give a better talk next time.

Notice that I'm not saying "take what you *like* and leave the rest." The most painful feedback can sometimes be the most enlightening. People have given me feedback that "murdered my darlings," a phrase that means "something I love doesn't work." A joke I laughed at that isn't funny, a point that was too vague, a slide that didn't convey my meaning. I've written many clever, oh so clever, lines of code that didn't make it through code review because they weren't as clever as they seemed.

Sometimes you won't simply murder your darlings; you'll change direction entirely. I have architected solutions that, in the end, would not have generated the results I intended. Trustworthy feedback showed me where I went wrong. Not every goal we want to pursue is viable; not every idea is a good one. Negative feedback is as valuable as positive feedback if the feedback is helpful. "You suck" isn't helpful. "You might create a bottleneck if you do this" is helpful.

When we seek feedback, we *want* to know what doesn't work, as well as what does. This doesn't mean, however, that we must believe (or even deeply consider) that our talk sucks or our idea won't work or we are wrong about a systems challenge just because someone tells us so. Inherent in the feedback process is consent. You get to consider the input and decide what to accept and what to appreciatively ignore.

For example, when you have a cold, people might tell you to take lots of Vitamin C. This advice was made popular by Linus Pauling in the 1970s. Vitamin C won't have any effect on your cold. This erroneous idea was believed by experts for decades. Ideas are organic—we prune and transform them, even the well-established ones, as we learn and grow. We are all part of a system of ideas that are evolving. I wasn't just told to take Vitamin C, I consented. And now that I know better, I wouldn't consent. I would recognize that the person giving the advice was incorrect.

I don't mean disregarding expert advice (during, for example, a pandemic) or valid science because you've decided, without reason, to disregard it. You can't have expertise in everything, to some extent we need to trust each other's expertise.

I am advocating for thoughtful discernment and the understanding that you will experience the impact of your choices. So take feedback that you need in order to strengthen your systems thinking insights…and leave the rest.

One final note on the golden rule: not only does it describe a single instance, but it can also describe a pattern. If someone you rely on for feedback only gives you critical feedback, no matter what you improve, that person's feedback is inherently unreliable regardless of their level of expertise. They can't, as they say, see the forest for the trees. Find someone who can.

Feedback Loops Include Learning

Imagine you recommend a change and all the feedback you get confirms that your idea is the best idea ever. Three hours after your recommended change is pushed to production…chaos ensues. It was, it turns out, a terrible idea that nobody predicted correctly.

Conversely, imagine you prototype an idea that everyone said won't work. Lo and behold, it works! New software is built based on the prototype, pushed to production, and the company generates unexpected revenue. Everyone forgets they said it was a bad idea.

Imagine you push a change to production and hackers figure out a way to exploit it. Or users do something totally unexpected with it.

Regardless of how sound our reasoning is and how expertly designed our feedback loops are, we don't know what will happen. How will you know that your recommendation had the intended impact? How will you measure that impact? What are you looking at to see change? What are you trying not to change?

When you design a feedback loop, extend the feedback you get past the decision-made point. Include methods for measuring the idea once it becomes a living, breathing change in the world. Learn from your experience and apply that learning to subsequent thinking. That's, fundamentally, the core systems thinking practice.

Four Core Skills

Whenever two or more people engage in systems thinking and feedback together, there are four steps involved.

1. Listening
2. Thinking and considering
3. Engaging with the reasons
4. Looking for logical fallacies

You might imagine you already know how to do those obvious things. No doubt you do! But we can also improve them as our knowledge worker skills improve.

How to Listen

Healthy feedback loops depend on how well we listen to each other. When engaging with someone else's recommendation, we deeply consider other people's points of view and look for ways to affirm and acknowledge them. This means challenging our common technology-culture habit of listening for what's wrong or listening with a resistant mindset.

Listening is an active activity. We lean in and listen with self-awareness. We notice what happens in our own minds, reactions, and responses, and we also seek to understand what is happening in other people's minds. How did they reach this conclusion?

For example, say someone has recommended a change to the API structure. To indicate you are listening well, your first response might be: "I appreciate your thinking about this API change; I agree it's important."

Respectfully acknowledge what you've heard. Repeat back your summarized understanding so other people have an opportunity to correct it. "What I understand is that the current database-to-database communication is problematic for a number of reasons, and you want to shift the two software parts to communicating via an API?"

Listening does not mean you agree with what you hear. Listening is learning, and it's building trust in systemic reasoning. We listen as part of knowledge work, and we can learn to demonstrate that we are, in fact, listening.

Change Your Own Mind

When we think together, we are willing to change our own minds. We are all willing to see things differently. We are especially willing to hold ambiguity.

There is often no single, concrete answer to systemic challenges. Our thinking is usually partly right and partly wrong. We can work together to build well-reasoned theories about what is best to do, under the circumstances. Just like we work together to build well-structured software.

Giving and receiving feedback is a process of investigating your own mental models. Do they hold up? Do they need deeper consideration? When you engage in feedback loops, you are willing to learn and grow and change. If you aren't, feedback isn't worthwhile. You are also missing out on the fun of systems thinking, which is learning together.

In our API recommendation example, you no doubt have opinions about how APIs should be implemented. The goal is to discern if those opinions are relevant, valuable, and well-reasoned under these circumstances. If not, be willing to change them.

Engage with the Reasons

Strengthening the reasons is the point of collective systemic reasoning. You are listening for helpful ways to engage with the reasons. Here are some possible responses to the API example:

- "My understanding of the data structure is slightly different; may I show you where I think the labels need changing?"

- "I'm concerned about performance; let's model how it will handle critical load, shall we?"

- "This approach was taken because, at the time, there was a blocker to securing access roles in our current stack. Can we walk through how that will work here? I'm not sure it's resolved."

- "Another reason that supports this approach is..."

It is relatively easy to dismiss ideas that do not agree with yours. Systems thinking is developing the ability to share *why* you think differently. How did you reach a different conclusion? Then, sharing that perspective.

Building conceptual bridges through collective reasoning also includes noticing flaws in reasoning. These are the bugs in our thinking code.

Look for Fallacies

He who establishes his argument by noise and command shows that his reason is weak.
—Michel de Montaigne, French essayist

A logical fallacy is a flaw in reasoning. The further we move away from linear, incremental reasoning, the more space we create for logical fallacies to flourish. Like weeds in a vegetable garden, logical fallacies will arise, and you'll need to be vigilant about pulling them out.

Erroneous leaps of logic trigger a spiral of fallacious thinking. If you pay close attention, you'll see that when people share logical fallacies, rather than sound recommendations, they trigger a maelstrom of noise. In other words, people freak out but nothing productive comes of it.

Fallacies are inherently emotional and make it difficult to stay on track. You can't respond to fallacies with logic because once they are part of the reasoning, the logic is broken.

Advertising and politics *depend* on the use of logical fallacies to control discourse. We are exposed to them constantly. A politician tells you what's wrong with the opponent, rather than making a case for themselves. Beauty product ads make us afraid to grow older. Ads that begin with "Everybody knows that..." are always fallacious.

There is nothing that everybody knows. Movie trailers touting "from the producer of *A Great Movie You've Probably Liked*" aren't giving you any evidence that *this* movie is great.

Fallacies are powerful; they appeal to our baser instincts and feel important for convincing people.

 We are trained to use logical fallacies rather than to spot them. Systems thinking is learning to spot them.

Bugs in our reasoning will inevitably lead to poor systems design. They are a form of reactive reasoning. As you can see from the following examples, logical fallacies influence our software systems thinking in ways that are so familiar, you might not be aware of the negative impact they generate.

Strawman

Hollis recommends offloading complexity by using cloud-native tools. Briar responds: "Hollis hates open source."

Briar has shifted the discussion away from the benefits and drawbacks of cloud-native tools. "Hates open source" is an exaggerated misrepresentation of Hollis' view, and it's beside the point. A strawman refers to a fake version of the person's argument that replaces what the person actually said. This fake version is a distraction; usually it is more emotionally loaded and easier to attack. In this example, Briar knows that the teams involved in the decision value open source. By upsetting them with "Hollis hates open source" he has hijacked the discussion rather than respond with reasoning. Instead, Briar could help Hollis consider the benefits of open source alternatives and compare them to the benefits of cloud-native tools. "Have you explored open source alternatives? What are the drawbacks?"

Anecdotal

Hollis recommends building a new capability using microservices, with detailed reasons supporting the recommendation. Briar says: "We tried microservices, and it was a disaster."

Briar is using personal experience and an isolated example to dismiss, instead of engage, Hollis' reasoning. As they say in finance, "Past performance does not predict future results." The insights gained last time might improve the odds of success this time.

Either way, Briar needs to demonstrate why past experience is relevant now.

Appeal to authority

Hollis recommends building a new capability using microservices, with detailed reasons to support it. Briar says: "Our CTO said that microservices won't work for us."

The fact that an authority thinks that something is true…does not make it true. This isn't a sufficiently valid response. What were the reasons supporting the CTO's conclusions?

A better response would be "The CTO is concerned about X, Y, and Z in our circumstance. Can we discuss those concerns?"

Bandwagon

Hollis says: "We need Kubernetes; everyone is using it now."

Popularity is not validation. Hollis needs to show why Kubernetes is a valuable priority in this context right now.

Black or white

"If you can't pass this whiteboard test, you can't succeed at this job."

Be wary whenever anyone argues a binary reality…the world is full of possibilities. Unless your entire job involves passing whiteboard tests in stressful interview scenarios, this is a dubious claim. A famous American example of this fallacy is the New Hampshire state motto: Live free or die. Maybe, move to a different state?

Middle ground

Product team A says the organization needs a car. Product team B says the organization needs a boat. So, the organization builds a carboat.

A compromise between two extremes is not always the truth…or the best solution. Compromise can be a sneaky way of avoiding difficult, collaborative decisions. What does the organization most need? (Hint: It wasn't a carboat.)

Burden of proof

In response to a recommendation shared by Briar in a Google Doc, Hollis commented: "This looks like a graph, and graphs don't scale."

We see this fallacy so often that it might feel normal. The comment shifts the burden of proof onto the recommender. Hollis needs to say more. What reasons justify the claim that graphs don't scale? How are those reasons directly correlated to the context and reasoning in Briar's recommendation?

Ad hominem

Hollis makes a compelling recommendation for adopting event-based interactions. Briar says, "Hollis overcomplicates everything!"

Attacking someone's character in an attempt to undermine their argument does not undermine their argument. It avoids their argument. (And it's mean.) Even if Hollis habitually overcomplicates things, Briar still needs to describe how *this* recommendation is overly complicated.

Appeal to emotion

An architect shares a recommendation with the engineering team and asks for feedback. The lead engineer tells the team not to respond because "architecture is a bull&*#$ role that doesn't respect our expertise!"

This is an emotionally loaded response meant to influence the feelings and actions of the team. This scenario is so common, you might be thinking, "Hell yes, the lead engineer is right!" Or, at least, you might imagine a scenario in which the architect deserves this reaction.

Doesn't matter. This is a fallacious response because it has nothing to do with the recommendation's validity. Architecture might be a bull&*#$ role, and the recommendation might still be valid and worthwhile.

Logical fallacies seem effective, but they rarely get us what we really want. The lead engineer wants more respect for their expertise. Does that reaction earn the team more respect? Unlikely....

Slippery slope

"If we host parts of our system in AWS, we will be locked in and paying exorbitant fees."

You cannot negate a recommendation simply by predicting catastrophe. If there is a connection between one microservices hosted in AWS and bankruptcy, you need to explicitly describe it.

Your Practice: Get Some Feedback

Using your proposition from the previous chapter, consider who can help you improve it. Then design feedback loops:

- What feedback do you need?
- Who might give it to you?
- How will you measure the impact and learn from the outcome?

Once you collect this feedback, discern what you will take and what you will leave. Do you need to gather more?

Use the feedback to improve your recommendation.

Also, offer to give feedback to someone else. Practice the core principles of engaged listening, noticing your own mind and being willing to change it, strengthening the reasons (if you can) and noticing logical fallacies.

MAGO: Helpful Conceptual Bridges

Building conceptual bridges between parts of the system will help MAGO design a software system that meets their emerging needs. As a great first step, cross-functional teams can work together to describe how the system works. They can also describe their pain points and areas where systems-level integration would help them.

Here are some subject matter expert (SME) groups that could work together with adjacent team(s) and technologists to improve knowledge flow. Their goal is to uncover leverage points by creating a shared understanding of the system from multiple points of view.

Helpful, integrative insight	SME team	Adjacent team(s)	Technology
Information flow: How do graphic and image assets flow across the system? What software do they rely on? Where do these assets interconnect with text? How does a change in context (different devices or platforms) impact asset files?	Graphics and images team(s)	Content developers across the software system, production team(s)	Engineering teams across the software system
Information sharing: What information does the social media team need when sharing published content? What software tools do they use? Do the newsletters include published information? How does that information flow?	Social media team	Graphics and image team(s), content developers who originate content, video team(s)	Anyone who develops these tools
Data structure: Is there consistency in content structure across different contexts? Could MAGO content developers create content that can display anywhere?	Information or system architect(s)	Content developers across the system, social media team, production team(s)	Teams who are building apps or APIs that display information in different contexts
User analytics: What information does MAGO want to collect about readers, subscribers, and people who engage with their content?	Data analytics	Content developers across the system, social media team, marketing teams for all products	Team(s) who build tools for tracking user behavior and engagement

Helpful, integrative insight	SME team	Adjacent team(s)	Technology
Revenue: How does advertising integrate with information across the platform? What software tools are involved? How do people pay for access across the system? What software tools and flows are needed to support it?	Advertising teams across the system, subscription team(s)	Business revenue tracking team(s)	Engineers across the system who build integration tools
Outliers: What products and services exist outside of the MAGO flow of content? Why did people build them that way? Are they using information generated elsewhere?	Product or other teams that went rogue	Content developers working on those products or platforms	Vendor or external teams that are building tech in the system, internal engineering leadership team

Support for Your Practice: Strong Conceptual Bridges

How do you know if collective decision making is improving technology initiatives?

Here are some indicators, some patterns in a technology culture, that help you discern whether or not there is a healthy process of building conceptual bridges.

Strong feedback loops that create conceptual bridges	Weak feedback loops with few conceptual bridges
Proactive communication.	Reactive communication.
Different parts of the software ecosystem have a similar feel.	Different parts of the software ecosystem are unnecessarily dissimilar.
Solutions are argued at the conceptual level, "Portability is valuable and a priority because…."	Solutions are argued at the implementation level, "We need microservices."
Constraints strengthen the outcome.	Constraints control the outcome.
Tradeoffs are made.	Blame is shifted.
Mission-driven teams.	Power-driven leadership styles.
Transparency is the norm.	Information is strictly "need to know."
Decisions can be traced to priorities.	Decisions can be traced to authority.
Communication is considerate and respectful.	Communication is derisive and frustrating.
There is elegant simplicity in the system.	There is mounting technical debt and workarounds in the system.

Pattern Thinking

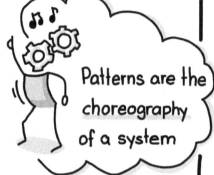

ℹ Pattern Thinking
- ▷ Discover, discern, and describe patterns in your circumstances
- ▷ Transform patterns to steer a system in a different direction

Patterns are the choreography of a system

TIME

CONTEXT

OTHER PARTS

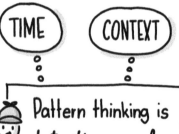

Pattern thinking is *detective work* in relationship to...

STRUCTURES

OWN THINKING

Modeling together makes patterns VISIBLE

3 TYPES OF PATTERNS (in software dev)

→ External Patterns

→ Patterns in tech system

→ Process Patterns

"Counterintuiveness can keep you stuck in old patterns while trying to form new ones

Pattern Thinking

No pattern is an isolated entity. Each pattern can exist in the world, only to the extent that is supported by other patterns: the larger patterns in which it is embedded, the patterns of the same size that surround it, and the smaller patterns which are embedded in it.

—Christopher W. Alexander et al., *A Pattern Language* (Oxford)

I confess, I am a pattern thinker by nature. When I catch a cold, I think about the factors that contributed to getting sick. Have I been stressed or overtired? Was I exposed to groups of people or someone sick? I compare my symptoms to colds I've had in the past and to not-colds like seasonal allergies or Covid. I research, and by "research" I mean Google. Are there new, better treatments available? Would my symptoms benefit from a doctor's visit? What has helped me get well in the past? I alter my schedule to accommodate a few days of recovery.

Then…I try to "just power through!" My longstanding reactive pattern to getting sick is to ignore it, despite being fully aware of the inevitable outcome. Like the Friday afternoon, early in my software engineering career, when I was brain-foggingly sick and didn't want to admit it. I pushed a small JavaScript change to production that broke the entire e-commerce process.

I use viruses as an example because they are a good example of systemic patterns.

> The application of complex systems theory to viral dynamics has provided new insights into the development of AIDS in patients infected with HIV-1, the emergence of new antigenic variants of the influenza A virus, and other cutting-edge advances.
>
> —Ricard Solé and Santiago F. Elena, *Viruses as Complex Adaptive Systems* (Princeton)

What happens in a person's physical system after exposure is interrelated to factors like physical condition and diet. I have an autoimmune disease that wreaks havoc with my immune system if I eat certain foods. For a long time, doctors were not looking for those types of patterns, so they didn't make the connection between my diet and recurring illnesses.

Characteristics of each virus plays a role. Your body behaves differently if you've been exposed to a virus before. (Sometimes.) Outcomes after exposure are unpredictable. Not everyone exposed to Covid, for example, gets sick. A leading expert, who was waiting in line with me to board a plane at the Reykjavik airport, said that there aren't just superspreader events—there are superspreader people. Some of us exposed to Covid will transmit it to nearly everyone we come in contact with. Some of us get Covid and no one else gets sick. We don't know why this happens or even if, by the time you read this, we still understand transmission patterns this way.

In all systems, we watch patterns, and some of those patterns are surprising. This is life in systems. The closer you look, the more complexity you discover.

What Is Pattern Thinking?

> *Systems thinking often involves moving from observing events or data, to identifying patterns of behavior over time, to surfacing the underlying structures that drive those events and patterns.*
>
> —Michael Goodman[1]

Like most phrases in systems thinking, there are multiple definitions of pattern thinking. A common definition of pattern thinking is "Has this event happened before, and were the circumstances similar?" But be careful: if you imagine patterns only along a linear timeline, you will stay entrenched in linear thinking even as you apply systems thinking approaches.

Patterns that repeat are also, often subtly, changing as they repeat. When you are able to spot a repeating pattern and understand the ways the pattern is reinforced and consider the forces reinforcing it (or not) and the ways the pattern changes…you are pattern thinking.

When you look at a pattern, you are mentally isolating it from the complexity in which it operates. This means that the definition of pattern thinking depends on your perspective, the frame through which you look at a pattern.

---

1 "Systems Thinking: What, Why, When, Where, and How?" (*https://oreil.ly/8R-Qh*) *The Systems Thinker*, accessed May 1, 2024.

In software, interest in patterns was popularized by books like *Design Patterns*[2] (1994) and *Pattern-Oriented Software Architecture*[3] (1996). We have framed the word "patterns" to describe object-oriented approaches to software development, like the factory pattern or state. We continued to evolve our thinking about patterns, describing relational patterns in software, like client-server and event bus.

Enterprise integration patterns arose with software system complexity.[4] Interface development using design systems and components is, fundamentally, applying pattern thinking to create reusability and consistent user experiences.

When we talk about DevOps, stream-aligned teams, and microservices architecture, we are talking about patterns.

In systems, we expand the scope of our definition—we use bigger or different frames. System patterns depend on the circumstances, so there are fewer generic patterns we can apply and significantly more observations are needed to understand how the system operates.

Patterns in our software systems are always evolving. At the end of this chapter, I will give you pattern examples using our fictitious MAGO system, which is facing a profound pattern-change problem. You will likely recognize some of the patterns. You are also guaranteed to be facing pattern challenges that are different from MAGO's.

 Pattern thinking is not simply learning patterns you can apply. It is learning to discover, discern, and describe patterns in your circumstances. And it is learning to transform patterns to steer a system in a different direction.

Patterns Produce Events

To illustrate, let's use the example "There's a bug in production." The bug is a syntax error that a linter would have caught. Your team has been extra busy, pushing changes faster than usual. You are missing little things because you have less time for peer review. You decide to add a linting step to the merge process. For a while, this decreases the bugs.

2 Erich Gamma, Richard Helm, Ralph Johnson, and John Vlissides, *Design Patterns: Elements of Reusable Object-Oriented Software* (Addison-Wesley Professional).

3 Frank Buschmann, Regine Meunier, Hans Rohnert, Peter Sommerlad, and Michael Stal, *Pattern-Oriented Software Architecture Volume 1: A System of Patterns* (Wiley).

4 Gregor Hohpe and Bobby Woolf, *Enterprise Integration Patterns: Designing, Building, and Deploying Messaging Solutions* (Addison-Wesley Professional, 2003).

This is an example of pattern thinking: rather than viewing each bug as its own discrete event and reacting to it, you see the pattern—a repeating event with a common feature (syntax errors). You see that the circumstances are encouraging it. You intervene (prevent or alter the course of events) with a relatively small change that improves the system as a whole (by keeping it tidy with linting).

Here, though, is the no man's land between linear and nonlinear: does linting change the root cause of the problem?

Perhaps. There is nothing wrong with adding a linter and calling it good. We don't need to overthink everything, all the time, and overly engage in root-cause analysis. Many teams use linters because they are helpful. A valid concern about systems thinking is that it adds conceptual load onto people who are already at capacity. There's no need to overdo it. You can, however, look deeper into the situation and see what you see.

According to the Iceberg Model, underneath events are patterns, and looking at them is a great first step toward systems thinking. Underneath patterns are structures… forces acting on patterns to cause or reinforce them. Structures arise from our mental models and, as we've said previously, if you don't transform the mental models, you won't effectively change the patterns.

Why is the team pushing code to production faster? Why has their peer review process become strained and sometimes ineffective? Why wasn't linting already part of the delivery process; was there a reason?

Perhaps the team was ready to move faster and syntax errors in production simply reflect that they've been overcautious. They were perfectionistic in their approach, unwilling to accept that it's perfectly normal to miss errors in code. We all want to believe that we can write perfect code, but the mind doesn't work that way. When we are generating something novel, we miss things. Everyone does; it's unavoidable. A linter might be the safety net that allows the team to take more risks and increase their pace.

Perhaps they had a manager who was reinforcing this perfectionistic structure. The manager's core mental model was "Good developers write perfect code quickly." Patterns of blaming and micromanagement were slowing the team down. They were rarely pushing bugs but they were also rarely pushing code.

Now they have a new manager, who encourages them to stretch more and try harder things. They have more bugs because they also write more code. At first, they make more mistakes, but over time, they make fewer mistakes. A linter supports them as they grow. Perhaps they are also improving test coverage, supporting the change in multiple ways. From a systems point of view, for the moment, I would call the root problem solved.

Perhaps the team is under pressure to deliver faster. In my experience, this is the most common cause and not always a bad thing. Teams have crunch times, when they are down in the weeds together trying to hit a launch deadline. Sometimes, despite their best efforts, things get messier than usual. They might tolerate a leftover TODO that they wouldn't under normal operating conditions. Once the crunch time passes, they tidy up. Meanwhile, they add linting.

In this case, their structures and mental models are flexible enough to adapt to circumstances. Overall, they do excellent work and they know that sometimes it's harder to find low-level errors than other times. Their work over time is trustworthy, so they don't worry too much about the crazy days.

More often, though, the pressure isn't coming from the natural rise and fall of activity in software development. When I ask people to identify the core mental models and structures that lie beneath bugs in production, the most common theme is fear. An organization, for one reason or another, is reinforcing their own chaos. Some examples include the following:

- Believing they are a ship at sea during a storm and constantly fearing they might sink, they drive everyone to row faster.
- Believing that they can only gain competitive advantage, be first to market, through sustained authoritarian leadership, bullies are promoted and rewarded.
- C-levels are constantly fighting each other for control, which translates into constant drama and distraction for the teams. People begin their week working on one thing, only to be told they also need to work on three other Priority One issues simultaneously—without missing their deadlines.
- The frailty in the software system has, over time, created an "always on fire" culture that has become the norm.

A sustained core mental model of "Deliver quickly or we die" will rarely deliver anything faster over time. Nobody thinks well when they are constantly on fire. When delivering as fast as possible is the only goal, a syntax-error bug in production acts like oil on the fire of fear that's already raging. More pressure is put on the team—the bugs are perceived as their fault, not the natural outcome of fearful mental models.

Adding a linter won't solve this core problem. It's just a Band-Aid. What happens next? Harder-to-spot "bugs" in the system arise from poorly architected relationships, the team gets burnt out, products are quickly brought to market untested by users (who are unpredictable at the best of times). More managerial oversight is added, increasing the conflicting expectations on the team.

This is a vicious cycle I've seen time and time again. Whenever we make changes in a system, the impact of the change depends on *why* we are making that change. What are the mental models and reinforcing structures involved? The efficacy of our changes depends on how well we understand the patterns that are acting on the system and how well our change addresses core mental models.

Over the years, I've gotten tired of never-ending solutions that don't solve the core problems. Perhaps you've felt this too? As relational complexity increases, our command and control approaches become more noise than signal. Pattern thinking can help us amplify signal rather than amp up the noise…if we are watching how relationships produce effect.

How Relationships Produce Effect

> *We can't impose our will upon a system. We can listen to what the system tells us, and discover how its properties and our values can work together to bring forth something much better than could ever be produced by our will alone.*
>
> *We can't control systems or figure them out. But we can dance with them!*
> —Donella Meadows[5]

Patterns are the choreography of a system. Everything is in relationship to everything else and patterns we don't explicitly design will emerge, despite our best efforts to control them. Behaviors in systems arise from relationships among parts and the way those parts share information. Structures, networks of relationships that create behavior, reinforce thinking and behaviors, in software systems and in people.

Pattern thinking is looking beneath the surface of events to discern how relationships produce effects. Relational patterns are, perhaps, more familiar to us outside of technology. You, as an individual, have patterns of thinking and behavior. When you get into a relationship, you, as a couple, have patterns of thinking and behavior that neither of you exhibit alone. Patterns you might discuss in couples therapy. When you have children, the relational patterns have an increasingly complex and long-term impact. Psychologists call this a "family system" because familial relationships produce effects beyond what any one person says or does.

Not just direct effects, but indirect as well. A family system is in relationship to external systems, like employers, grandparents, schools, religious beliefs, and the communities in which the family lives. All of these relationships will influence the way a family thinks and behaves. When you can't sleep because you are feeling stressed about work and family pressures, you are experiencing how relationships produce effects.

---

5 "Dancing With Systems" (*https://oreil.ly/Y3Uy9*), *The Donella Meadows Project,* August 2012.

The same is true for software systems. Pattern thinking is understanding how the system of software, the people building it, and the organizations around them produce effects. Pattern thinking is also discerning ways to improve patterns in order to improve the system as a whole.

This is a messy subject to explore because each software system will have unique patterns. And each software system will share common patterns with other similar software systems. At the intersection of these unique and shared patterns is systems architecture—the process of figuring out how to improve relational patterns in a particular system.

When we shift into pattern thinking, we move away from demanding concrete answers to complex challenges and into the whitewater world of interrelationships. When you understand patterns, you understand that everything is in flux. Like a sailor, you learn to navigate toward your destination while respecting the forces acting on you. You can't ignore the ocean, the weather, or the need to provision regularly. You can discern how to operate wisely in whatever circumstances you find yourself in.

System patterns aren't usually visible at the code level. Modeling is essential for pattern thinking. Modeling together makes patterns visible and synthesizes disparate views about what happens in a system. I always use a whiteboard (digital or physical) to facilitate discussions about patterns. Collective modeling shifts people away from their usual mindset into the world of bounded shapes and interrelationships.

We can use frameworks to structure patterns. Software frameworks, like Spring Boot, Symphony, or Angular, save us design time by enforcing patterns. In my experience, though, wholesale adoption of any one framework is insufficient to support systems thinking. You'll still need to model, and understand, the patterns in your system. You'll still need to synthesize other people's expertise and experience while designing in a way that will support your situation. Sometimes, that work will lead you away from a framework; sometimes it will lead you toward one.

We more often draw on metaphors to describe patterns, as I do in this chapter. This can be frustrating for those of us who equate metaphor with "too abstract." I understand that frustration. To understand and model patterns, we need "just enough" abstraction to make patterns visible and sufficient data-driven observations to ensure we are describing reality.

In Chapter 10, we'll dive deeper into modeling. Modeling patterns is both an art and a science, an opportunity to generate insight in both traditional and novel ways. As you read this chapter, I encourage you to imagine how you might model the types of patterns we are exploring.

Same Event, Different Patterns

In the previous "bug in production" example, I showed how the same event can be caused by very different patterns, structures, and core mental models. Here is another example of how the same event can be influenced by very different patterns and sociotechnical structures.

An organization experiences a major, unpredicted outage in a business-critical part of the software system. Everyone who can get the system back up and running is put on high alert. They triage the problem, figure out its root cause, and resolve it. The outage was a rare occurrence, triggered by a cascade of outages in third-party dependencies. There was very little they could do to prevent it, though they recommend some changes to reduce impact if it happens again (which is unlikely).

Conversely, an organization experiences a major, unpredicted outage in a business-critical part of the software system for the 32nd time this year. Everyone is on constant high alert, and leadership wants to know who is to blame. They put increasing pressure on the development teams to write perfect code in a software system that is increasingly frail and unpredictable.

This is a self-reinforcing pattern, but not in the way you might expect. Figuring out the root cause of recurring outages requires deep knowledge and experience with the software system. Because of the blame-driven culture, people aren't staying long enough to develop that expertise. They leave for roles that treat them more respectfully. The people who stay become reticent to share ideas. Patterns within these outages are clues to the causes, but new developers are re-climbing the same learning curves as their predecessors. The few senior people with sufficient expertise are burnt out and condescending to new developers, so they are avoided whenever possible.

Design patterns emerging in the industry would improve the performance of the system as a whole. The developers are not to blame. The current frailty is caused, in large part, by trying to scale software suited for one paradigm into a world that's changed. Unfortunately, the long-term engineers reinforce "this is how we do things here" patterns and structures, strongly resisting changes suggested by newer people they feel don't understand their problems.

The whole system is dead in the water despite constant drama and activity.

HR is told to find top talent, the elusive 10x developer who can solve their problem… but top talent recognizes toxic delivery patterns and steers clear. Top talent also want to build with modern tools. Until the organization changes its core mental models, and builds structures that support cooperative evolution, the outages in production are going to continue—regardless of how many 2 a.m. patches are pushed to production.

Where to Look for Patterns

Pattern thinking is detective work, watching what is observable and sussing out the (sometimes invisible) connections among events. There are often multiple forces acting on observable events. We use pattern thinking to help us decide which ones have the most impact, under the circumstances.

When there is a bug in production, for example, that event has four important relationships: to time, context, other parts, and the structures it exists in.

Relationship to time

Does the event repeat? If so, when? Has the repeating event changed over time? Has the frequency changed? Are the bugs in different parts of the code that always reveal themselves during a deployment?

Some patterns help us to improve a system over time. Best practices, when done well, establish healthy patterns for code quality, delivery, and interactions among parts. Some of the same patterns can later degrade the system over time. We see the symptoms of this decline in what we call "tech debt."

Time is always a factor in systems thinking. As things change, the value of our established patterns change. The best way of doing things yesterday might be the worst thing to do today. Our past selves have generated challenges for our future selves… sometimes we are cleaning up a mess, and sometimes we are pleasantly surprised by the good results.

Relationship to context

Context is an understanding of the circumstances. A system serves a purpose in relationship to the context. In every context, circumstances are changing. The purpose of Netflix's system has always been to provide movies on demand. But the circumstances in which it operates has changed dramatically. Imagine the differences between a system designed to mail DVDs to monthly subscribers and one designed to provide streaming movies on demand. Operating well in the context of distributing movies depends on understanding, and responding to, the ever-changing circumstances.

At the software level, we are used to thinking about context. Does an event happen in one context but not in others? A bug that appears only in Safari indicates a relational problem between the source code and the browser.

On a systems level, leverage points, the most-impactful changes to make in a system, completely depend on the context. What works for Netflix or Spotify or Facebook won't work for any other company, at least not in the same way they worked for Netflix, Spotify, and Facebook. The patterns in each circumstance will be, at least somewhat, different. Also, what works for Netflix, Spotify, or Facebook today might not work for them next year.

What we prioritize depends on context. Some software systems need to be fast; some need to be perfectly accurate; others need to be exceptionally easy to change. We might want all three, all the time, but we prioritize the patterns that matter most based on our context.

Relationships to other parts

Decoupling and modernization have become common phrases over the last 10 years. These are pattern changes that happen, primarily, in relationships among the parts. You'll find many resources that help you understand API design, event-driven interactions, microsites, and microservices. Conferences and talks increasingly include domain-driven design[6] and Wardley Mapping[7] topics to help us design parts of a software system, and their relationships, to match the context (the domain) in which we are building them. We are encouraged to use domain language to describe technology parts and interactions. Popular books like *Team Topologies*[8] and *Accelerate*[9] integrate people relationship design with technology design.

Despite all this attention to relationships between parts, I rarely see project or program management approaches that support emergent systems design. By emergent, I mean the whole becomes greater than the sum of its parts. Generally, we "manage" by breaking down the parts and adding control structures, like SaFE, rather than orchestrating interrelated but somewhat-independent activity.

Control structures are partly necessary: we need to coordinate what an individual works on today with the overall goal of the system. We need relational patterns, in the people and the system, that are, whenever possible, self-organizing and deeply aware of context.

I've also seen groups figure out how to apply "just enough" control in the midst of their system design and delivery process. We need to amplify that thinking, wherever we find it, so that we can improve the way we structure relationships among people and technology parts for the systems age.

Relationship to structures

A pattern is always held in place by structures of thinking, behavior, information sharing, etc. Sociotechnical structures reinforce patterns and keep them from changing. Hierarchical leadership is a structure. Delivery methods and project management

---

6 Modeling software to match the domain using input from domain experts.

7 An approach to mapping business strategy and value streams.

8 Matthew Skelton and Manuel Pais, *Team Topologies* (*https://teamtopologies.com*) (IT Revolution Press, 2019).

9 Nicole Forsgren, Jez Humble, and Gene Kim, *Accelerate* (IT Revolution Press, 2018).

processes are structures. Test-driven development is a structure. Templates defining the ways we should communicate thinking (or not) comprise structures.

In a technology system, there is, of course, infrastructure. Infrastructure is deeply involved in establishing and governing patterns in a technology system. It can also be a leading source of hard-to-find-and-fix systemic issues. In systems I've worked on, for example, the caching structure was both keeping the system running efficiently and the leading cause of unpredictability.

Decision making is also always interrelated to structure. Here is an example:

Developers working in a legacy system want to build test coverage so they can decrease bugs in production. They invest too much time, they say, fixing problems when their code inadvertently impacts code elsewhere in their Big Ball of Mud codebase. A short-term investment in tests will pay off in the long term.

But decisions about where the team invests their time are made by product managers who are pressured by leadership to deliver more change, faster. Improving the system is rarely prioritized because each initiative has a budget that only covers new development. The organizational decision-making structure leaves no space to resolve these competing needs.

Remember the carboat example? One team wants a car, and one team wants a boat, so the engineers build a carboat, which nobody wants. Groups within an organization are pushing and pulling technology decisions in different directions. How we grapple with decision-making patterns will inherently architect the system. Few organizations structure teams to operate cross-functionally, but that is where the patterns we want to improve usually exist.

In your own thinking

The most important place to look for patterns is in your own thinking. When I was an engineering lead, I helped build linear thinking approaches that worked for us, at the time. However, as relational complexity increased, I realized that I wasn't practicing sufficient pattern thinking in my work.

That's not a bad thing. In the world before "modernization," my teammates and I delivered code that was well encapsulated by the software's framework. For example, pushing PHP code into an ever-expanding CMS framework didn't require as much pattern thinking as designing an event-driven microservices platform. My need for systems thinking reflected the changes in the world around me.

The pattern thinking that enables me to design software in one context is different from the pattern thinking that enables me to succeed in another. Imperative patterns, like setting A as equal to B + C, differ from reactive patterns, like changing the value of A whenever B or C changes. The differences aren't just in the code; *they are in the entire structure of the system.*

Sometimes, the hardest thing to change in a system is your own thinking.

Three Types of Patterns

As software professionals, we can shift our thinking toward patterns in numerous ways. One way is to look at the three groups of patterns involved in software development.

External patterns

Software is being influenced by patterns that exist beyond the boundary of our software-building experience. We tend to imagine that our users have static needs that we can understand and design toward. This is somewhat true. But those needs are constantly being influenced by experiences they are having in the world outside of our domain.

There was a time, for example, when the user interface could be scrunched and boxy, in frames, with limited fonts and perhaps even an animated gif. Now users would view that as an untrustworthy scam. They expect white space, responsiveness, variation in visual shapes, and high-resolution images. Fifteen years ago, a user might wait two minutes, perhaps even longer, for something to load. Now they'd be long gone.

Expectations change as users experience emergent patterns, which weren't necessarily what any one company determined.

We build software that fits a paradigm, and then, the paradigm shifts. When that happens, our software thinking is especially vulnerable to misidentifying what matters to change. We need more than modern infrastructure tools; we need to think about the mission, purpose, and patterns impacted by external changes.

External patterns can also be social forces that reinforce (or not) hiring practices, the way we define leadership and follow "authority," who gets money to develop things (and who doesn't), and how we are all taught software skills in educational institutions. The social culture at technology conferences influences the way teams build software and vice versa. External trends, like DevOps practices, interrelate with our internal patterns.

Patterns in the technology system

Patterns govern where we put new code. Layers are patterns—the application layer is where we put software logic, and the presentation layer is where we put look-and-feel logic. We use patterns to make our code reusable. We design patterns that structure parts in relationships, services, for example. Patterns are formed by the relationships among those parts, when and how and what they communicate to each other. Patterns are formed by when and how and what they *don't* communicate to each other. Events form patterns—every relationship in a technology system is governed by patterns.

Nearly everything related to data management follows some agreed-upon patterns of queries and storage.

Process patterns

As I've said in previous chapters, systems are sociotechnical. We can see this clearly in our day-to-day experience of patterns. What is the process governing delivery? How are decisions made? How are roles defined and bounded? What is the definition of "done"? What tools and structures do people use to communicate?

Nowadays, I see thinking divided into "product" and "tech" in ways it wasn't early in my career. I've seen a huge variety of thinking patterns. Waterfall decisions trickling down from leadership. Self-organizing, cross-functional teams architecting their own software. Weekly releases. Continuous deployment. I've seen groups that help and support each other and groups that despise and sabotage each other.

To illuminate people-process patterns, follow the money. If you model how money is allocated to technology initiatives in an organization, you will learn a lot about why the system is how it is. Much of what you experience every day will be related to how money flows.

All of the human aspects of software and systems development are subject to patterns that we can (potentially) consider and improve. This book focuses a lot on process patterns not because they are the most important, necessarily…but they are the ones that will need to change if we want to change other types of patterns.

When we are thinking in systems, are we thinking about external patterns, internal (to the software) patterns, or process patterns? Yes! Systems thinking, for us as software professionals, is thinking about how these three types of patterns *intersect and interact* so we can discern where to intervene.

Discernment is the key word. You can't change all patterns at once…you wouldn't want to, but even if you did, you wouldn't succeed. Patterns exist as a confluence of thinking, behaviors, mental models, and longstanding socially conditioned structures. They rarely change easily. When we think in patterns, we are looking for small changes that will have a big impact.

Patterns can be hard to find and confusing. To simplify, there are seven questions you can ask that might help you uncover them.

Seven Pattern Thinking Questions

When you are trying to identify patterns in a software system, here are some good questions to explore, model, and consider:

- *How does information flow?* How and where is it created, shared, stored, and shaped? If it's in motion, is it transformed? Does the information change as the context changes? Is this flow monitored? Should it be?

- *What are the events* that happen in the system? When one thing happens, what happens next? What core activities define the system's purpose? When do these activities happen, and what do they change? (In my experience, changing patterns related to events is an impactful place to intervene.)

- *What are the boundaries* in the system? What are the encapsulated parts, and why do they exist? Do they mirror the capabilities of the domain? How strong (or not) are these boundaries, and how strong (or not) are the relationships among them?

- *What are the building blocks* in the system? Are there components, widgets, modules, classes, or other ways to reuse logic? How do they interrelate and form structures?

- *What is the delivery process?* How are priorities set? Quality ensured? How are decisions about what matters, and what doesn't get made? What are the core mental models and structures supporting this process?

- *How are people organized?* What are the hiring practices? How are teams structured? What groups exist in the organization, and how do they interact with each other? What are the practices expected from a manager? How is leadership defined?

- *How is discourse structured?* Who is involved in decision making? Are reasons given for decisions? Does information flow across teams? Up and down the organizational hierarchy? Do teams communicate as peers? Do people listen to each other?

When there are blockers and stuck places that you can't see, because of counterintuitiveness, exploring these questions can often help you see what you are missing.

MAGO: Looking at the Patterns

MAGO is in the midst of a vast sea of pattern changes. As the world became increasingly interconnected, MAGO's system patterns could not keep pace. For example, in 10 short years, MAGO's weekly publishing rhythm became asynchronous, 24/7 multi-channel, multimedia content delivery. Software parts and people were quickly becoming both independent and interdependent.

Even though they aren't a technology company, MAGO teams built a lot of software. But they had little control over the relational patterns among software parts. Over time, an ad hoc collection of mostly dissociated software parts were "glued" together by people moving information by hand.

Nobody in the organization understood how the system patterns worked together to form a whole. But pattern design is where the most pain *and* the most opportunity lie for MAGO.

Patterns in Relationship

In relationship to time, the entire organization had a synchronous structure set up to support weekly delivery of content. Digital content, at first, stayed within this structure, including a weekly release schedule.

But as the paradigm shifted, development and delivery schedules became asynchronous. As did user engagement, advertising strategies (as they shifted from static to dynamic), product design approaches, and team interactions. The system became a patchwork of time-driven processes in silos.

In relationship to context, the mission of MAGO hasn't changed. The system's purpose—to provide captivating and relevant content that people are willing to pay to read—has stayed the same. But as the contexts in which that mission was accomplished expanded into many realms, including personalized experiences in the browser or app, their ability to understand and track user behavior in multiple contexts has been non-existent.

When someone comments on an article shared on social media, for example, MAGO doesn't know if that person is also a subscriber or someone who watches videos or someone who reads the newsletter. The relationship patterns between MAGO and readers became disjointed.

In relationship to other parts…well, here's where chaos reigns. Software parts, and the teams who build them, and the content creators who need them, came online in a haphazard way. When there was communication between software built in-house, by vendors and SaaS solutions, rickety duct-taped bridges were built using exports or batch processes, or someone just did it by hand. There was so much siloing that no one person knew what all the technology parts involved were. Where there wasn't good encapsulation, the software became a Big Ball of Mud rather than parts in relationship.

In relationship to structure, there was constant intrigue. Budget was given to teams building new products and initiatives that potentially generated return on investment. There was no mental model, yet, for investing in a *digital distribution system*. The organization valued "sweating their equity," making capital investments in technology that would last 10–20 years or more. They were resistant to seeing themselves as a technology innovator (even as their position in the industry meant that the technology teams were often ahead of the curve). They approached digital transformation as yet another project, another capital investment, rather than rethinking their core mental models. When transformation initiatives failed, which they inevitably did, the people leading them were blamed, and more "management" was added.

For each individual involved in the sociotechnical system, the internal thinking patterns they'd learned over a decade of working in the old paradigm (for many, that was CRUD software) did not translate well into the new one paradigm. People who did make the conceptual leap left for organizations who were leveraging modern approaches to systems design, event-based interactions, decoupling, continuous deployment. New leadership was hired to drive change but struggled to communicate the change to minds looking for solutions that fit into the current structure.

External, Technology System, and Process Patterns

Over the course of time, these three types of patterns changed around MAGO. The external pattern changes, for the most part, were not triggered by MAGO's system goals. They represent how MAGO is a subsystem within a broader information system. The technology and process patterns reflect MAGO's attempts to adapt.

External patterns

The external situation has changed dramatically, with key impacts in MAGO's core area of concern. Information flows and changes context much more readily, and the landscape is less predictable.

Then	Now
Information was difficult to get unless you went to the library or bookstore. Timely information was shared on evening news programs, in magazines or newspapers, which had a daily, weekly, monthly rhythm. People waited for it.	Information is ubiquitous and always at your fingertips. Timely information is shared constantly, in streams that readers can't keep up with. Multiple information sources can be scanned and cross-referenced quickly and for free.
Revenue from subscriptions and advertising was dependable and sufficient.	Subscriptions and advertising continue to be revenue sources but MAGO now competes with a world of free content and ubiquitous information. The revenue processes are transmuting so fast, nobody knows what a sustainable and sufficient future for MAGO looks like.
Staff roles were coveted and long held. Everyone worked in the office. Teams, even technology teams, were stable, with little turnover.	Staff roles increasingly manage relationships with contractors, freelancers, and vendor teams. The organization has staff all over the world, with only a core group that works full-time in the same office. People stay for 2–5 years on average.
Information was organized on pages.	Information could take any length and form and be in any kind of digital relationship with other information.

Technology patterns

There has been a shift in technology from patterns that are static to those that are dynamic, asynchronous to synchronous, analog to digital.

Then	Now
Enterprise software with batch export scripts was used to share information to other enterprise software when necessary. Data was stored in multiple data stores.	A system of software reacts to asynchronous events. There's an increasing desire to stop copying data from one place to another and have a single shared source of truth.
Relationships among information parts were structured by a single, hierarchical taxonomy.	Relationships among information parts are dynamic and evolving.
There was one technology team; no such thing as a systems architect.	Many teams and multiple systems architects.
Analog tools were intertwined with digital tools in the content generation and delivery process.	Fully digital process with automation when possible.
No test coverage.	Layers of test coverage.
Weekly releases.	Many siloed release processes.

Process patterns

Patterns in the process of creating MAGO's product have shifted from being centralized and consistent to more responsive and distributed. Their linear approaches don't fit their emerging people system.

Then	Now
The sole focus was on delivering the magazine itself, supported by technology.	The focus is on delivering technology initiatives to support content and reader engagement.
Weekly planning meetings took place for both content creators and technology teams. Agile teams delivered in bi-weekly sprints.	Ad hoc team creation and delivery processes with little integration among them.
Hands-on production of materials.	Hands-on migration of content and assets across the digital ecosystem.
Budget supported better content.	Budget supports better technology.
"The way we've always done it" still worked.	"The way we've always done it" is a blocker.
Ad sales were king.	Social media engagement is king.

Applying the Seven Questions to MAGO

In order to understand how the patterns have changed, we can use the seven questions to ask "What are the patterns in the world that MAGO now inhabits?" This will help them design patterns to stay viable in that world. I would use these answers to begin modeling systemic relationships that will generate these patterns:

- *How does information flow?* Information that once flowed in a closed system, or one that could be understood as closed, now flows in an open system. It is consumed by many types of software as it flows.

- *What are the events* that happen in the system? Whenever content or assets are published, there are multiple destinations that shape and consume them. Users are engaging all over the ecosystem.

- *What are the boundaries* in the system? The boundaries in the system match the evolution of digital tools. The website, the app, the social media team. A rethinking of boundaries is critical.

- *What are the building blocks* in the system? Layers, information, and storage are some of the building blocks across the system. Each layer has its own logic and components. The look and feel always needs to match the brand. The information needs to be structured for consumers and context. Storage needs to be fully secure. Some storage needs to be highly performant, and some storage will be rarely accessed.

- *What is the delivery process?* It depends on what is being delivered.

- *How are people organized?* People are organized according to what type of technology product they produce. An app team, a web team, a video team, etc.

- *How is discourse structured?* There is more politics than collaboration. Who has a voice totally depends on both charisma and the power structure they are in.

Now that we understand something about the patterns in the MAGO system, where do we begin? There are, in fact, many ways to begin. As long as the approaches are pattern-aware, there isn't a right one...only options that align MAGO with the patterns they need to succeed.

Your Practice: The Seven Questions

In Part III, you've developed a proposition and strengthened the reasons that support it. Next, turn your attention to the patterns influencing your circumstances. Can you find patterns, using the seven questions, that help you expand your thinking about how to improve your circumstances?

- *How does information flow?*
- *What are the events* that happen in the system?
- *What are the boundaries* in the system?
- *What are the building blocks* in the system?
- *What is the delivery process?*

- *How are people organized?*
- *How is discourse structured?*

You can write the answer to these questions. You will, however, likely gain more insight if you try to model them. Make pictures of how these patterns work and ask for feedback in areas where you need more information.

Support for Your Practice: Pattern Thinking Outside of Technology

I have learned valuable lessons about technology patterns from people who are not technologists. My personal favorite book on pattern thinking, and the book that many systems architects geek out about, is *A Pattern Language* by Christopher Alexander and others. This book has nothing to do with software. Yet Alexander triggered the pattern language movement in computer science, which led to changes in object-oriented programming and Agile development.

Mark Bittman's *Animal, Vegetable, Junk* and Michael Pollan's *The Omnivore's Dilemma* (Penguin Press, 2006) describe patterns in our food system. I have used many quotes from Bittman's book to describe technology system patterns. The overlap is intriguing.

Another personal favorite is *Design Unbound: Designing for Emergence in a White Water World* by Ann M. Pendleton-Jullian and John Seely Brown. Dr. Pendleton-Jullian has taught at MIT and Stanford and writes about architecture—of literal buildings, not software—yet her thinking reflects many of the challenges we face. Your pattern thinking practice will be well supported by learning about patterns beyond software.

Designing a System of Thinking

When we shift our linear thinking toward systems, we are shifting away from top-down thinking structures, ideas about management, and our usual definitions of success. Instead, we practice modeling, thinking well cross-functionally about how a system works and where it will benefit from our interventions. We provide systems leadership, encouraging an ecosystem where knowledge flow generates valuable impact. And we redefine our definitions of success to include the system as a whole.

In Part IV, you'll practice modeling (which is not the same as diagramming). You'll understand the paradigm we currently work in and how systems leadership shifts that paradigm. And you'll look at systems success from a systems perspective, including the technology industry, a system we are all part of designing.

Modeling, Together!

> "You need other people to shine a light on your blindspots and illuminate biases that skew your insight

Act of modeling unifies people's thinking

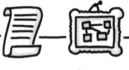

Models can be text as well as visuals

Modeling to generate INSIGHT

There is no one right way to model

HOW we model is more important than WHAT we model!

Transform common artifacts into models encouraging systems thinking.
e.g., ADR → Systemic Reasoning

Strong overlap between DESIGN THINKING & SYSTEMS ARCHITECTURE

MODELING → understand circumstances from multiple perspectives

CHAPTER 10

Modeling, Together

Remember, always, that everything you know, and everything everyone knows, is only a model. Get your model out there where it can be viewed. Invite others to challenge your assumptions and add their own.

—Donella Meadows, *Thinking in Systems: A Primer*

In Chapter 3, you used the Iceberg Model to shift your perspective. In Chapter 6, modeling was part of your learning plan. In Chapter 7, modeling was a tool for improving your systemic reasoning. In Chapter 8, modeling was one way of getting feedback. In Chapter 9, you used modeling to think about patterns in systems.

In an organization, "systems thinking" isn't happening without modeling. When people model together, they make relevant concepts—and the relationships between them—visible. Structuring collaborative exercises that encourage systems thinking is systems leadership.

Systems thinking work is rarely done by one person. You can't possibly understand circumstances from multiple perspectives without...multiple perspectives. Remember, in systems, you are crafting conceptual integrity—synthesizing knowledge and experience. Modeling bridges gaps in people's points of view by framing circumstances in ways they can look at together.

This chapter isn't, and can't be, a comprehensive description of all the models you might make. No template, tool, approach, or framework fits all circumstances. While writing this chapter, whenever I included a specific model, I left out others that might be equally useful. There are too many options to catalog in one chapter of a book on systems thinking.

Systems thinking is discerning which templates, tools, and frameworks fit your circumstances. I encourage you to experiment, try different approaches, and become familiar with a sufficient portfolio of options. Or just open a digital whiteboard and play with the concepts.

Instead of giving you concrete "go do this" examples, I will nudge you toward taking a systems perspective on modeling. How does taking a systems perspective change your approach to modeling and what you might model?

As a systems thinker, you are part of a community of people learning to think together about software systems. Invent modeling approaches that fit your needs. When you do, share them with the rest of us.

What Is Modeling?

All models are wrong, but some are useful.
　—George Box

Modeling is conceptualizing some aspect of a system: framing questions in a way that enables people to think about them together. The goal of modeling, for software professionals, is to generate knowledge that helps us build more impactful software systems.

When I say "modeling," you might think of UML, ArchiMate, or C4. You might imagine cloud architecture, use case, sequence, or class diagrams. You might think of frameworks like TOGAF or SAFe. You might have strong feelings about which modeling approaches are helpful and which are designed to torture software engineers.

When I say "models," you probably think of diagrams. Most software professionals, most of the time, have six types of artifacts in mind:

- *A diagram of software interactions* (like an API response).
- *Infrastructure* models, describing how the software works (or will be built) in AWS.
- *An architecture decision record* (ADR), request for comments template, or RACI matrix.
- *Work to be done and when it's due* (requirements documents, Gantt charts, milestones, burn downs). Agile teams might include a ready backlog.
- *Wireframes or design docs* to show how an interface should look and how users interact with it.
- *Machine learning models* for reading and parsing data.

These artifacts are valuable communication tools. They get thinking out of our minds and into a shared space, where it can be reshaped and worked with. Diagrams are valuable, but making them is not what I mean by modeling.

 How we model is more important than *what* we model.

In systems thinking, we aren't capturing an image. We are generating insight. Peter Senge says, "Systems thinking [...] is a framework for seeing interrelationships rather than things, for seeing 'patterns of change' rather than 'static snapshots.'"

In systems, everything is in flux; we aren't looking for concrete answers. The value of systems thinking, of understanding concepts like leverage points, is most obvious in modeling. We've all had the experience of having to choose between multiple good options. The process we go through to discern and decide is modeling.

Models are conversations.
There is no right way to converse. Establishing a vibrant, healthy, and impactful modeling process is far more important than which tools, templates, or approaches you use.

Modeling is framing questions and exploring answers.
Like systems thinking, modeling depends on discovering the best questions to ask. We aren't trying to model "reality." There is no way to perceive the whole of reality; we can only frame circumstances in helpful ways. Modeling explores what exists and envisions what might be.

Models exist in relationship with other models.
A component diagram, for example, reveals the structural relationships between components in a software system. It doesn't show how those components are useful to people. For that, we need other models.

Modeling helps us find leverage points, impactful places to make changes.
To find leverage points, you have to enter the murky world of shifting paradigms. In most cases, we need to change a shared belief that is holding the system back. Reality isn't something outside of a software system; it is also baked into the system by the people who built it.

A Model Doesn't Unify—Modeling Does

Systems folks would say you change paradigms by modeling a system, which takes you outside the system and forces you to see it whole. We say that because our own paradigms have been changed that way.

—Donella Meadows[1]

A systems architect was hired by an organization to modernize their legacy system. Modernize and legacy had become overused buzzwords, but they were relevant to the information system's struggle to meet emerging needs.

The architect was asked to make a "north star" model. "We want to show engineers what they will be building." The architect's response was "If a systems architect says yes to that request, fire them."

They were partly joking, of course. The lack of shared agreement about the system's core purpose and value, its north star, was a big blocker. The organization couldn't adapt their software to meet modern needs because people in the organization held many conflicting and antagonistic points of view about the system's purpose.

This was holding them back. The teams responsible for delivering change were spending more time fighting change than delivering any. The leadership team needed to create cohesion and they were failing. They hoped a model could get people rowing in the same direction.

Shared vision is a good thing, a necessary thing. What's the problem with this approach? The organization was making two common mistakes:

- Trying to fix social relationships with a technology model
- Trying to lead systems change with a top-down approach

What was missing wasn't a model. What was missing was *the willingness and ability to model together.*

 A model doesn't unify—modeling does.

---

1 "Leverage Points: Places to Intervene in a System" (*https://oreil.ly/4QWaT*), The Donella Meadows Project, accessed on May 1, 2024.

Modeling together requires proactive engagement, respect, cooperation, and the willingness to change. Groups can't row toward their "north star" if everyone in the boat refuses to row together.

> *Dangers lurk in all systems. Systems incorporate the unexamined beliefs of their creators. Adopt a system, accept its beliefs, and you help strengthen the resistance to change.*
> —Frank Herbert

Some people were willing to model together, and they did good work. Inevitably, the established patterns of fighting for control, sabotage, and resistance overwhelmed their nascent willingness to think together. Backchanneling was so entrenched in the people system patterns, newcomers eventually joined in. As W. Edwards Deming said, "A bad system will beat a good person every time."

The architect made a collection of models and some of the recommendations ended up in production. But the interpersonal challenges got worse rather than better over time.

This example demonstrates counterintuitiveness. The organization knew the problem was a lack of mutual respect. But they pushed it in the wrong direction by trying to control, rather than change, that pattern.

Fortunately, even when modeling isn't successful, the process teaches us valuable lessons. The architect, and the leadership team, learned that designing software systems is also, always, architecting organizational communication patterns. You'll struggle to accomplish the former unless you are able to influence the later.

Modeling is not a great tool for governance; diagrams are better for this. Modeling does, however, integrate design thinking into software development.

Design Thinking

> *Design is not just what it looks like and feels like. Design is how it works.*
> —Steve Jobs

I learned about design thinking when I developed a workshop, *Tools for Systems Thinking*, with Dawn Ahukanna. Dawn is currently a design principal at IBM. Through our work together, I discovered that there is a strong overlap between design thinking and systems architecture.

Dawn and I use different vocabulary to describe the same thing. (Which is why, I presume, it can be challenging for engineers and designers to communicate.) She and I rely on different approaches when thinking with others. We use many of the same tools for thinking and modeling but we use them very differently.

Yet, there is deep synergy between our thinking processes. In ways that matter, we are more alike than different. Through this experience, I realized that "design thinking" is so similar to systems thinking, they are often the same thing.

As an exercise, Dawn and I described our process as a systems architect and designer. The question we asked ourselves was "When you face a choice, how do you come to a conclusion and develop a recommendation?" This is what we said:

Diana (systems architect)	Dawn (interface designer)
1. Understand the context.	1. Understand the operating context.
2. Summarize my understanding of the problem.	2. Is this the "right" problem to solve?
3. Seek diverse perspectives.	3. Ideate collaboratively.
4. Free write.	4. Co-create and collaborate on the next solution—10x faster.
5. Construct a recommendation from the multiple perspectives/expertise gathered.	5. Converge to a recommendation.
6. Get feedback.	6. Get feedback.
7. Tailor my conclusion for my audience.	7. Play back and tell the story to the target audience.

When Dawn and I think and discern, we go through nearly identical processes.

If you understand that designing isn't just making wireframes, then you also understand that modeling isn't just making diagrams. As Dawn says, it's "working in EX spaces: Exploration, Experimentation, Explanation, and Execution." Each requires different tools and models.

And there's no one right way to do it.

There's No One Way

> *The system, to a large extent, causes its own behavior! An outside event may unleash that behavior, but the same outside event applied to a different system is likely to produce a different result.*
>
> —Donella H. Meadows

Taking different perspectives *while* modeling also means taking different perspectives *about* modeling. There is no single modeling course you can take and BAM! all of your modeling challenges are solved.

Solving modeling challenges is similar to solving coding challenges. You think strategically about the problem, consider which tools and approaches might help you solve it, and then try things. Same with modeling. We are not trying to fit our problems into a tool or approach; we are trying to choose tools and approaches that fit our problems.

Your cognitive biases will inform your choices about which approaches to adopt. Everyone tends to adopt experiences they like and avoid ones they don't like. We reach for what is familiar. Once I learned to build UML models in Confluence, I wanted to do that on my next project because I knew how. Even though, next time, UML models weren't particularly helpful.

Nowadays, my default approach is using sticky notes in Miro for everything. This drives my visually skilled colleagues crazy. They want more orderly visual information. They help me, through sharing their expertise, continue expanding my portfolio of approaches.

Through trial and error, I've learned that three things are always true:

- *My personal preferences don't help me discern what helps other people*, in a specific circumstance, design their system.
- *What works in one circumstance might not work in another.* The thinking and communications patterns are different in different groups. Even when the same modeling exercise, like EventStorming, helps multiple groups of people, the challenges each group faces when they model collectively will be different.
- *I can learn something from all modeling approaches.* I don't always agree that a modeling approach solves the problem it claims to solve. But every modeling approach was invented to solve a problem. Why did people need this? What was missing?

Models are conversations. We can get ideas for modeling from everywhere. Frameworks like TOGAF, ArchiMate, C4, and Lean Architecture Framework highlight knowledge that might be valuable to your circumstances. Domain-driven Design and EventStorming take a systems perspective. Making business and product models together can integrate perspectives in a cohesive way.

 Systems thinkers discern how any artifact can be used as a thinking and learning tool.

Organizations sometimes adopt a Big Framework as a first modeling step, especially when facing a big systems challenge. This is usually a mistake. We can start small when shifting toward a systems perspective.

Start small

You can use familiar tools with a systems thinking mindset. Many of our common approaches are a good starting point. You can transform common artifacts into models that encourage systems thinking. An artifact can accomplish the same goal (conveying ideas, decisions, or work to be done) but from a more integrated perspective. Here are a few examples:

Common artifact	Systems perspective
A wireframe as a design definition	A wireframe as a shared understanding of how parts (people and tech) interact
A requirements document	A model of where a change fits into a system, what is changing (in people and tech), and how those changes impact the system
Architectural Decision Record (ADR)	Systemic reasoning (these can be the same thing but they often aren't), as described in Chapter 7
Diagrams	Interrelate one diagram with other diagrams by linking them (ideally, making them clickable)
A backlog of tasks assigned to developer	A backlog of work, organizing and describing impactful changes understood holistically by the team, who also understand why they matter to do

Though you might cringe when I say this, I use Jira for guiding software system development, even across teams. Not because Jira enables systems thinking—it decidedly does not. Even though my cohorts and I are good at cross-functional modeling and systemic reasoning, we still need a system that enables us to focus on one, high-priority thing. We summarize and prioritize our activities in Jira (linking to other artifacts) without abandoning systems thinking.

"Do you use Jira?" isn't the question. The question is "How does a Jira ticket relate to the overall systems development process?"

Teams with a good process can use almost any tool to organize their work. Teams without a good process aren't helped by any tool they might adopt. Including Jira.

Ideally, every story in the backlog (or however you communicate work to be done) links to why the work matters.

In Chapter 7, I introduced the top-down elaboration (TDE) as a tool for systemic reasoning. I'm including it again here as a modeling example. Models can be text as well as visuals. A TDE is a one-page artifact that interconnects the problem being solved with the solution being considered. It keeps the "how" connected to the bigger picture.

It includes:

Summary
An optional paragraph to set the context, describe any needed background, or summarize the following sections.

Why
Why does this system exist, and why does this work serve that purpose?

What
What, exactly, are we doing to serve that purpose?

Who
Who is impacted, and how do they benefit? How will you measure that benefit?

How
How will we build, design, or continue to explore the "What." (This could be a link to the backlog or wherever evolving "How" discussions happen.)

When
How does time impact this work?

The circumstances
The value of our solutions depends on understanding the circumstances. Here is where you can talk about the gray areas. What alternative options did we consider but not choose? What assumptions have we made? What is unknown? How will we know the purpose has been served?

A TDE can interweave other models. You don't need to repeat information that is found elsewhere, in mission statements, system models, meeting notes, ADRs, etc. Link to them, using the TDE to make relevant information easy to find.

Interlinking models is a systems thinking superpower.

Link models to show relationships

Creating a systems perspective involves developing relationships among our artifacts. Of all the things I do professionally, developing these relationships is the hardest part. I need to interrelate thinking and perspectives to form a cohesive whole that describes the system and leads into the code. And the space needs to evolve as things change.

In every system I've worked on, one thing has always been missing: a space that describes the system as a whole.

> *Me:* "Where can I look to understand your system?"
> *Everyone:* "Um...."

Many of my systems design colleagues have said the same.

There are excellent models that help me understand one perspective, like the user journey or the cloud infrastructure or the delivery pipeline. But there is rarely a relationship between these models; *they are dissociated from each other and the context.* Teams create models in siloed spaces. Artifacts describe the same system, but they don't reveal the relationships between parts and perspectives.

The solution isn't to make one constantly updated system model. One model will rarely be sufficient. The solution is to link models together so people can find higher-level thinking or dive down into the parts.

Describing a system means designing a system of artifacts. The artifacts don't need to be created or controlled by one person (like an architect), but it can help to have someone creating relationships between artifacts. Someone (or a group of people) willing to think about the system as a whole (which is what I do as a systems architect).

Creating relationships among models is a whole book by itself. For now, start small and practice interlinking artifacts. Don't try to squeeze your thinking into one model. Show a higher-level view that links to more detailed views. Link your ADRs to the overall description of why a decision mattered. Experiment with second brain tools like Notion, Obsidian, or acreom to help you design relationships among concepts.

These relationships are a first step toward taking a systems perspective.

Taking a Systems Perspective

> A document shouldn't try to do what the code already does well. The code already supplies the detail. It is an exact specification of program behavior. Other documents need to illuminate meaning, to give insight into large-scale structures, and to focus attention on core elements. Documents can clarify design intent when the programming language does not support a straightforward implementation of a concept. Written documents should complement the code and the talking.
>
> —Eric Evans, *Domain-Driven Design: Tackling Complexity in the Heart of Software*
> (Addison-Wesley)

Throughout this book, you've seen that systems thinking is a shift in perspective. A shift in how we communicate thinking. As a systems thinker, we enable people to think about a system together, in ways that support impactful change.

When we approach modeling, we ask ourselves, "Does this modeling exercise help us understand how relationships produce effects? Does it help us understand the system as a whole?"

Shifting toward a systems perspective can seem quite subtle, but the experience can be quite different. Here is a recent example from personal experience.

Working on a new platform, the UX team asked me for an outline of requirements they could wireframe. What's in early release? What's in the launch?

The challenge was that we didn't yet understand the system sufficiently to define requirements for each part. I could invent a list of requirements but didn't trust that they would *actually* generate the software system we were designing.

Rather than dive right into requirements, we did this…

We made a capabilities model, adapted from business capabilities mapping, that described the core behaviors the software system (platform) will support. At the highest level, there were behaviors like "Access the Platform," "Engage in the Platform," etc. We used sticky notes in Miro so we could move them around.

Beneath this level, we put the (still high-level) activities that make up each capability. One of them was:

Access the Platform
1. Create an Account

2. Log In and Log Out

I reviewed and iterated on the model with the team, including the business owner, UX lead, and the engineers. We asked ourselves, "Can you think of any behavior that wouldn't fit under one of these headings?" We made some changes and agreed it was sufficient. Then I described the behaviors in more detail.

Access the Platform
1. Create an Account

   - Enter [specific fields] account information

   - Add avatar image

   - Validate identity

   - Edit account information

     Note: Should this capability be "create and manage an account" or should managing account data be a capability at the same level?

2. Log In

   - Log in with [specific data]

   - Log out

We had already built a prototype that showed the minimum viable functionality for this capability. (Prototypes are models!) We'd chosen Firebase as our backend development toolset, and it included authentication. We employed that service for basic account creation and login. We'd also expanded the data model with a user object in the noSQL database.

The long-term vision was to create a more robust account creation process with better verification, alternative authentication workflows, and visible user profiles. Also, we weren't clear yet on how the user model would vary depending on roles and permissions. These will become more complex as the platform grows. We needed to do some modeling to understand that aspect.

The UX lead and engineers collaborated to describe the models and diagrams we needed. We agreed that modeling means "think together and produce artifacts." Diagram means "make a picture of something." We model to understand what a system does, we diagram to describe our understanding so it can be validated and implemented. We also captured decisions in architecture decision records.

Access the platform	Already built	Prioritized	To-do
Create an Account	• Enter account information	• Add avatar image • Edit account information	• Diagram identity validation workflow • Model account permissions and roles (across the platform) • Diagram the user account object to reflect that model • Wireframe user profile page • Build user profile page
Log In	• Log in with email and password • Log out		• Based on account model(s), identify authentication options beyond current

The team gathered together again and walked through each item with the business owner. We clarified what each release name meant, defining the goals of users in each release. We highlighted items for early release and MVPs, leaving the rest as launch items. Some of those would likely be moved to post-launch, but for our purposes, this was sufficient. (Knowing how far ahead to think is also part of systems discernment.)

Access the platform	Already built	Early release	MVP	Launch
Create an Account	• Enter account information	• Add avatar image • Edit account information • Model account permissions and roles (across the platform)	• Diagram the user account object to reflect that model • Wireframe user profile page • Build user profile page	• Diagram identity validation workflow
Log In	• Log in with email and password • Log out			• Based on account model(s), identify authentication options beyond current

Voila! We had a framework for building requirements. People could dive into coding, modeling, and diagramming while maintaining conceptual integrity. The complexity is still there, but we could work within it.

We also used the capabilities model to organize our artifacts. Each capability, Create an Account and Log In, links to a Confluence page where I can see links to models, diagrams, prioritized stories, and the repository of working code. The page also links to the Epic in Jira that groups use to organize work to be done. We can zoom in and zoom out our focus without getting lost or being overwhelmed by complexity.

Like I said earlier, taking a systems perspective is less about *what* you model and more about *how* you model. But we still need to decide what to model.

What Do We Model?

A systems perspective relies on models I've already introduced in this book. Systemic reasoning is modeling. We use it to construct sound recommendations supported by strong reasons. The Iceberg Model, introduced in Chapter 3, gives us a framework for changing the mental models, structures, and patterns that generate visible events in a system.

The Iceberg has been my most valuable systems thinking model. I've adapted many other types of models and frameworks, depending on circumstances, but so far, that one applies to all circumstances.

The Domain

Another valuable modeling activity is domain modeling. To understand a software system, we need to understand the domain—the main area of activity that encapsulates the interconnected concepts of a software system.

For example, courier delivery is FedEx's domain. All software used by FedEx supports courier delivery. The goal of software development is to improve courier delivery. Encapsulated by the domain are fine-grained activities, called *subdomains*. The FedEx software systems are made up of concepts like sending a package, moving a package, and delivering a package. Ideally, FedEx's software system is designed to mirror these concepts.

Even software systems like payroll and accounting serve FedEx's mission by supporting the people who support the mission. All software is part of the domain, but some doesn't directly impact courier delivery. Understanding the domain guides sound software decisions. In a buy versus build situation (deciding what software to build in house and what to buy "off the shelf"), FedEx would build software for package tracking and buy software for HR tasks.

If you Google "domain model," you'll see a variety of examples. There is no One Right Way. My favorite approach is described in Vlad Khononov's book, *Learning Domain-Driven Design*.[2] The modeling exercises he recommends have helped me detangle some challenging circumstances.

You don't have to adopt domain-driven design. You can begin with domain analysis, as Vlad describes in the first few chapters. This will help you "see" software from a domain perspective and understand what "domain" means. This is a great place to start, then see where it takes you.

Causal Loops

Most systems thinking books, articles, and courses prioritize causal loop diagrams as essential models for systems thinking. I haven't discovered a way, yet, to use them in software systems design. I suspect they are useful! I encourage you to Google "causal loop diagrams" and see what they do. You might discover a use for them.

The Seven Questions

In Chapter 9, I introduced seven questions to explore that help you identify patterns in a software system. These questions also represent good areas to model! You can use a more formal approach or open a digital whiteboard and experiment.

How does information flow?

- How and where is information/data created, shared, stored, and shaped?
- If it's in motion, is it transformed?
- Does the information change as the context changes?

What are the events that happen in the system?
- What core activities define the system's purpose?
- When do these activities happen, and what do they change?

What are the boundaries in the system?
- What are the encapsulated parts, and why do they exist?
- What are the relationships among them?

What are the building blocks in the system?
- What are the capabilities, the activities that the system supports? For example, the *NY Times* software system supports publishing an article and subscribing.
- How do the capabilities interrelate?

---

2 *Learning Domain-Driven Design: Aligning Software Architecture and Business Strategy* (O'Reilly, 2021).

- What tools, processes, and practices work across the capabilities? (Like monitoring.)

What is the delivery process?
- How are decisions about what matters, and what doesn't get made?
- How are priorities set? Quality ensured?
- What are the core mental models and structures supporting this process?

How are people organized?
- How are teams structured?
- How do cross-functional roles interact with each other?
- What are the hiring practices for software roles?
- What are the feedback loops expected from a manager and/or leadership?

How is discourse structured?
- Who is involved in decision making?
- How does information flow across teams? Up and down the organizational hierarchy?
- When solving a systems challenge, who engages with whom, and what is the outcome expected?

When we model these questions, we can also model better answers. If, for example, the engineering team increasingly needs to communicate well (in words, code, and models) but the hiring practices do not consider communication skills, model a hiring practice that does.

For a better understanding of what we model, let's return to MAGO.

MAGO from a Systems Perspective

Although you've read about MAGO in each chapter, you may have forgotten the challenges they are facing. Here is a quick synopsis.

Before the internet was ubiquitous, MAGO published the most popular, internationally distributed magazine in the world. Their state-of-the-art publishing software distributed each edition (physically) to millions of people worldwide every week.

They "went digital" by exporting pages from their legacy software system and importing them into extensible digital content management software, hosted on-premises. Every week, a custom script exported articles created for the printed page and transformed them into a web page. MAGO's data architecture, delivery workflows, and software choreography revolved around the concept of a "page."

Digital page views quickly rose to millions per day. An entire ecosystem of digital infrastructure arose to manage subscriptions, track behaviors, monitor availability, distribute image assets, support distributed teams. Mago built an app and expanded the script, importing the exported content into it.

Though "digital first" was becoming a buzzword, MAGO needed to go slowly. Their current system had to work without disruption. Revenue had been consistently flowing in for decades. They needed to cultivate new digital relationships while keeping their longstanding readers subscribing.

Their system was difficult to change without risking disruption. Everything—people processes and software tools—was designed around their current system.

In 10 short years, the paradigm had shifted around MAGO. Multichannel became the norm. The shape of information was transmuting. A single context—a page—became multi-contextual. People on their desktop wanted different information than people on their phone. A passenger on a plane was happy to spend an hour reading articles. The same person at home wanted to ask Alexa or Siri a quick question about a fact in the article.

MAGO's content needed to become increasingly ubiquitous, showing up on search engine results, social media platforms, news aggregators, video and audio platforms, etc.

MAGO hired staff to create extended video stories, podcasts, and custom interactive graphics. Each of these innovations required software systems (that didn't exist yet) to support them. Where there were once a few IT people, now there were international, cross-functional teams building *a lot* of software. The CTO's reports outnumbered content creators, yet they struggled to keep up with the relentless pace of modernization. A high percentage of MAGO's content was "distributed" by people cutting and pasting from one piece of software to another.

Product development was an emerging concept, one that overlapped with business, technology, and project leadership. At first, these various roles worked well together. But over time, they fought for control, causing constant conflict. One product person went rogue and built "their own" software to support a new product. Other teams followed, and soon the software "system" delivering the core value to customers had no conceptual integrity.

Meanwhile, the original print software, which still generated a high percentage of their workflow, was becoming obsolete. MAGO needed to restructure their system. Which meant that they needed to restructure their mental models.

The Problem and Solution Space

There is no sense in talking about the solution before we agree on the problem, and no sense talking about the implementation steps before we agree on the solution.
—Efrat Goldratt-Ashlag

One of the most valuable lessons I've learned is this: when a group is unable to solve a problem, they are usually solving different problems.

I've been in many engineering discussions where every problem was strictly a technology problem. The team wanted budget to build delivery pipelines or microservices, but they couldn't articulate how that investment solves business challenges.

"We need Kubernetes!"

"Why?"

"Because we don't have Kubernetes!"

I've been on teams where the product owner (or some version of that role) architected the technology solutions, rather than articulating the business problem the team was solving and letting them solve it.

In systems, it helps to discern the difference between the problem space and the solution space. In the problem space, we ensure that we all understand the problem—for the system as a whole. Is the problem we've identified keeping the system from serving its purpose? What is the impact? Who is impacted? How will we measure a meaningful change?

The value of a solution is directly related to how well it solves a high-impact problem. Without a shared understanding of the problem space, you'll create no valuable model of a solution. Ensure you are modeling the problem space, when necessary, before you model the solution space.

In MAGO's case, what is the problem?

- The people who think the problem is "obsolete software needs upgrading" want to research available options, evaluate user needs, etc.
- The people who think the problem is "we aren't digital-first" want to architect a digital-first workflow.
- The people who think the problem is "product does not have enough control" want to design a system that gives product control, beginning by defining what control they need.
- The people who think the problem is "we aren't leveraging the cloud" want to architect a move to the cloud, maybe even toward serverless.

- The people who think the problem is "our data is fragmented and trapped in SaaS software" want to begin by data modeling.

- The people who think the problem is decreasing ad revenue want to be able to expect any systems change to generate more digital revenue.

It's easy to imagine six members of the MAGO team in a room, talking about solutions, while each of them has these different problems in mind. If they don't work together to define the problem space, they will never arrive at a solution.

Because I think about the system, I would say that the problem is "the world has changed around us." The core mental models that gave rise to the current systems don't fit the new world. I would model the structures and patterns we need now, to meet our goals in this world.

That's not the right answer. None of these examples are the "right" answer. The truth is, most of the problems are a problem! They are also symptoms of a systemic problem. If the team invests the time to discover the systemic problem underlying their individual problems, they might actually solve the problem.

This work takes time, but it is worth the investment.

In previous chapters, we outlined shifting toward nonlinear and pattern thinking when looking at the MAGO challenge. Now let's add some modeling suggestions that will help illuminate that thinking.

Linear and Nonlinear, Revisited

In Chapter 3, I described some nonlinear approaches that might help MAGO move forward. Here is the same table again, with some examples of related modeling activities.

Linear	Nonlinear	Modeling
Model the solution that meets the need of a new channel.	Understand systemic pain points.	Model the underlying capabilities that support delivering content to emerging channels.
Decouple by designing an API that shares the "page" with other software parts.	Understand the system's information sharing needs	Create a data model that structures, and semantically names, the information distributed by the system.
Add an API that shares all information on a "page."	Enable the consumers to ask for what they need.	Model and structure information that is inherently interrelated and queryable.
Build services that leverage information from existing systems (through APIs or shared databases).	Design an event-based system that supports adding new services without direct integrations (loose coupling).	EventStorming.[a]
Replace old software parts.	Reconsider the context in which those parts operate.	The Value Flywheel with Wardley Mapping.[b]

Linear	Nonlinear	Modeling
Lift-and-shift migration to the cloud.	Maximize the benefits and opportunities of running in the cloud.	Explore the potential of cloud-native tools to solve the problem.
Design one-off features to meet short-term needs.	Design capabilities that will support the current feature needs as well as potential future needs.	Model the capabilities and, as far as possible, imagine them able to operate independently.
Decouple frontend and backend.	Build an information service that can gather information from backends and serve frontends that haven't been invented yet.	Model the consumer needs from that information and what triggers them. Model a flow of information and events that meets those needs.
Put an abstraction layer in front of legacy software to "modernize" and avoid making changes to a complex legacy system.	Use an abstraction layer to iteratively redesign software parts and bring them online, creating eventual obsolescence (strangler fig pattern).	Model the needs of external consumers.
Focus two teams on different initiatives.	Focus two teams on different parts that reflect the domain.	Team Topologies (*https://teamtopologies.com*).
Get everyone's opinion on decisions (or make all the decisions without getting feedback).	Separation of concerns: make "who owns the decision" clear from a systems perspective.	Systemic reasoning (Chapter 7).
Glue together applications by adapting the outputs of established tools owned by other parts of the organization.	Review the tools used across the organizational boundaries to ensure the tools integrate well.	Model the relationships among software parts, rather than taking what you get and stuffing it in a database.
There is a problem with a system not scaling. We identify an issue with the number of connections the system can handle. We increase the number of connections and the failure point shifts elsewhere.	Faced with a scaling change, we explore the problem holistically, including the human behaviors leading to the issue.	Model the multiple areas where the system would fail to scale and look for the core issue.

[a] EventStorming (*https://www.eventstorming.com*) has great resources.

[b] See David Anderson, Mark McCann, Michael O'Reilly, *The Value Flywheel Effect* (IT Revolution Press, 2022).

Patterns, Revisited

In Chapter 9, I outlined external, technology, and process patterns that are impacting MAGO. The table showed patterns "back then" and patterns now. Here are some modeling activities that might help illuminate those patterns and find leverage points.

External patterns

Here we consider how MAGO relates to the larger context it's in.

Then	Now	Modeling
Information was difficult to get unless you went to the library or bookstore. Timely information was shared on evening news programs, in magazines, or in newspapers, which had a daily, weekly, or monthly rhythm. People waited for it.	Information is ubiquitous and always at your fingertips. Timely information is shared constantly, in streams that readers can't keep up with. Multiple information sources can be scanned and cross-referenced quickly and for free.	Information flows across the system and how it's structured. Where is it stuck, missing, duplicated, or otherwise poorly structured?
Revenue from subscriptions and advertising was dependable and sufficient.	Subscriptions and advertising continue to be revenue sources, but MAGO now competes with a world of free content and ubiquitous information. The revenue processes are transmuting so fast, nobody knows what a sustainable and sufficient future for MAGO looks like.	Model the business process model for each revenue-generating activity. Do they have shared components? Are there more options available that are blocked by the current system?
Staff roles were coveted and long-held. Everyone worked in the office. Teams, even technology teams, were stable with little turnover.	Staff roles increasingly manage relationships with contractors, freelancers, and vendor teams. The organization has staff all over the world, with only a core group that works full-time in the same office. People stay for 2–5 years on average.	Interview teams to understand their communication process. What works and what doesn't? Model a process that encourages and supports collective reasoning and collaborative modeling.
Information was organized on pages.	Information can be in any length, form, and digital relationship with other information.	Model the current and anticipated consumers of information. Interrelate this model with the information flow models.

Technology patterns

The technology that supports MAGO's mission has changed and continues to, and that change is accelerating.

Then	Now	Modeling
Enterprise software with batch export scripts to share information to other enterprise software when necessary was the norm. Data was stored in multiple data stores.	A system of software reacts to asynchronous events. There's an increasing desire to stop copying data from one place to another and have a single shared source of truth.	Model the events.
Relationships among information parts were structured by a single, hierarchical taxonomy.	Relationships among information parts are dynamic and evolving.	Model information parts and the relationships among them. Explore decoupling and other approaches to make them easier to evolve.

Then	Now	Modeling
There was one technology team and no such thing as a systems architect.	Many teams and multiple systems architects.	Model the decision-making process. What works, what doesn't?
Analog tools were intertwined with digital tools in the content generation and delivery process.	A fully digital process with automation when possible is the ideal.	Model the places where "by hand" processes still exist in the system. Model alternatives. (Note: by hand is sometimes the right answer.)
No test coverage.	Layers of test coverage.	Model quality assurance needs across the system. Compare that to what exists.
Weekly releases.	Many siloed release processes.	Model continuous delivery. What are the blockers?

Process patterns

The ways that MAGO functions have shifted along with the larger context and technology. Some of those changes have been deliberate and considered, and others have just happened.

Then	Now	Modeling
The sole focus was on delivering the magazine itself, supported by technology.	The focus is on delivering technology initiatives to support content and reader engagement.	Model a system that delivers content to many, emerging consumers. Model a system that understands user behavior across the ecosystem.
Weekly planning meetings took place for both content creators and technology teams. Agile teams delivered in bi-weekly sprints.	Ad hoc teams are created and delivery processes have little integration between them.	Model the activities necessary to deliver change. What does everyone have in common? What needs to be different? Model a hybrid process that combines them.
Hands-on production of materials.	Hands-on migration of content and assets across the digital ecosystem.	Model the transformations and services that could perform them.
Budget supported better content.	Budget supports better technology.	Use the domain model to guide investment. What improves the system's core purpose?
"The way we've always done it" still worked.	"The way we've always done it" is a blocker.	Model the happy path for doing what needs doing now.
Ad sales were king.	Social media engagement is king.	Model the revenue and engagement streams. What do they have in common? How are they unique?

Now that your mind is brimming with ideas…go model! Don't worry too much about how "good" or "right" your approach is. Just enjoy the process.

Your Practice: Go Model

As you've read through this book, you've considered systemic challenges you face. You have probably made models, either as part of this practice or in your daily work life. Now I encourage you to invent one.

This is a big shift toward taking a systemic perspective. Rather than using a template, use modeling as a framing and thinking tool. Model, alone or with others, an aspect of a system you are familiar with. Begin with a question in mind: "how does this work?" or "how does this pattern operate?" or "what is the relationship between X and Y?"

If nothing immediately comes to mind, no worries. You can choose one of the pattern questions and explore it.

- *How does information flow?*
- *What are the events that happen in the system?*
- *What are the boundaries in the system?*
- *What are the building blocks in the system?*
- *What is the delivery process?*
- *How are people organized?*
- *How is discourse structured?*

Support for Your Practice: Resources

Here are some resources for approaches mentioned in this chapter. Explore them to help you envision modeling approaches that might be helpful in your circumstances.

- Cynefin Framework and Mapping (*https://thecynefin.co*)
- ArchiMate (*https://www.archimatetool.com*)
- The C4 model (*https://c4model.com*)
- The TOGAF Architecture Development Method (*https://www.opengroup.org/togaf*)
- The Unified Modeling Language (UML) (*https://developer.ibm.com/articles/an-introduction-to-uml*)
- Architectural Decision Records (ADRs) (*https://adr.github.io*)
- Design Thinking (*https://www.interaction-design.org/literature/topics/design-thinking*)
- The Digital Capability Framework (*https://robllewellyn.com/what-is-the-digital-capability-framework*)
- Business process modeling (*https://monday.com/blog/project-management/business-process-modeling*)
- Yurko, "Doman and Core Domain in DDD" (*https://levelup.gitconnected.com/domain-and-core-domain-in-ddd-c49733fa8c74*)

- Event Storming (*https://www.eventstorming.com*)
- Data modeling (*https://www.ibm.com/topics/data-modeling*)
- Wardley Mapping (*https://learnwardleymapping.com*)
- Team Topologies (*https://teamtopologies.com*)
- The Value Flywheel (*https://itrevolution.com/articles/using-wardley-mapping-with-the-value-flywheel*)
- *Collaborative Software Design* by Evelyn van Kelle, Gien Verschatse, and Kenny Baas-Schwegler (Manning, 2024)
- *Learning Domain-Driven Design* by Vlad Khononov (O'Reilly, 2021)
- *The Value Flywheel Effect* (*https://itrevolution.com/product/the-value-flywheel-effect*) by David Anderson (IT Revolution, 2022)
- *Fundamentals of Software Architecture* by Mark Richards and Neal Ford (O'Reilly, 2020)
- *Communication Patterns* by Jacqui Read (O'Reilly, 2023)
- *Technology Strategy Patterns* by Eben Hewitt (O'Reilly, 2018)

SYSTEMS LEADERSHIP

Systemic Leadership ≢ common understanding of leadership

SYSTEMS LEADERSHIP

- ≠ Management
- ≠ Unique to technology
- ≠ Subject matter expertise exclusively

Architecting communication structures

shared responsibility

Integrative leadership

CHARACTERISTICS OF SYSTEMS LEADERSHIP

Finding places to intervene

Systems Design

HEURISTICS ≠ RULES

7 LEARNING HEURISTICS

1. What you know is probably your blocker
2. Knowledge is more valuable than information
3. Devalue your opinion
4. One perspective is always insufficient
5. There's always another right way
6. Be Missouri. Show more than tell
7. Is the word in the glossary?

We are all, always, debugging a cat

CHAPTER 11

Systems Leadership

Great things in business are never done by one person; they're done by a team of people.
    —Steve Jobs

The primary blocker to providing systems leadership is that we are rarely given roles designed to provide systems leadership. Knowledge work is a paradigm shift for most organizations. The roles we apply for fit a linear-thinking world—predictable, procedural, concerned with control. *We are systems thinkers in a world that was not designed for us.*

The good news is that we can provide systems leadership regardless of our role. Systems leadership is integrative leadership, developing ecologies of change. We can influence, through our thinking and behavior and the ecologies we inhabit, and contribute experiences that give others a taste of systems thinking's benefits.

We are providing systems leadership whenever we do the following:

- Discern the difference between linear and nonlinear approaches, choosing the mindset that most fits the circumstances.
- Encourage healthy relationships among sociotechnical parts.
- Keep solutions connected to systemic goals and purposes.
- Shift perspectives proactively and see challenges from multiple perspectives.
- Express tolerance for ambiguity.
- Demonstrate and reinforce self-awareness.
- Whenever possible, champion learning teams and knowledge flow.
- Demonstrate and reinforce systemic reasoning.
- Design and demonstrate impactful feedback loops.

- Improve the patterns and structures we can improve.
- Develop a portfolio of modeling activities that support systems thinking.
- Describe to others what systems leadership means.

Systems leadership begins with envisioning a world that nourishes and supports systems thinking practices. We provide this type of leadership when we facilitate thinking experiences that improve the system.

In most organizations, leadership is synonymous with management. For our purposes, they are not the same thing. Leadership skills are also not, solely, advanced subject matter expertise. We provide systems leadership when we improve knowledge flow…not (simply) improve our own knowledge stock.

Leadership as the practice of coordinating and supporting knowledge flow is not how we usually define leadership. We have inherited a very different view.

The Paradigm We Work In

We will never transform the prevailing system of management without transforming our prevailing system of education. They are the same system.
    —Peter Senge

When I say "leadership," what you imagine is powerfully coupled to the social system you inherited. In the US, leadership practices arose from industrialization (defined by men like Henry Ford) and Taylorism. Many organizational norms that we consider necessary were generated by mental models that you might not have explicitly chosen to perpetuate.

Frederick Winslow Taylor, an engineer, arguably influenced how we work more than anyone else. When Taylor became a foreman, he said he was "constantly impressed by the failure of his [team members] to produce more than about one-third of [what he deemed] a good day's work."

Taylorism, aka Scientific Management, is based on his conclusion that most workers who are forced to perform repetitive tasks tend to work at the slowest rate that goes unpunished. He believed that we are all trying to trick our employers into thinking we are doing work.

He called this "systematic soldiering." People will avoid work (soldiering) to whatever extent is allowable by the organization.

Taylor had an apprentice named Henry Gant. Until the American Civil War, Gant's family depended on slave labor. When they lost their land as a result of the war, Gant moved to Baltimore, where he met Taylor. And, later on, he became a major proponent of Scientific Management.

Taylor and Gant believed that management is "knowing exactly what you want men to do, and then seeing that they do it in the best and cheapest way." Fastest, too. They would have been big fans of 10x developers. Taylor would have paid developers by lines of code.

Taylorism includes control over worker's bodies. "When a manager tells you to walk, you walk. When he tells you to sit down, you sit down." We see this ideology playing out in the post-pandemic "back to the office" tension between employers and workers. Business hierarchies are designed to prevent "systematic soldiering," adopting the slowest rate of work that goes unpunished. Traditionalists like Elon Musk say that remote workers "pretend to work." Microsoft found that 85% of leaders say they don't have confidence that hybrid employees are being productive,[1] even as multiple studies have demonstrated that hybrid work and working from home increase productivity.[2] Our beliefs about the value of control and the actual value of control do not, necessarily, align.

The structure, and history, of education is also tightly coupled to the way we work. By the time we reach the workforce, we are already conditioned to learn skills and meet expectations. The skills we need as knowledge workers, collaborative learners, and systems leaders are not, necessarily, part of the skillset we've been encouraged to develop.

What Systems Leadership Is Not

As you can see, our inherited mental models might not serve us as knowledge workers. Before I describe systems leadership, I want to describe what I *don't* mean when I say "systems leadership."

Management

Systems leadership and management can overlap, but they are not the same thing. You can contribute systems leadership without being a manager. Managers can be systems leaders. Managers can, and often do, work against systems thinking.

Regardless of our role, you can adopt practices that will improve systems thinking in yourself and the people around you. You will make better recommendations because you are integrating ideas and thinking critically with others. I have seen a correlation between systems leadership skills development and being given roles with more responsibility.

---

1 Microsoft, "Hybrid Work Is Just Work. Are We Doing It Wrong?" (*https://oreil.ly/P0P67*) *Work Trend Index Special Report*, September 2022.

2 Dr. Gleb Tsipursky, "Workers Are Less Productive Working Remotely (At Least That's What Their Bosses Think)" (*https://oreil.ly/3bTe2*), *Forbes*, November 2022.

I have not seen a direct correlation between becoming a CTO and providing systems leadership. CTOs don't magically become systems thinkers. For those who are, sometimes being the boss helps. Organizational power can, potentially, increase your ability to influence change at a systems level. But in most organizations, a management role and a systems leadership role are at cross purposes. Are we designing a healthy sociotechnical system, or are we judging performance and delegating tasks?

In systems, our ability to have a positive impact matters more than our title. Cultivating influence can, in some organizations, be more productive than seeking power. My role as a systems architect is to synthesize ideas, not dictate what to think. My goal is to empower people to thrive because I depend on everyone's knowledge to succeed (just like the system).

Unique to technology

Systems leadership is not unique to technology systems. I have learned a lot from people whose roles are so different from technology roles, you might not imagine we share anything in common. But systems are systems, and thinking about them and leading them are experiences with similar patterns, regardless of the details.

For example, Kelly Shine. Kelly is a talented hairdresser, entrepreneur, and a natural systems thinker. When someone sits in her chair, she engages with them in multiple dimensions; psychology, science, skill, intuition, and strategy. She listens to what they ask for and translates it into actionable meaning.

She balances constraints with context. What will this person look like on a normal day? She observes—watches facial expressions and speech patterns for a sense of personality. How does this person want to feel about themselves?

She thinks about chemistry. What combination of processes are needed here? Kelly specializes in fantasy colors (purple-haired people); there is a lot of chemistry involved. A multi-step process, where a lot can go wrong, precedes the result she envisions.

With an outcome in mind, she considers the cost. Does it match the client's expected financial investment? Are there other, less expensive options?

All this takes Kelly less than five minutes.

As a software professional, you probably don't think of hairdressing as similar to your work. But over the years, my discussions with Kelly have helped me navigate many challenges in my career. We understand each other.

Being a systems thinker does not enable me to do Kelly's job. She has proven skills, decades of experience, and talents that I don't have. She couldn't step into a technology role for the same reasons. Leadership depends on subject matter expertise. But too often, especially in technology groups, we confuse subject matter expertise with leadership.

Subject matter expertise (exclusively)

Systems leadership is not, necessarily, a promotion from lead engineer. Subject matter expertise in a particular technology toolset is insufficient preparation for systems leadership.

Knowing a lot about technology is, of course, instrumental in designing software systems. But your own expertise isn't what matters most. Systems leadership is building relationships with other people as experts, especially when you don't have their skills. Integrating other people's skills into your own increases your capacity for relationship design, pattern thinking, and communicating solutions to systemic challenges.

Here is a list describing the expertise a systems leader role might include:

- Facilitate a cross-functional communication structure that mirrors a technology system that meets our highest-value goals.
- Design highly effective knowledge flows in the organization.
- Synthesize knowledge and experience into reliable, relevant, and sound recommendations.
- Create an ecology of change, where teams innovate, learn, and deliver impactful solutions to systemic challenges.
- Build cross-functional teams that are high-performing because they think well together and understand the organization's needs.
- Architect an emergent information system that will continue to grow our reach and delight our users.
- Discover leverage points in our system and advocate for meaningful, structural change supported by sound reasons.
- Design and empower knowledge workers as a system of learning that generates valuable solutions to the problems we face.

As a systems leader, we are developing the characteristics that enable us to facilitate systems thinking.

Characteristics of Systems Leadership

> *Any fool can know. The point is to understand.*
> —Einstein

As software professionals, where do we focus our attention to develop systems leadership skills? We've covered them throughout this book. Here is a synopsis.

Architecting Communication Structures

(The practices in Chapters 1, 4, 5, and 8.)

Conway's Law inextricably links the communication structures in an organization to the systems they design and deliver. Systems leadership is systems design, which means, also, always designing communication structures. Specifically, communication design involves:

Communication skills
Using text, code, and visuals to share the thinking behind your ideas.

Systemic reasoning
Crafting ideas that are supported by sound reasons and continuous learning. In other words, doing the work required to have a trustworthy opinion.

Effective partnership
Improving the impact of your ideas by partnering with people who think differently or have relevant expertise, regardless of your partners' positions on the organizational hierarchy.

Proactive listening
Asking questions to ensure you understand. Giving helpful, productive feedback and advice.

Empathy as a technical skill
We write code with and for people.

Integrative Leadership

(The practices in Chapters 2, 3, 6, and 7.)

In systems, leadership is a shared responsibility. I don't mean that everyone plays the same role, and I don't mean creating a "flat" organization. Systems rely on hierarchy to organize themselves. But the qualities of that hierarchy are quite different from our familiar org chart structure.

Hierarchy is a communication structure rather than a management structure. For example, as a systems architect, I might focus on the relationship between our internal software system and an external software system like Salesforce. In partnership with others, I am likely responsible for many of the decisions made about that relationship.

An internal team might focus on one capability of the systems, like order processing. This subsystem includes a group of microservices. In partnership with others, they are responsible for many of the decisions made about that subsystem.

Our roles are hierarchical. I am concerned with system-to-system design; they are concerned with lines of code in individual services inside one of those systems. Yet my leadership does not supersede their leadership; they exist in relationship to each other.

In integrative (systems) leadership, higher-level functions serve the needs of lower-level activities (not the other way around). My goal as a systems architect isn't to tell the team what to do. My goal is to ensure that they know—and I know—what we need to know to have a positive impact on the system. Leadership, unsurprisingly given how often we talked about it so far, is creating conceptual integrity. Orchestrating activity rather than rigidly controlling it.

Integrative leadership is *creating ecologies of change*. Designing a space where people have permission to see, think, understand and operate. In ecologies of change, people are encouraged to think differently from the norm, to have agency, and change their approaches as the patterns around them change. Rather than rely on rigid, linear, task control workflows, leaders design workflows that integrate activity across the system.

The most successful systems thinking systems operate with little need for executive control. Success in this type of leadership is, as far as possible, making yourself obsolete. This is something you'll never do, because sociotechnical systems need executive functioning, but that need is lightweight and flexible.

Other integrative leadership skills include the following:

Curation
Design and structure information that frames systemic understanding and empowers people to collaborate on challenges.

Collaborative modeling
Processes to think well together.

Respect for knowledge work
Create an environment where people thrive in complexity because they know how to work together and innovate.

Servant leadership
Make the growth and well-being of the sociotechnical system your goal.

Integrative leadership creates space for systems thinking to happen. Then, we need to actually design software systems.

Systems design

(Practices from Chapters 9 and 10.)

I am writing this book because we are moving from building software to building systems of software. Where once I added lots of code to tightly coupled software, now I choreograph events and information flows asynchronously across a system of software parts. Increasingly, we will all do more of this in the future.

You don't have to be the architect or the Kubernetes Person to think about system design. Tools like Kubernetes and Kafka and microservices help us implement a systems design, but they do not generate a system. A system is emergent…a whole that is more than the sum of its parts. We design for emergence when we design the boundaries, patterns, relationships, and structures in a system.

Systems leadership is focusing on the following:

Integration

Combining one thing with another to form a whole, rather than breaking everything into silos and defining boundaries and the relationship between them. This includes designing smart integration patterns.

Relationship design

Understanding how parts of the system act in relationship to each other and how those relationships produce effect. What do decoupled parts give you that tightly coupled parts can't? Knowing when that effect is helping (or not) the system's purpose and considering what to do about it.

Pattern design

Understanding the forces acting on sociotechnical systems and how those patterns can be changed to produce impactful, meaningful change. When recommending change, articulate why a change in external patterns requires a change in internal patterns. This inevitably requires developing a pattern language, a vocabulary for patterns (event-based versus event-driven is one example).

Information structure

Systems are communication structures. Sharing information among parts, following patterns, is systems design. Deeply considering the structure of information (its shape) and how to supply just enough information across the system at the right time.

Orchestration

Systems are a dance. Activities in the system are acting in their own time. You can't provide systems leadership without, also, thinking deeply about time. How do you choreograph interrelationships among parts in ways that serve the needs of those parts and the system as a whole?

Rather than tweaking this API or that network speed, systems leaders go deeper into patterns and relationships to discover the root causes of events. They don't Band-Aid problems; they look for leverage points, places to intervene in patterns and relationships.

Finding Places to Intervene

As a systems leader, our most valuable contribution is discovering leverage points. This is not a skill unique to technology work. Here is a relatable example, one in which two people with very different expertise could communicate about patterns and potential places to intervene.

One afternoon, I found my cat, Mauritia, behind the sofa, struggling to breathe. Her body expanded and contracted, as if taking a breath was like pulling a stubborn weed from the garden. I put her in a carry case and hurried to the vet. The vet did tests but didn't find a definitive answer. She worried that it was Mauritia's heart, so she sent us to the emergency clinic.

For two days, while Mauritia was in the kitty intensive-care unit, three different veterinarians gave me conflicting diagnoses. Each vet was sure, like the previous vet, of their veracity. The third vet sent Mauritia home, saying, "It's not her heart or lungs; she'll be okay."

The next morning, Mauritia was near death (again). I called the clinic, and they told me to hurry back.

The chief medical officer was waiting for me. He said, "I am taking over her care." He sat down with me and shared his thinking. He told me what he knew and what he didn't know. He explained the theories he was investigating, the reasons that supported them, and how he'd test them.

I didn't understand all of the medical vocabulary, but I could follow the reasoning. I asked a few clarifying questions, and we discussed the tradeoffs. For the first time in days, my panic eased.

"We are debugging the cat," I said. He blinked. "I don't know feline physiology, I'm in tech, but I know how to investigate systemic problems."

For the next few days, he gave me honest, detailed updates. We didn't know if Mauritia would survive, but tolerance for uncertainty was required. On the fifth day, the CMO called to tell me she had recovered. "Come pick her up!"

He never figured out exactly what was wrong, except that it was viral and not a virus he'd seen before. In systems, there isn't always a concrete answer. But we can understand enough of the patterns to act effectively, rather than randomly stab problems with needles full of guesses.

He knew where to intervene. Mauritia lived another nine years.

Looking for places to intervene is a universal skill. The first three vets didn't employ it. They diagnosed the problem and gave me their solution. They were wrong, yes, but in the end, nobody was "right." Their mistake, one that we software professionals often make, was to form a linear, concrete solution for a systemic problem. Then act on the solution, without respect for counterintuitiveness. Remember, because of counterintuitiveness, the first actions we take are likely to make the problem worse.

That's okay…we are all, always, debugging a cat.

The chief medical officer, like every systems leader, did four important things:

- He kept the full equation in his mind. He knew he was choosing the best option from among viable options, not finding "the" solution. He talked to me in equations, not linear statements.
- He was always learning; everything he discovered helped him shift his thinking about the situation.
- He drew on experience and expertise. I could not have saved my cat; I don't have the training or experience. Being a systems thinker is inextricable from studying your subject area.
- He used intuition and imagination.

You are already finding places to intervene, even though you might not know it was systems thinking. You are debugging cats. And you also already know famous people who found major leverage points that changed the world's thinking.

Be like Albert and challenge paradigms

Arguably, the most skilled systems thinker of the 20th century was Albert Einstein. His $E=mc^2$ equation isn't a straightforward leverage point. It didn't point us to a change that will effectively lower greenhouse gasses or avoid climate change. His ideas aren't helping us transform a complicated software monolith into a complex, fast, and efficient system of software.

His equation was the highest-value leverage point though, according to Donella Meadows' list of 12 places to intervene in a system.[3] He embraced the power to transcend paradigms.

Paradigms are shared social agreements about reality. Systems thinking is understanding that no paradigm is "true." When we think critically about paradigms, we change our mindset about the structure of reality. Our goals, rules, and behaviors arise from this mindset. Lasting change arises from restructuring "reality."

---

3 "Leverage Points: Places to Intervene in a System" (*https://oreil.ly/4QWaT*), *The Donella Meadows Project*, accessed May 2, 2024.

Einstein, like the veterinarian, can teach us about finding leverage points:

- "The one who follows the crowd will usually go no further than the crowd. The one who walks alone is likely to find themselves in places no one has ever been before."
- "The important thing is not to stop questioning. Curiosity has its own reason for existing."
- "The only source of knowledge is experience."
- "The true sign of intelligence is not knowledge but imagination. Logic will get you from A to B; imagination will take you everywhere."

Finding leverage points is a skill we develop nonlinearly. Discovering leverage points is a process, like debugging the cat, done with a mindset comfortable with uncertainty. We develop the ability when we practice looking. Einstein summed it up best: "I have no special talents. I am only passionately curious."

Learning Leadership

The only thing that interferes with my learning is my education.
—Albert Einstein

"I am only passionately curious." This describes many of the people I've worked with in tech. We are curious about different things, but generally speaking, the industry attracts curious people. Systems leadership depends on the quality of your own learning practice (Chapter 6), as much as anything else. Being a learning leader is, first and foremost, being a learner.

What does systems leadership add to what we've already explored about learning? Systems leadership is a form of knowledge work design. It is structuring discovery, questioning, framing exploration; organizing, orchestrating, and applying (as a group or organization) learning.

Learning leadership is the art and science of increasing knowledge flow.

Some of us may need support for recovering our joy in learning and discovery. We are knowledge workers who have been taught that passing an exam is more important than learning. We need encouragement to learn for learning's sake and not simply to meet expectations.

As a systems leader, your success depends on how well people learn, so providing support and encouragement to the "passionately curious" is a great investment. You can shape the experience of learning in ways that encourage systems thinking. Software systems are all, in some way, novel. Novel thinking is a welcome and expected part of building teams.

Draw out the joy of learning. Structure and protect that type of thinking and learning.

Developing Learning Heuristics

Systems leaders are more likely to develop heuristics than rules. Heuristics are principles developed by observing and recognizing patterns. They are mental shortcuts, spiffy little sayings that help you remember good practices. Heuristics don't dictate what to do; instead, they help people share a guiding principle. Heuristics help us decide what to do when we get confused or competing priorities make decisions difficult.

Heuristics aren't rules. When we turn heuristics (or any type of constraint) into a Rule, we limit the system's ability to evolve and change as the paradigms around it shift. Rules are sometimes helpful. They can also limit people's ability to challenge mental models that no longer serve them (or perhaps never did).

We are used to rules. We are used to preparing for the exam. We are taught to follow rules because they are rules.

In systems, we learn so that we can understand and apply that understanding in useful ways. We learn so that we can create knowledge (in the form of software) and a knowledge flow that enables people to do matterful things. We learn so that we can grow and develop our expertise. The veterinarian could make recommendations because he's learned from lots of sick cats. He understands patterns in that system.

We need to learn leadership because nobody knows how to build the technology solutions we'll rely on 10 years from now. We are figuring it out. As in all forms of science, we are also figuring out what we were wrong about yesterday. Our path is not a ladder of exams; it's a spiral of evolving what we know while also re-examining what we think we know.

Seven Learning Heuristics

There are no guarantees. Heuristics can fail. The tenacity that defines an engineer is when she steps back, regroups, and finds a different heuristic to try next.
—Rebecca Wirfs-Brock

Here are some shortcuts, ideas that help us to create learning-driven environments:

- What you know is probably your blocker.
- Knowledge is more valuable than information.

- Devalue your opinion.
- One perspective is always insufficient.
- There's always another right way.
- Be Missouri. Show more than tell.
- Is the word in the glossary?

What you know is probably your blocker

Systems problems are often created by the systems themselves, like the ending of a horror movie where "the call is coming from inside the house." We know how to fix a problem; we fix it and the problem gets worse. What we knew last time isn't helping us this time.

If you dig deep and consider what you know, you'll discover that much of what you believe came from someone else. The tech industry is full of people giving talks and writing books (uh, hmmm, yes, like me). Sometimes, in some situations, we are correct and helpful. Other times, in other situations, our advice is incorrect and can even make things worse.

Remember, before you go searching for a newfangled solution to a problem, to consider whether what you "know" is causing the problem.

Sometimes, it isn't what you know but how you are communicating it. People don't understand, so they can't make use of your knowledge.

I couldn't count how many times I thought I was perfectly clear, describing my ideas as reasonably as possible, only to discover that I'd left out an important bit of knowledge. I'd jumped into an idea without giving context. (I have a bad habit of starting conversations out loud that are half over in my mind.) When a discussion becomes blocked, check to ensure you've made your knowledge visible and understandable.

Knowledge is more valuable than information

In Chapter 6, we've talked about how difficult "knowledge" is to define. We learned about knowledge from Larry Prusak, an Ivy League professor, consultant for NASA, and founder of the Institute for Knowledge Management.

He's expressed some key insights:

- Knowledge gives meaning to information.
- Knowledge is a social attribute, not an individual attribute. It is socially constructed.

- No one person or organization can know enough. You have to build alliances. Knowledge is in the space between people.

- No one does anything great by themselves. Well, maybe…nah. No one does.

We aren't simply knowledge stock, an encyclopedia of retrievable information about JavaScript syntax, IAM configuration, or bubble sort algorithms. We organize, collate, prioritize, and apply information to make it mean something. We are part of knowledge flow.

Knowledge is forming relationships between information stores and (re)defining the ephemeral meanings that arise from those relationships. Information helps us build a car. Or a boat. Knowledge helps us avoid building a carboat.

Knowledge is not an object, a testable chunk of information we store in our mental collection. Knowledge is a living, growing, changing experience we share within an ecosystem of information. Information is "eating less red meat reduces your cholesterol levels." Knowledge is "my cholesterol levels are a systemic challenge impacted by my lifestyle, genetic predispositions, and other factors we don't yet understand."

Larry says, "Knowledge is what a knower knows." Knowledge is you; you are intrinsic to the knowledge you create.

As systems leaders, you craft knowledge. Which means that you look for ways to form relationships among "what people know" that help them understand the systems they are designing.

Devalue your opinion

My opinion is not knowledge. It is a judgment that I've made. It's a thought. Some of my opinions are awesome. People should definitely trust them. But my opinions are not my knowledge work.

When I share my opinion with someone else, they've learned what my opinion is. "Diana thinks X." They might, at that point, adopt my opinion. Maybe they already agreed with me. Maybe they hadn't thought about it before. Maybe they trust that my opinion is based on expertise. But this adoption is not learning, except in its most basic opinion-forming mode.

Systemic reasoning, as described in Chapter 7, is structured learning. Rather than simply share an opinion, I share the reasons that convinced me. Others can consider my reasons and add some of their own. I also share the context because very few ideas are Right All The Time.

I do the work necessary to transform opinions into helpful knowledge.

For example, I believe in being honest. My default is to accept repercussions rather than tell a lie. Experiencing the harm a lie causes, in multiple scenarios, has taught me to be wary. Professionally, even when I tell a hard truth that nobody wants to hear, the outcome (long term) is that people trust me.

I don't have an opinion about honesty. In a discussion, I wouldn't say "lying is wrong" and leave it at that. I would lie to someone trying to cause harm. If I did choose to lie, I would have reasons.

This heuristic reminds us to share our thinking process, experience and reasons…not our opinions.

One perspective is always insufficient

If you craft a recommendation that only describes your point of view, or the technology point of view, there is not nearly enough learning behind your recommendation. In systems approaches, we integrate multiple points of view. This can be done lightly, like describing "why" (from a business perspective) the solution matters. We can describe the positive impact of a change on users. Learning means not staying in your lane when understanding a challenge.

This applies to improving your skillset. If you are learning about a subject, like systems thinking or Vue.js, from one source, you gain skill and information but not (arguably) knowledge. You have only one point of view, the picture of a subject through one window. The more you explore multiple points of views, the more you'll understand the core principles, the things that come up again and again, and the flexible parts that change from person to person.

Yes, I am encouraging you to also read other people's books on systems thinking.

There's always another right way

I am not always as flexible as I think I am. Perhaps that's true for you too. This heuristic reminds me that if I haven't come across more than one "right" answer, I probably haven't learned sufficiently. When I'm busy, I tend to grab the first right solution, especially when coding, and this is not a bad thing. I can discern a good solution from a bad one, usually. But I'm not stretching my perspective, which is learning.

When I consider a system's challenge, I want to consider other options, then explain why I recommend the option I recommend. I make my discernment visible. People learn more when they aren't debating right versus wrong, but instead focus on choosing the best answer under the circumstances. There's always another right way, but perhaps it's not "right" for this problem at this moment.

Be Missouri

In the United States, every state has a nickname. New York is the Empire State (presumably because the Empire State Building is here). Arizona is the Grand Canyon State, because that's where the Grand Canyon is. Delaware is the First State because… it was. Missouri's nickname is the Show-Me State.

In 1899, Missouri Congressman Vandiver said to an audience: "I come from a state that raises corn and cotton and cockleburs and Democrats, and frothy eloquence neither convinces nor satisfies me. I am from Missouri. You have got to show me."

Everyone benefits from being shown, rather than simply told. By shown, I mean visual enhancements, like models and diagrams. I mean graphics that sum up an insight. I also mean telling a story to illustrate a point.

The Golden Rule in writing is "Show, don't tell." Wikipedia describes this (*https://oreil.ly/ifTKt*) as "a narrative technique used in various kinds of texts to allow the reader to experience the story through actions, words, subtext, thoughts, senses, and feelings rather than through the author's exposition, summarization, and description."

In technology artifacts, we scrape off everything that isn't concrete: exposition, summarization, and description. While I'm not suggesting that we write poems in our ADRs or describe the breeze blowing through your hair in a code review, I am reminding you, with this heuristic, that showing is more powerful than telling. We need more than concrete to help us learn.

Is the word in the glossary?

In the previous chapter (Chapter 10), we explored modeling. Kenny Baas-Schwegler has a helpful heuristic when we use multiple models to frame the same software system: "Use consistent language between visual collaboration tools."

Every organization speaks its own language. We want our artifacts to reveal that language. Ubiquitous language creates conceptual integrity in the software. Create a glossary to capture this language.

Whenever people don't share the same definition or understanding of a word, like "user," "customer," "Agile," or "artifact," add it to a glossary. Make the glossary visible to everyone and include variations of understanding. This little practice makes a big difference.

I admit, I have always failed to do this consistently. Which is why I know how many troubles you'll avoid if you do. The biggest blocker to consensus that I encounter is people using the same word but describing different things.

MAGO: Systems Leadership

Given the complex challenge MAGO is facing, what could a systems leader do? Here are some examples of activities that would help lead MAGO toward a more sustainable software systems design.

Understand the Pain

You might know some of the pain points in MAGO's system; you are probably correct about some of them. But you need to understand from multiple perspectives. Interview internal users of the system, readers, product people, and technology developers to understand their pain points. Watch them do their jobs. What patterns in the system are illuminated by the pain points you've gathered?

Identify the System's Highest-Value Purpose

Identify MAGO's core domain. How does their system provide competitive advantage to the organization? How does this system serve that purpose, and how is it failing to mature as things change? What changes will have the *biggest* impact on this purpose? If they want to be viable in 10 years, what do they need to do now?

Model the Current System

Like in many organizations, nobody at MAGO knows how the whole system works. Everyone is focused on their part. Modeling the current system enables everyone to begin with a shared mental model.

There are many ways to do this (I once wrote a story to describe a system). Consider the people who need to understand the model and what they need to understand. (AWS cloud architecture models won't help everyone understand what a system does.) How does information flow across the system, where is it needed, and how it is transformed?

Model the activities the system must support. MAGO must create, edit, publish, and distribute multiple types of assets to many types of consumers (including social media platforms). Do the relationships among software parts and teams enable these activities to change as they need to change? Where do the activities fail?

Create a Shared Space for Thinking Together

You modeled MAGOs current system to overcome the siloed thinking within the organization. How can you help people continue to create shared understanding? Perhaps there is a working group of volunteers willing to help improve the sociotechnical patterns. Where can people create artifacts, discuss challenges, and integrate links to other relevant information? Can you integrate artifacts that help people see the big picture?

Articulate and Justify the Core Problem(s)

Remember, systems are counterintuitive! The problems people are focused on at MAGO may or may not be the core problem. Use the Iceberg Model to test ideas about core problems. The organization is also, likely, making the problem worse. Challenge "that's how we do things here" reasons for doing things the way they are done.

Recommend Pathways Toward Improving the Systems

You are looking for leverage points, places to intervene in the MAGO system that will improve the system as a whole. For example, they may prioritize replacing one piece of core software, but you suspect that's a Band-Aid. The problem is that the system isn't designed for digital distribution. Use systemic reasoning to explore and justify other options for changing the system.

Inherent in this work is understanding the scope of investment MAGO is facing. For this, a systems leader becomes comfortable with integrating money discussions (and accountants) into thinking about how to move forward.

Design a System of Communication and Encourage Thinking Well Together

Your goal as a systemic leader within MAGO is to encourage conceptual integrity. Do not seek opinions; demonstrate systemic reasoning, and ask others to engage. Listen to other points of view. Be wary of "because I said so" approaches, and create artifacts that demonstrate the thinking behind decisions. Identify blockers to effective change and decision making. Learn from others in the industry. Encourage friendly helpfulness, especially when people are talking about the code.

Take Excellent Care of Yourself

Remember that this work is hard—like pushing against the tide. Nourish your body and mind. Rest in creative and energizing play. Partner with people who understand you and help you improve your thinking. Take breaks, let people go off in the "wrong" direction. You are there to be of service. That can be difficult to remember when you are frustrated and tired.

Encourage Systems Thinking

Systems leadership is necessary, but MAGO does not yet understand its value. Which means the work will sometimes be invisible. Even if you are not interested in systems leadership, you can be an ally. That shift, toward systems thinking, would be powerful. Who knows, you might just enable a shift in perspective that creates lasting, meaningful change.

Your Practice: A Systems Leadership Cohort

Whenever I teach workshops, one question is always asked: "How do I encourage other people and my organization to think differently?" Even if your role gives you authority and power, you cannot control what other people think. You can, however, influence thinking (and behaviors) by demonstrating and exploring alternative approaches.

A powerful, and often necessary, practice for systems leadership is building a support system for your practice. Over the last 10 years of my career, I have always been part of groups of people figuring out how to encourage systems thinking approaches. In the beginning, I knew one or two people practicing systems design. Now I know many talented people who understand my challenges and improve my ability to navigate them.

I encourage you to build your own support system. This can be as simple as setting up a monthly discussion with one person who is thinking in systems. I have monthly one-on-ones with people who work across the industry, and yet we share common frustrations and goals.

You can create a stealth group of people in your organization who are working toward collective reasoning and collaborative modeling. Nourish and support each other's efforts, share ideas, and create workshops for interested people. Or you could join communities that champion systems design skills, like virtual domain-driven design (*https://virtualddd.com*), who hold talks, workshops, and open spaces.

While writing this book, I began the SystemCrafters Collective (*https://mentrix.systems*). The goal is building a community of people developing systems thinking practices together. It's free to join, and you are welcome.

REDEFINING SUCCESS

SUCCESS from a **SYSTEMS** point of view:
not measured by how well we dominate a system, but how well we thrive in it.

Success for who?

Success is rarely measurable by ONE thing

In systems knowledge is power

 Learn more, dictate less

Respect your teammates and your own integrity

OBJECTIVES FOR SYSTEMS LEADERS

 Cultivate conceptual integrity in solution recommendations

 Improve knowledge stock

 Improve knowledge flow

DANCE WITH SYSTEMS

"My goal has been, and will continue to be, improving our ability to do hard things TOGETHER.

CHAPTER 12

Redefining Success

Systems are the essential building blocks of every successful business.
—Ron Carroll

We are nearing the end of our journey together. It's time to ask ourselves two questions:

- How do I know that I'm learning systems thinking?
- What is success, from a systems point of view?

If we envision success for you, the systems thinker, we are also envisioning success for an organization. You are becoming comfortable with uncertainty and experimentation. So is an organization. You are developing a mind in which systems thinking flourishes. An organization's ecosystem nourishes and supports systems thinking. You can shift perspective, discover root causes, and understand the reasons that support your propositions. So can an organization.

You contribute more signal than noise, engage in deep learning, and think well with others. A successful organization, from a systems point of view, benefits from these activities, so actively encourages them.

What about the system itself? How can we tell a successful system from one that needs our intervention?

Success Is a System

We do not rise to the level of our goals. We fall to the level of our systems.
        —James Clear

If there is no single way to measure success in a system, how do we measure it? We look at a system from multiple points of view, examining it using a system of criteria that help us identify whether or not a system is thriving. Here are a few of those criteria.

Successful Systems Have Enabling Constraints

In the US, we generally equate success with wealth. A wealthy person is a successful person. A company that generates huge profits is successful. Is profit the measure of systemic success?

As with everything in systems, it depends. Using a single measure of success, like profit, is a form of reductionism. We are measuring one aspect of the system (revenue) and ignoring the impact on other systems (and on the earth's system as a whole).

Let's use McDonald's as an example. McDonald's has a gross annual profit of 13 billion US dollars a year. It also has a negative impact on individual physical systems (our bodies) and the healthcare system (treating diseases caused by diet). McDonald's generates three tons of packaging waste every minute.[1] Deforestation to support cattle grazing weakens the planet's climate regulation system.

The US tobacco industry was staggeringly successful until people reconsidered its systemic impact. Will we someday look at fast food like we look at tobacco?

Like all things systems, there is nuance. I occasionally smoke tobacco and enjoy it. My work generates sufficient revenue to pay my mortgage, feed my family healthy food, drive a safe car, and buy medicine when I'm ill. I want my initiatives to do the same for others. Profit is part of success in most circumstances. I don't eat fast food, but I love gluten-free cake. (I could not live in Vienna, where there is transcendent gluten-free cake.)

Success is keeping our measurements and the impact interrelated, seeing circumstances as a whole, not just a bottom line. A systemic view includes the full impact on the world around a system and the people who are part of it. It includes the things we ignore.

Successful systems have enabling constraints: limits on growth or impact that enable the system to scale while still containing the impact of that scaling. Enabling constraints slow down system growth so that we can observe impact and adapt our design. A successful system is one in which the growth serves the needs of the system as a whole.

---

1 Takeaway Packaging, "The Facts: Fast-Food Packaging Waste Statistics 2023" (*https://oreil.ly/GUYzT*), July 2023.

From a systems point of view, success is not measured by how well we dominate *a system, but by how well we* thrive *in it.*

Successful Systems Solve Root Causes

As I write this, 1 in 100 United States citizens is in prison. That is the highest percentage rate in the world. (Russia is second.) Does this outcome describe any of the following?

a. Success

b. A successful system of law enforcement

c. A failed system of prevention, parenting, or education

d. A country with more criminals than anywhere in the world

e. The success of the prison industry as an enterprise

f. The core mental models generating this structure

g. Some combination of many factors

The answer is, of course, g.

This high number of prison inmates is likely an example of intervention dependance. Rather than solving problems at the root cause, we are applying fixes and Band-Aids and an increasing amount of control. We put a lid on circumstances rather than dive in and discover the root causes.

What would we find if we used the Iceberg Model to explore this system? Successful systems address root causes, then recreating the structures and patterns that generate the outcome they hope to create.

Intervention dependance is a form of counterintuitiveness—over-reliance on the intuitive, easy-to-accept solution that feels right in the moment. We know where a problem is in a system, but we push the problem in the wrong direction.

Successful Systems Equalize Impact

When considering success criteria, we need to answer this question: "success for whom?" Success for one group is not systemic success. Successful systems equalize the impact of advantages and privilege.

Using our earlier prison example, 30% of the prison population has white skin, compared to 64% outside the prison system. Fifty-six percent inside identify as Black or Hispanic, 28% outside. Ten percent of the prison population is female, compared to

50.4% in the outside world. People living under the poverty line are significantly more likely to go to prison.

Imbalances in a system, like most things in systems, arise from the Death by a Thousand Papercuts problem. A system or, more likely, the people in a system, are ignoring small recurring problems that, by themselves, don't seem to have much impact. But these problems scale to have a massive impact on the system as a whole.

That is why we need to pay attention to those small, recurring problems and change the rules of a system. This is why practices in this book—responding rather than reacting, designing better feedback loops, and contributing system reasoning—can have a powerful, lasting impact on organizational systems.

Successful Systems Generate Knowledge Flow

In systems, knowledge is power. The more knowledge flow there is in a system, sometimes called *transparency* in technology cultures, the higher likelihood of that system's success. We've explored the practices that generate knowledge flow, the most important one being continuous learning. But the way we structure hierarchy is also a major encouragement, or impediment, to knowledge flow.

In systems, hierarchy serves subsystems. It exists to coordinate the overall system toward its goals while ensuring there is sufficient autonomy for lower subsystems to carry out their functions and flourish. Information flows from the bottom up, not the top down, as subsystems' needs are either managed or require coordination. As we discussed in the previous chapter on leadership (11), our approaches to management are often antithetical to designing flourishing systems.

Your Practice: Success Is a Paradigm Shift

> You keep pointing at the anomalies and failures in the old paradigm, you keep coming yourself, and loudly and with assurance from the new one, you insert people with the new paradigm in places of public visibility and power. You don't waste time with reactionaries; rather you work with active change agents and with the vast middle ground of people who are open-minded.
>
> —Donella Meadows

According to a study done in 2022, 91.88% of software engineers worldwide are men.[2] Predominantly, white, straight, American or European men under the age of 40. In systems, a lack of diversity is rarely a natural occurrence. As we've learned throughout this book, three things are usually true:

---

2 Lionel Sujay Vailshery, "Software Developer Gender Distribution Worldwide as of 2022" (*https://oreil.ly/rRwqX*), Statista, March 2023.

- The system itself is generating its own outcome.
- We are blaming the wrong things.
- We are making the problem worse when we try to fix it, because of counterintuitiveness.

There is no easy or single answer to the question of "Why?" As a systems leader, hoping to generate system success, you are looking for root causes. If you apply the Iceberg Model to this systemic challenge in technology (see Figure 12-1), what do you discover?

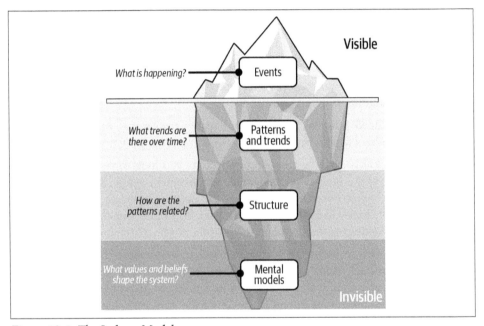

Figure 12-1. The Iceberg Model

As a systems leader, hoping to improve systems, you are also debugging the system to avoid common systemic pitfalls. A pitfall that may be in play here is called "success to the successful." This means that people who experience success in a system also benefit from that success in ways that generate more success (for them). The problem, as Donella Meadows says, is the structure of the system, not the morals of the people in it.

How might you balance out this systemic challenge? When does it come into play? You might want to research suggestions to see if approaches to this pitfall could be applied to technology systems.

Qualities of Success

You've come this far in the book without any templates or checklists to apply. Thank you for staying with me. Here, at the end, is a checklist of qualities you can use to measure your systems thinking practice.

☐ You practice thinking. You and your knowledge-working cohorts make this practice part of your daily life—whether it's writing, artifact crafting, collective modeling, coding, or improving feedback skills. You talk about these practices as essential technology skills (not "soft skills" that aren't "hard").

☐ You and your cohorts can describe the difference between reductionistic, analytical thinking (linear) and taking a systemic perspective (nonlinear). You can discern when to apply one or the other (or both).

☐ You and your cohorts know that people systems are inextricable from technical systems. You view challenges as inherently sociotechnical and always describe technology solutions' impacts on people.

☐ You've developed your own understanding of "conceptual integrity" and can describe to others what it means and how you are developing it.

☐ Because you know systems are counterintuitive, you look for ways that you and your cohorts might be inadvertently making a problem worse. Knowing you will face pushback, you nevertheless describe the negative impacts and recommend improvements that will have a positive impact. You know this takes time and are (generally speaking) patient enough to help others who are trying to understand.

☐ When faced with recurring problems, you seek to understand the systemic structures and feedback loops that block change. You know that blame, around you and in your own mind, is a distraction and unlikely to point you in the right direction. You discourage others from taking the easy path, blaming leadership, adopting what Netflix does, blaming product, or solving complex challenges with a tool (like Kubernetes as a magic bullet).

☐ When you look at a software system, you try to understand how interrelated and interdependent parts act together to create a whole. You can describe the patterns and processes that form relationships among these parts. You investigate how these patterns are reinforced. When possible, you recommend changes to both social and technological patterns, whether or not they are social or technological patterns (or both).

☐ When challenges arise, you take a systemic perspective. For example, you use the Iceberg Model to understand the "invisible" structures, patterns, and mental models impacting the situation.

☐ When faced with a recurring problem, you look for leverage points, places to intervene, rather than reacting to every instance, to every problem.

☐ You and your cohorts accept that uncertainty is a natural, welcome, and inevitable part of software development. You comfortably shift your mental models as the circumstances around you change.

☐ You and your cohorts shift perspective easily to explore challenges from different points of view. You proactively synthesize other people's knowledge and experience in order to understand a challenge or change. You include nontechnologists and people who don't agree with your thinking.

☐ When faced with a difficult situation, you can describe what you think. When you don't know what you think, you invest in deep work to develop your thinking.

☐ When faced with a difficult situation, you demonstrate high levels of self-awareness. You can describe what you think, feel, and experience. When you notice yourself reacting to other people's thinking, you create space to reflect before responding. You are familiar with your own reactive patterns and have practices that let them settle down.

☐ You recognize thinking patterns that are reactive, fallacious, or biased. You practice helping people improve these patterns, strengthening the integrity of the thinking, rather than joining the fight.

☐ You approach your work with an "always learning" mindset. You regularly structure discovery, learning, and exploration with others proactively. When something fails, you explore what you learned.

☐ You and your cohorts make systemic reasoning the default communication structure. You create well-reasoned ideas, recommendations, and theories. You articulate the reasoning behind your conclusions.

☐ You helpfully work with others to strengthen their reasoning rather than giving them your opinion or derision. Changing communication patterns and behaviors is a high priority. You've seen the truth of Conway's Law: systems are inherently designed by communication structures.

☐ Your solutions are meaningfully and explicitly connected to the context, the "why." When you deploy code, you understand how it supports the system's purpose and can describe it using ubiquitous language.

☐ You regularly create conceptual models, alone and with others, to guide impactful decisions. You make artifacts and talk about artifact creation as an essential technology skill. You understand, and explain, how this work is different from (but related to) documentation and diagramming.

- ☐ You are developing a portfolio of "systems thinking" approaches and sufficiently diverse modeling techniques. You use them improvisationally, discerning what helps you, your cohorts, and your current circumstances. You use a systems thinking vocabulary when you talk about change. (You might even be developing a glossary.)
- ☐ You encourage knowledge flow. You create an ecosystem for knowledge work.

Success for MAGO

Like everything in systems, success for MAGO depends on your point of view. Which part of the system do you focus on? They need a system for curating and developing quality content that people want to consume. This includes subsystems for graphics, video, editing, layout, planning, etc. They need a system for attracting new consumers and analyzing engagement behavior across a wide variety of platforms and media types. They need a system for collecting revenue and another for running the company economically. They need a technology-driven system for distributing and displaying information to people in various contexts.

More importantly, they need to understand how these systems work together to combine into a whole. And how changes in one subsystem, or in the world around them, will impact other areas they use to measure success.

Despite the challenges they face, the core purpose of MAGO's system hasn't changed: publish information products that people pay to consume. No doubt, their mission statement describes deeper values. For example, people pay to consume pornography, but MAGO does not publish pornography. But from a technology system point of view, publishing, consuming, and paying is what the system must support.

What is limiting their success is rather straightforward: information systems have become ubiquitous, omnichannelled, and interconnected. MAGO's sociotechnical system no longer fits the world around them.

Every word of their purpose has shifted:

Purpose word	Previous meaning	Current meaning
Publish	Print media migrated to a digital version in a mechanistic assembly process, usually following a predefined schedule.	Distribute to a wide variety of existing, and emerging, digital platforms (while still supporting print media for some products). Asynchronous processes are running 24/7.
Information	The data object structured by, and wholly governed by, the publishing software: a page, an article, an image, a video. (Generally speaking, CRUD.)	Data in motion, structured for creation, then restructured by the software/platform consuming it. An "article" is a group of characters organized by display information like headline or paragraph. Web software consumes it all and changes display settings depending on the context (desktop versus mobile). A social media platform consumes the summary. Another platform consumes a different summary and a different image. One smaller part (a sentence) can be consumed to answer a "Hey Siri" question or feed an LLM. Each information part can be interrelated with other data objects, like graphics, video, or annotations. The relationships may or may not be consumed.
Products	Information packaged by software into a predefined shape, like a magazine article, navigable website, book, or film.	Product is unbounded; it can mean one digital property, an information stream of interesting headlines sent via SMS, a film, a YouTube channel, a paid newsletter, a social feed...anything, really. All derived from the same information source.
People	Subscribers, "traffic," consumers of books, movies. Each demographic with preferences that are relatively easy to measure.	Everyone, everywhere. Communicating with a target audience member browsing magazines in the airport is quite different from communicating with a target audience member browsing the internet. Establishing relationships with consumers is an omnichannel, multimedia process.
Pay	Comsumers purchase the product, e.g., MAGO at the newsstand, or bookstore, a ticket to a movie theater, a DVD purchase. Publish ads to support the products.	Most organizations are still figuring this out. Is Kobo.com the new bookstore? Is Netflix the new movie theater? Is the *New York Times* a newspaper—what about Wirecutter, Wordle? Is ad revenue still worth pursuing? There is a lot of free information available. Now there is ChatGPT. What makes information worth paying for?
Consume	Browse the magazine, at home or on a flight. Read the book while lying in bed, hoping to fall asleep. Watch the movie, sitting in your theater seat or on the couch next to your date. (There is a physical relationship between the consumer's attention and the product being consumed.)	Glimpse on any device, in any context, anytime, anywhere, on demand. Can be physically doing one thing (cooking dinner) while consuming (audiobook, video streaming, asking Alexa for recipe information).

Every piece of information has nearly infinite contexts in which it can be consumed. Yet, MAGO still needs to design a system that distributes information and, in return, generates revenue. Replacing outworn pieces of CRUD software, or adding new ones, won't help them publish information products that people pay to consume…and not just today, but also in tomorrow's world. They've duct-taped their system together, but is that "success"?

From a systems perspective, success for MAGO would be designing and building a sociotechnical system that meets emerging needs. *Success for MAGO is changing the system's goal:*

 Asynchronously create and distribute well-structured and interrelated information to products and platforms where people will engage and pay for more.

To meet that goal, align MAGO's activities, success measures, language, structures, patterns, and mental models with the goal.

Support for Your Practice: Objectives for Systems Leaders

Earlier in this chapter, I told you stories about organizations that headed toward "transformation" and then turned back. This happens for many reasons; one of them is lacking systems objectives. They aren't embracing small habits that will scale to transformation. And they didn't act against old patterns when they reinforced themselves.

Imagine you are a brand new systems leader. Here are some ways to measure whether the team(s) is developing systems thinking skills.

Objective: Cultivate Conceptual Integrity in Solution Recommendations

Goal 1: Team members describe why a recommendation serves the system's purpose in a high-priority way.

Goal 2: Team members describe multiple cross-functional perspectives on the recommendation, including one (when possible) that disagrees with the recommendation.

Goal 3: Team members describe at least one other considered option and why their recommended option is preferable.

Goal 4: Team members model system patterns and recommend changes that have positive impact. Whenever possible, use the Iceberg Model.

Goal 5: Team members collectively improve the people processes and understand how you will support (and reinforce) changes in thinking, communication, and behavior.

Objective: Improve Knowledge Stock

Goal 1: Whenever a team member gives advice or shares an idea, they also share the reasons that support their thinking. They do their best to ensure the reasons are true, relevant, strong, and cohesive.

Goal 2: Before responding to other people's thinking, team members respectfully acknowledge what they've heard and understood. They engage with the reasons shared and help strengthen them (especially when they disagree).

Goal 3: Team members share thinking in artifacts and create them collaboratively. They are curious and improvisatory in their approach.

Goal 4: When expertise is needed from outside the team, team members partner with others to think about the problem together.

Objective: Improve Knowledge Flow

Goal 1: Create consistent experiences that encourage team members to learn together and build sound recommendations.

Goal 2: Leverage the skills, experience, and judgment of the team members when facing hard challenges. Synthesize their knowledge and experience into recommendations based on valid reasons.

Goal 3: Create relationships among models and other artifacts. Cultivate a knowledge system where the team's thinking and learning generates success for the organization.

Goal 4: Approach technology development as a sociotechnical system that adapts as things change. Whenever you restructure a team, technology system, or process, describe the patterns of thought, action, and behavior that you are changing and the mental models you are encouraging.

Goal 5: Reinforce, through feedback loops, behavior you want to encourage (especially learning). Discourage, through feedback loops and improved structures, behavior you don't want to encourage (especially derision).

If I had to sum up the practices of a software professional who is a systems leader, I would say: learn more, dictate less. Respect your teammates and your own integrity.

Dancing with Systems

Here we are, at the end of our journey. I sincerely hope that you've found value here. My fondest wish is that you will enjoy knowledge work more. And know that you are not alone (even when you feel you are).

My goal has been, and will continue to be, improving our ability to do hard things together. I look forward to all the knowledge you will contribute and all I have yet to learn. I hope you will come to love, as I do, dancing with systems.

> We can't control systems or figure them out. But we can dance with them!
>
> —Donella Meadows

Further Resources

Throughout this book, I have mentioned or quoted systems thinkers who have contributed knowledge we need. Here is a list of those resources. You can find them all—and more—in the resource center (*https://systemslibrary.com*). Join the System-Crafters Collective (*https://mentrix.systems*) to learn with other systems thinkers.

Books

Ackoff, Russell. 1978. *The Art of Problem Solving: Accompanied by Ackoff's Fables*. John Wiley & Sons.

Ackoff, Russell. 1999. *Ackoff's Best: His Classic Writings on Management*. Wiley.

Alexander, Christopher, Sara Ishikawa, Murray Silverstein, Max Jacobson, Ingrid Fiksdahl-King, and Shlomo Angel. 1977. *A Pattern Language: Towns, Buildings, Construction (Center for Environmental Structure Series)*. Oxford: Oxford University Press.

Anderson, David, Mark McCann, and Michael O'Reilly. 2022. *The Value Flywheel Effect: Power the Future and Accelerate Your Organization to the Modern Cloud*. IT Revolution.

Bittman, Mark. 2021. *Animal, Vegetable, Junk: A History of Food, from Sustainable to Suicidal*. Mariner.

Brooks, Frederick P., Jr. 1975. *The Mythical Man-Month: Essays on Software Engineering*. Addison-Wesley.

Buschmann, Frank, Regine Meunier, Hans Rohnert, Peter Sommerlad, and Michael Stal. 1996. *Pattern-Oriented Software Architecture Volume 1: A System of Patterns*. Wiley.

Campell, Joseph and Bill Moyers. 1988. *The Power of Myth*. Doubleday.

Carreyrou, John. 2020. *Bad Blood: Secrets and Lies in a Silicon Valley Startup*. Vintage.

Clear, James. 2018. *Atomic Habits: An Easy & Proven Way to Build Good Habits & Break Bad Ones*. Penguin.

Davenport, Thomas H. and Laurence Prusak. 1998. *Working Knowledge: How Organizations Manage What They Know*. Harvard Business Review Press.

Dreyer, Benjamin. 2019. *Dreyer's English: An Utterly Correct Guide to Clarity and Style*. Random House.

Evans, Eric. 2003. *Domain-driven Design: Tackling Complexity in the Heart of Software*. Addison-Wesley Professional.

Ford, Neal, Pramod Sadalage, Zhamak Dehghani, and Mark Richards. 2021. *Software Architecture: The Hard Parts: Modern Trade-Off Analyses for Distributed Architectures*. O'Reilly Media.

Forsgren, Nicole, Jez Humble, and Gene Kim. 2018. *Accelerate*. IT Revolution Press.

Forrester, Jay W. 1969. *Principles of Systems*. System Dynamics Society.

Gamma, Erich, Richard Helm, Ralph Johnson, and John Vlissides. 1994. *Design Patterns: Elements of Reusable Object-Oriented Software*. Addison-Wesley Professional.

Gell-Mann, Murray. 2023. *The Quark and the Jaguar: Adventures in the Simple and the Complex*. Santa Fe Institute of Science.

Gleick, James. 2011. *Chaos: Making a New Science*—the enhanced edition. Open Road Media.

Harmel-Law, Andrew. 2025. *Facilitating Software Architecture*. O'Reilly Media.

Heifetz, Ronald A. 1998. *Leadership Without Easy Answers*. Harvard University Press.

Hewitt, Eben. 2018. *Technology Strategy Patterns: Architecture as Strategy*. O'Reilly Media.

Hohpe, Gregor and Bobby Woolf. 2003. *Enterprise Integration Patterns: Designing, Building, and Deploying Messaging Solutions*. Addison-Wesley Professional.

Hoque, Faisal. 2023. *Reinvent: Navigating Business Transformation in a Hyperdigital Era*. Greenleaf Book Group.

Joko Beck, Charlotte. 1989. *Everyday Zen: Love and Work*. HarperOne.

Kahneman, Daniel. 2011. *Thinking, Fast and Slow*. Farrar, Straus and Giroux.

Kelle, Evelyn van, Gien Verschatse, and Kenny Baas-Schwegler. 2024. *Collaborative Software Design: How to Facilitate Domain Modeling Decisions*. Manning.

Khononov, Vlad. 2021. *Learning Domain-Driven Design*. O'Reilly Media.

Meadows, Donella H. 2008. *Thinking in Systems: A Primer*. Chelsea Green Publishing.

Mitchell, Melanie. 2010. *Complexity: A Guided Tour*. Oxford University Press.

Newport, Cal. 2016. *Deep Work: Rules for Focused Success in a Distracted World*. Grand Central Publishing.

Parrish, Shane and Rhiannon Beaubien. 2018. *The Great Mental Models*. Latticework Publishing.

Pendleton-Jullian, Ann M. and John Seely Brown. 2008. *Design Unbound: Designing for Emergence in a White Water World*. MIT Press.

Pollan, Michael. 2006. *The Omnivore's Dilemma: A Natural History of Four Meals*. Penguin Press.

Read, Jacqui. 2023. *Communication Patterns*. O'Reilly Media.

Rechtin, Eberhardt and Mark W. Maier. 1817. *The Art of Systems Architecting*, 1st edition. CRC Press.

Richards, Mark and Neal Ford. 2020. *Fundamentals of Software Architecture: An Engineering Approach*. O'Reilly Media.

Senge, Peter M. 1999. *The Fifth Discipline: The Art & Practice of the Learning Organization*. Crown Currency.

Skelton, Matthew and Manuel Pais. 2019. *Team Topologies: Organizing Business and Technology Teams for Fast Flow*. Revolution Press.

Solé, Ricard and Santiago F. Elena. 2018. *Viruses as Complex Adaptive Systems*. Princeton University Press.

Sweeney, Linda Booth and Dennis Meadows. 2010. *The Systems Thinking Playbook: Exercises to Stretch and Build Learning and Systems Thinking Capabilities*. Chelsea Green Publishing.

Taleb, Nassim Nicholas. 2012. *Antifragile: Things That Gain from Disorder*. Random House.

Tune, Nick and Jean-Georges Perrin. 2024. *Architecture Modernization: Socio-Technical Alignment of Software, Strategy, and Structure*. Manning.

Vonnegut, Kurt. 1981. *Palm Sunday*. Delacorte Press.

Weinberg, Gerald M. 1986. *Becoming a Technical Leader: An Organic Problem-Solving Approach*. Dorset House.

West, Geoffrey. 2018. *Scale: The Universal Laws of Life, Growth, and Death in Organisms, Cities, and Companies*. Penguin Books.

Young, Scott. 2019. *Ultralearning: Master Hard Skills, Outsmart the Competition, and Accelerate Your Career*. Harper Business.

Zinsser, William. 2006. *On Writing Well: The Classic Guide to Writing Nonfiction*. Turtleback Books.

Articles

Academy for Systems Change. 2024. *A System Leader's Fieldbook* (*https://oreil.ly/YVkVm*), academyforchange.org.

Ackoff, Russell. "A Lifetime of Systems Thinking" (*https://oreil.ly/O1SVm*). *Systems Thinker*. Accessed on May 3, 2024.

Ackoff, Russell. "From Data to Wisdom" (*https://faculty.ung.edu/kmelton/documents/datawisdom.pdf*), from *Ackoff's Best*, pp. 170–172.

Ackoff, Russell. 1993. "From Mechanistic to Systemic Thinking" (*https://oreil.ly/mmYLw*). *The Library of Consciousness* (November).

Dreier, Lisa, David Nabarro, and Jane Nelson. 2019. "Systems Leadership for Sustainable Development: Strategies for Achieving Systemic Change" (*https://oreil.ly/-WYgh*). The Corporate Responsibility Initiative at the Harvard Kennedy School.

Goodman, Michael. "Systems Thinking: What, Why, When, Where and How?" (*https://thesystemsthinker.com/systems-thinking-what-why-when-where-and-how*) *Systems Thinker*. Accessed on May 3, 2024.

Martinez-Moyano, Ignacio J. 2024. "The History of the Beer Game" (*https://oreil.ly/4uDtA*). *System Dynamics Review* (February).

Meadows, Donella. "Leverage Points: Places to Intervene in a System" (*https://oreil.ly/rS1rX*). *The Donella Meadows Project*. Accessed on May 2, 2024.

Senge, Peter, Hal Hamilton, and John Kania. 2015. "The Dawn of System Leadership" (*https://ssir.org/articles/entry/the_dawn_of_system_leadership*). *Stanford Social Innovation Review* (Winter).

Tools & Approaches

Acreom (*https://acreom.com*) and Obsidian (*https://obsidian.md*)

ADRs (*https://adr.github.io*)

ArchiMate (*https://www.archimatetool.com*)

Business process modeling (*https://monday.com/blog/project-management/business-process-modeling*)

The C4 model (*https://c4model.com*)

Core Domain (*https://levelup.gitconnected.com/domain-and-core-domain-in-ddd-c49733fa8c74*)

The Cynefin Framework (*https://thecynefin.co*)

Data Modeling (*https://www.ibm.com/topics/data-modeling*)

Design Thinking (*https://www.interaction-design.org/literature/topics/design-thinking*)

The Digital Capability Framework (*https://robllewellyn.com/what-is-the-digital-capability-framework*)

EventStorming (*https://www.eventstorming.com*)

Team Topologies (*https://teamtopologies.com*)

TOGAF (*https://www.opengroup.org/togaf*)

UML (the Unified Modeling Language) (*https://developer.ibm.com/articles/an-introduction-to-uml*)

Value Flywheel (*https://itrevolution.com/articles/using-wardley-mapping-with-the-value-flywheel*)

Wardley Mapping (*https://learnwardleymapping.com*)

Glossary

When we talk about systems, we often use the same words but mean very different things. Throughout this book, I have used these concepts or keywords to convey what I mean by "systems thinking." Some of the general definitions are different from the way I mean them in this context. To help clarify, here is what I had in mind when I used these terms in *Learning Systems Thinking*.

Abstract thinking
The act of understanding concepts that are real but not exclusively describing a specific experience or object that can be observed directly

Ambiguity
The quality of being open to more than one interpretation

Architecture
Knowledge, experience, and sound judgment synthesized into systems-sound recommendations based on valid reasons

Argumentation
Systemic reasoning

Artifact
Any knowledge object created to structure and convey thinking

Asynchronous
Relational interactions in a system that happen in their own time, based on their own logic

Backchanneling
Reacting to ideas and events indirectly (like gossip) rather than directly (like engaging with someone's idea)

Big upfront design
The attempt to create a perfect, comprehensive software or system design before development begins

Bikeshedding
Focusing on trivial matters (noise), which are easier to solve and likely at the top of the iceberg model, rather than focusing on more complex matters like patterns, structures, and mental models (signal)

Blind spot
Ideas we can't generate because they don't occur to us or root causes we can't see

Boundaries
Delineated conceptual or physical borders between system parts (or a system and the rest of the world) that help us understand and design the relationships among those parts

Cat herding
> Attempting to control people, thinking, or circumstances that are resisting control or are uncontrollable

Circumstances
> Conditions inside of a system boundary, including the impacts of forces acting on the system

Cogent
> Convincing, clear, and relevant

Cognitive biases
> Ideas that reinforce core beliefs, personal experiences, or preferences

Coherence
> The quality of ideas that are logically consistent and connected

Collection
> A group of parts that do not form a system because they are not in relationship to each other

Collective systemic reasoning
> Building relevant and impactful ideas, actions, or theories supported by sound reasons through the integration of multiple points of view

Complex system
> A system is complex when relationships among the parts generate impacts and patterns of behavior that the individual parts do not produce on their own

Concept
> An idea that has shape, meaning, relevance, and a strong relationship to context

Conceptual integrity
> The quality of interdependent and well-reasoned abstract ideas generating relationships, parts, patterns, and structures that work together to serve a system's purpose

Concerned with control
> Prioritizing the ability to plan and predict precise outcomes

Concrete thinking
> Thinking and communication exclusively about physical objects, immediate experiences, and exact interpretations

Condescending
> Responding to ideas using tone, words, or mannerisms that indicate that your ideas are more important, insightful, or intelligent

Consent
> Agreeing to an idea, action, or theory (as opposed to being forced to accept it)

Constraint
> A limitation or restriction

Context
> The circumstances within a system boundary that can be considered and understood

Counterintuitiveness
> The quality of changes that may not "make sense" to a person, group, or organization because they do not match what we already think and know. Systemic changes might not be "intuitive" or visible to us, because they are counter to what we "know."

Critical thinking
> The ability to analyze and evaluate circumstances

Data
> Raw materials that make up information, facts

Deep work
> Concentrating deeply on a difficult task or concept for prolonged periods of time without getting distracted

Derision
> Ridicule, mockery, or disregarding something that should be considered

Diagram
> A simplified drawing showing the appearance, structure, and/or workings of software

Discernment

The ability to comprehend situations in ways that enable prioritizing ideas and actions that will have positive impact on the system as a whole

Ecosystem

An environment where parts (human and technological) interdepend and interrelate in ways that form patterns and structures

Effective

Able to produce a result that improves the system's ability to serve its purpose

Emergent

Coming into existence as a result of relationships among parts (not the parts themselves), or when changing systemic patterns generate new relational behaviors

Empathy

The experience of feeling, thinking, and perceiving things from an internal frame of reference in order to understand a point of view, rather than from an external, analytical, or objective frame of reference

Empowered teams

Teams with the skills, responsibility, and authority to make impactful decisions by relying on, and generating, knowledge flow

Enabling constraints

Intentional limits on growth that enable the system to scale while still containing the impact of that scaling

Engage

Become involved in the thinking and discernment process

Equalize impact

Attain a quality in a system wherein positive and negative impacts are experienced by everyone in the system

Experience

Be part of a changing situation before a desired change is identified and until the impact is clear

Feedback loop

Output that is used to improve future input; also, thinking contributed in response to shared thinking

Framework

A predefined structure underlying software or concepts

Framing

Creating conceptual boundaries around a systemic challenge, potential decision, or aspect of a system's behavior

Generative learning

Increasing our capacity for proactively synthesizing knowledge and experience

Hard versus soft skills

The idea that what we do (job-specific skills) can be separated from how we do it (interpersonal skills)

Heuristics

Principles developed by observing and recognizing patterns that aid thinking, learning, discovery, discernment, and problem solving

Hierarchy

In systems, hierarchy describes the information-sharing relationships between self-organizing subsystems. It does not describe power, rank or importance.

Iceberg Model

A systems thinking tool that can be used to understand the underlying causes of a problem or event

Information

Data expanded to have shape, meaning, inference, and conceptual relevance

Inquiry

The seeking of truth, information, and/or knowledge

Insufficient

An inadequate amount of reasoning, learning, or perspective taking

Integrative leadership
The development of ecologies of change

Interconnected
Parts of a system being connected to or relating to each other without having to be explicitly linked or tightly coupled

Interdependent
Parts of a system depending on each other without having to be explicitly connected

Interrelated
Parts of a system affecting other parts even when they are not explicitly coupled

It depends
Shorthand for "correct answers will vary depending on the context"

Justify
To give good, relevant reasons to support an idea, action, or theory

Knowledge
A sophisticated integration of data, information, and experience. It is the conceptual materials we use to create laws and theorems; best practices and heuristics (mental shortcuts for solving a problem); strategies and predictions based on patterns (like during a pandemic); *and* is our ability to generate artifacts (models, documents, code, software), routines, processes, practices, and cultural norms that are insightful and valuable in a particular context.

Knowledge flow
The ability to transfer knowledge between people (or between people and technology) in ways that improve the system

Knowledge stock
The store of knowledge you have developed or can access

Knowledge work
The understanding and application of knowledge (experience, values, contextual information, expert insight, and grounded intuition) in ways that enable organizations to evaluate and incorporate new experiences and information

Learning
Increasing our capacity for synthesizing knowledge and experience into knowledge stock and applying it as knowledge flow

Legacy software
Software that may still meet the needs of the system but cannot grow to meet emerging needs

Leverage points
Places to intervene in a system where a small shift in one thing will produce big changes in the system as a whole

Linear thinking
A sequential thought process generating concepts that are predictable, rational, repeatable, procedural, dualistic, top down, and concerned with control

Logical fallacies
Bugs in our thinking, faulty reasoning used to justify an idea or assertion

Magic bullet
A straightforward, single solution adopted to solve a complex problem (that rarely does)

Manage
Be in charge of other people's thinking and behavior

Mental model
An internal representation of an external reality (regardless of whether or not the representation describes reality)

Metacognition
Critical awareness of your own thought processes

Mindshift
Changing core mental models

Modeling
Framing a point of view and making relevant concepts—and the relationships among them—visible

Modern software

Software exhibiting increasing relational complexity among its parts and the information flow across those parts

Nonlinear

Can't be arranged in a straight line

Nonlinear approaches

Ways of working that generate value by coordinating thinking and action without exerting command or linear control over the activities

Nonlinear thinking

Seeing conceptual connections and patterns by shifting perspectives and forming new relationships among ideas

Nuance

A degree of difference that represents reality more accurately than either/or binary descriptions

Opinion-driven

A style of thought and communication characterized by sharing, debating, and acting on assertions without reasons to justify them

Orchestrating

Arranging harmonious activity in a system that produces a desired effect while still enabling parts to act according to their own timing and goals

Outcome

Demonstrated impact of work done (generally measured against the intention)

Paradigm

The deepest set of beliefs about how the world works; the mindset out of which the system (its goals, patterns, structure) arises

Paradox

A situation that combines contradictory qualities

Pattern

A combination of qualities, attitudes, recurring events, reinforced concepts, etc., forming a trend over time

Pattern thinking

Recognizing small qualities, attitudes, recurring events, reinforced concepts, etc., that scale to generate impact over time and across contexts

Personal mastery

A deep understanding of your learning process and how to improve it

Perspective

Point of view

Practice

The regular exercise and application of activities that develop (systems thinking) mastery

Principle

A fundamental proposition that serves as the reasoned foundation for a system of behavior

Proactive

A type of action that causes something to happen, initiates rather than reacts

Proposition

An idea, action, or theory supported by justifying reasons

Psychological safety

An absence of interpersonal fear; a quality enabled by proactive communication of trust and respect

Purpose

The intentions of system designers may convey a purpose, but the purpose of a system is what it does (POSIWID)

Rationality

Concepts arising from reason or logic

Reaction

Thoughts, action, or feeling experienced in response to a situation or event

Reductionism

Reducing complex data and phenomena to simple terms; understanding the whole as exclusively the sum of its parts

Relational complexity

The number of interrelated concepts needed to construct a mental model of a pattern, circumstance, or problem

Relevant

Directly related to the matter being considered

Reliable

Trustworthy

Resistance

The act of refusing, overtly or covertly, to accept or comply with something regardless of its veracity

Respectful

The quality of proactively expressed consideration or regard for something or someone (regardless of rank)

Root cause

The core mental models that give rise to events and are reinforced by systemic structures and patterns

Self-awareness

Critical awareness of your own thought processes, cognitive patterns, feelings, physical sensations, core beliefs, mental structures, habitual behaviors, future expectations, and past experiences, etc., and how they influence each other

Self-organizing

The quality of order and generative momentum that arise from local interactions (a self-organizing team can solve its own problems)

Shifting perspective

Considering the same circumstance from different points of view

Signal versus noise

Signal is an idea, information, insight, or concept that points your attention in a matterful direction. *Noise* describes all the information that, despite its seeming importance, distracts you from what actually matters (e.g., bikeshedding).

Silos

Barriers that prevent teams and/or software from communicating or cooperating with other parts of the system; can also refer to the teams or software themselves

Sociotechnical

Having interactions among people, infrastructure, technology, culture, processes, and goals that generate software systems; the system cannot be effectively understood by dissociating these parts

Software

Instructions and data that carry out a particular task

Sound

Justified by reason, strong inference, and judgment

Structuring inquiry

Planning an approach to learning something relevant and valuable to the circumstances

Subject matter expert

Someone with knowledge and relevant experience in a particular subject

Synthesize

Forming knowledge by combining knowledge and experience generated by different points of view

System

A group of interrelated hardware, software, people, organization(s), and other elements that interact and/or interdepend to serve a shared purpose

System dynamics

Nonlinear behavior in a system over time

System of software

An interrelated and interdependent collection of software that serves a purpose and is more than the sum of its parts

System structures

Physical things like software or office space, organizations like companies or governments, policies like laws or rules, rituals like habitual behaviors or "how we do things"

Systemic patterns

Related events that happen over time and influence how the system operates

Systemic reasoning

The art and science of reasoning systematically in support of an idea, action or theory. When you practice systemic reasoning, you move beyond sharing your opinion. You construct ideas by integrating the reasons that convinced you that the idea is sound, relevant, and matterful. You synthesize your own thinking with the thinking of others, arriving at *the best possible conclusion, under the circumstances, when conditions are uncertain.*

Systems age

Acceptance of nonlinear insights: nothing can be understood independently of its environment; analysis produces knowledge, but synthesis is needed to produce understanding; cause and effect is just one way of looking at reality

Systems design

Understanding, defining, or improving the relationships among parts of a system (human and technology) so that they generate desirable and purposeful effects

Systems leadership

Development of ecologies of change

Systems perspective

An understanding of the behaviors of a system as a whole in the context of its environment

Systems thinking

A system of foundational thinking practices that, when done together, improve nonlinear thinking skills

Taylorism

Also known as scientific management, processes and procedures based on the idea that people will avoid work unless managers enforce increased efficiency and productivity

Technology professional

Anyone whose thinking ends up in production

Thinking

Using one's mind to consider or reason

Top-down and bottom-up

A style of directive thinking that moves up or down a ranking hierarchy

Transformation

A shift in paradigm (the mental models, structures, patterns, and concepts that give rise to a system)

Transparency

A quality of knowledge flow that enables open access to relevant information that supports self-organization and problem solving

Uncertainty

Understanding that what is known is not all there is to know

Understanding

The ability to discern knowledge that will be most effective in a particular context

Wisdom

The ability to discover true leverage points in the systems we inhabit and push them in a valuable direction

Index

indicators of success, 153
conceptual integrity, 19-35
    changing nature of systems, 27-30
    counterintuitive MAGO, 35
    counterintuitiveness, 25-27
    cultivating in solution recommendations,
        230
    front of the train thinking, 33-34
    relational complexity in, 21-22
    sociotechnical systems thinking, 22-25
    time as factor of, 31-33
    writing as thinking, 34-35
concern with control, defined, 240
concrete thinking, 5
condescending, defined, 240
consent, systemic reasoning's reliance on, 113
constraint, 222
context
    circumstances and, 163
    events and, 163
    understanding, 101
counterintuitiveness
    basics, 25-27
    of MAGO problem, 35
critical thinking, defined, 53

D

data
    defined, 90
    integrating, 90-93
deep work, as core practice of systems thinking,
    40
Deep Work: Rules for Focused Success in a Dis-
    tracted World (Newport), 40
derision, defined, 240
design thinking, 181-182
diagrams, value of, 42
discernment
    ambiguity versus, 57
    difficulty with, 58
    process patterns and, 167
domain modeling, 189

E

ecosystem, defined, 241
effective partnerships, 206
Einstein, Albert, 210
emergent systems design, 164
empathy, as core skill, 75-76

empowered teams, defined, 241
enabling constraints, 222
engagement
    with reasons, 148
    respectful, 40
experience
    as component of knowledge, 90, 92
    empathizing with, 86
    motivation from, 97
external patterns
    basics, 166
    in modeling, 196
    relationship to other patterns, 170

F

feedback loops
    basics, 135-153
    conceptual bridge building, 137-142, 153
        bridges, 141
        gaps, 139-141
    four core skills, 146-151
        engaging with reasons, 148
        listening, 147
        looking for fallacies, 148-151
        thinking and considering, 147
    in learning systems, 103
    MAGO: helpful conceptual bridges, 152-153
    practical application, 151
    systems thinking, 142-151
        asking for feedback, 142
        feedback from people you need, 143-144
        golden rule of feedback, 144-146
        learning in feedback loops, 146
Fifth Discipline, The (Senge), 46-48
five core practices of systems thinking, 39-43
    changing patterns of behavior, 40
    doing deep work, 40
    learning, 39
    respectful engagement, 40
    structuring inquiry, 39
Forrester, Jay, 26, 46-48
four core skills of feedback loops, 146-151
    engaging with reasons, 148
    listening, 147
    looking for fallacies, 148-151
    thinking and considering, 147
framework, system as, 9
framing, of ambiguity in systemic reasoning
    structures, 123-125
front of the train thinking, 33-34

G

generative learning, 89
golden rule of feedback, 144-146
groupings, creating without reductionism, 102

H

hard skills, soft skills versus, 11
heuristics, 212-216
hierarchy
    in integrative leadership, 206
    in sociotechnical systems, 24

I

Iceberg Model of system analysis, 43-46
    collective systemic reasoning, 132
    events, 44
    mental models, 45
    patterns and trends, 45
    practical applications, 48
    structure, 45
information
    defined, 90
    knowledge versus, 213
    structure as characteristic of systems leadership, 208
inquiry
    investment of time, 122
    observation and, 96
    relationship to observation, 96
    structuring, 39
    systemic reasoning and, 121-122
insufficiency
    description of reasons, 128
    of one perspective, 215
integration, defined, 208
integrative leadership, 206-208
interconnections, in Iceberg model, 133
interdependence
    between people and software, 32
    in systems, 112
interpersonal skills development, 103
interrelatedness of programming skills, 105
intervention dependence, 223
it depends, defined, 242

J

judgment, sound, 102

K

knowledge
    collective systemic reasoning and, 112-114
    components of, 90-91
    generating artifacts with, 95
    increasing through observation and inquiry, 96
    information versus, 213
    motivation of, 94
    synthesized activities and, 96
    through experience, 97
knowledge flow
    generating, 224
    improving, 231
    knowledge stock versus, 92
    leadership support, 202
    learning leadership and, 202
knowledge stock
    improving, 231
    knowledge as measure of, 55
    knowledge flow versus, 92
knowledge work/knowledge workers, 92

L

language, consistent, 216
leadership, 16
learning
    as core practice of systems thinking, 39
    in feedback loops, 146
learning activities
    describing, 98
    designing, 95
    experience-building activities, 97
    generating artifacts, 95
    generating questions through observation and inquiry, 96
    synthesizing knowledge, 96
learning leadership, 211-216
    heuristics, 212-216
    knowledge flow and, 202
learning systems, 89-106
    describing activities, 98
    designing activities, 95
    designing feedback loops, 103
    finding help, 104
    learning-driven careers, 93
    MAGO's learning opportunities, 105
    motivation, 94
    outcomes, 99-103

creating groupings and boundaries
without reductionism, 102
designing, 98
developing interpersonal skills, 103
identifying patterns and structures, 101
increasing tolerance for ambiguity, 100
perspective shift, 100
thinking critically and applying sound
judgment, 102
understanding context and relational
impact, 101
using life experience, 105
learning-driven careers, 93
legacy software, defined, 242
leverage points
counterintuitive situations, 25-27
finding through modeling, 179
theory of relativity as, 210
linear thinking
as default mode, 5-7
linear and nonlinear approaches to modeling, 194-195
logical fallacies
ad hominem, 151
anecdotal, 149
appeal to authority, 150
appeal to emotion, 151
bandwagon, 150
black or white, 150
burden of proof, 150
looking for, 148-151
middle ground, 150
slippery slope, 151
strawman, 149
as triggers, 83

M

magic bullet, defined, 242
MAGO (fictitious organization)
applying seven questions of pattern thinking
to, 171-172
blind spots, 63-66
counterintuitive nature of problems, 35
helpful conceptual bridges in feedback
loops, 152-153
learning opportunities, 105
looking at patterns, 168-172
mental models, 45
quandary faced by, 14-16
reaction to event, 83

success at, 228-231
systems leadership at, 217-219
viewed from systems perspective, 191-197
Meadows, Donella, 225
on alternatives to control, 59
on counterintuitiveness, 26
graphic depiction of system, 27
on leverage points, 25
on resistance to systems thinking, 8
on systems, 9
on systems thinking, 21
mental models
blind spots in, 63-66
feedback loops and, 137-142
Iceberg Model as example, 45, 55, 158-160
metacognition, 54
middle ground fallacy, 150
mindshift, away from linear thinking, 13
modeling, 177-199
basics, 178-186
as core practice, 41-43
design thinking, 181-182
different perspectives, 182-186
finding leverage points through, 179
linear and nonlinear approaches, 194-195
MAGO from a systems perspective, 191-197
patterns, 195-197
practicing, 197
problem and solution space, 193-194
resources, 198
systems perspective, 186-191
causal loop diagrams, 190
domain modeling, 189
modeling choices, 189
seven questions of pattern thinking in,
190
as unifying action, 180-181
modern software, 7
motivation in learning systems, 94
Mythical Man-Month (Brooks), 20, 26

N

Newport, Cal, 40, 61, 62
nonlinear approach
beginning with observation, 60
difficulty, 8
to modeling, 194-195
nonlinear systems, 7-8
nonlinear thinking
importance, 14

Iceberg Model, 132
  idea building and, 115
  identifying ideas/actions/theories, 117
  identifying reasons, 117-119
  MAGO's Proposition, 132
  as method of inquiry, 121-122
  other names for, 114-115
  reason-strengthening components, 119-120
    cogency, 120, 131
    cohesiveness, 120, 130
    relevance, 119, 130
    reliability, 119, 130
    understandability, 129
  structures (and frames) ambiguity, 123-125
  top-down elaboration (TDE), 125-127
  as worthwhile investment, 122
systems (generally)
  changing nature of, 27-30
  dancing with, 232
  defined, 244
  identifying highest-value purpose, 217
systems age, 4
  defined, 245
systems architecture, defined, 161
systems design
  defined, 245
  leadership skill, 207
  mediation of top-down and bottom-up
    approaches, 24
  orchestration, 208
systems leadership, 201-219
  application beyond technology, 204
  articulating/justifying core problems, 218
  characteristics, 205-211
    architecting communication structures,
      206
    finding places to intervene, 209-211
    information structure, 208
    integration, 208
    pattern design, 208
    relationship design, 208
  cohorts, 219
  defined, 245
  designing system of communication for, 218
  encouraging systems thinking, 218
  learning leadership, 211-216
    heuristics, 212-216
    knowledge flow and, 202
  MAGO and, 217-219
  overlap with management, 203

paradigm, 202-205
recommending pathways toward improving
  the systems, 218
self-care, 218
subject matter expertise, 205
understanding pain points, 217
systems perspective, 186-191
  causal loop diagrams, 190
  choices for, 189
  defined, 245
  domain modeling, 189
  MAGO viewed from, 191-197
  seven questions of pattern thinking, 190
systems thinking, 3-16
  basics, 1
  defined, 8-10, 245
  designing, 175
  difficulties, 55
  feedback loops, 142-151
  five core practices, 39-43
    changing patterns of behavior, 40
    doing deep work, 40
    learning, 39
    respectful engagement, 40
    structuring inquiry, 39
  linear thinking as default, 5-7
  MAGO's quandary, 14-16
  nonlinear nature, 7-8
  personal, 51, 107
  practice, 10
  qualities, 11-14
  systems leadership, 218

T

Taylor, Frederick Winslow, 202
Taylorism, 202
technology patterns, in modeling, 196-197
technology professional, defined, 245
thinking
  alternative practices, 62-63
  creating shared space, 217
  critical, 102
  flowing, 61-62
  observing, 59-63
time
  events and, 163
  factor in systems, 31-33
  relationship to patterns, 163
top-down and bottom-up, defined, 245
top-down directive thinking, 23

top-down elaboration (TDE), 125-127
transformation, defined, 245
triggers, as clues, 83
24-hour rule of responding, 81

U

uncertainty
    constant nature of, 125
    discomfort with, 56
understandability, of propositions using collec-
    tive systemic reasoning, 129
understanding
    empathy and, 75
    knowledge work as, 92

    relationship to empathy, 75
    wisdom and, 91

W

wisdom
    defined, 91
    understanding and, 91
writing, as tool for practicing systems thinking,
    34-35

Y

"yes, and" method of improv, 79-81

About the Author

Diana Montalion has 20 years of experience delivering transformative initiatives, independently or as part of a professional services group, to clients including Stanford, the Gates Foundation, and Teach For All. She has served as principal architect for *The Economist* and the Wikimedia Foundation. She founded Mentrix Group, a consultancy providing technology architecture, systems leadership, and workshops on nonlinear approaches. Writing, teaching, and thinking about thinking are her favorite hobbies.

Colophon

The animal on the cover of *Learning Systems Thinking* is a giant kingfisher (*Megaceryle maxima*), native to Africa (mostly south of the Sahara Desert).

The giant kingfisher's diet consists primarily of insects, reptiles, and fish. When in search of dinner, it sits on a perch waiting for prey. Once it has successfully snared its initial prey, it moves on to another location. The giant kingfisher is territorial and monogamous, with the timing of breeding dependant on location. Its nest is actually a tunnel in the side of a river bank, created by both the male and the female. After the mother lays the eggs, the parents take turns incubating the eggs until they hatch, and the cycle begins again.

The giant kingfisher is one of many kingfisher species. Kingfishers in general were the inspiration for the Japanese bullet train: engineers studied the shapes of their beaks for the design. The current conservation status (IUCN) of the giant kingfisher is "Least Concern." Many of the animals on O'Reilly covers are endangered; all of them are important to the world.

The cover illustration is by Karen Montgomery, based on an antique line engraving from *English Cyclopedia*. The series design is by Edie Freedman, Ellie Volckhausen, and Karen Montgomery. The cover fonts are Gilroy Semibold and Guardian Sans. The text font is Adobe Minion Pro, and the heading font is Adobe Myriad Condensed.

Milton Keynes UK
Ingram Content Group UK Ltd.
UKHW032108281124
451746UK00005B/15